FOR ALL THE SAINTS

FOR ALL THE SAINTS

Changing Perceptions
of Martyrdom and Sainthood
in the Lutheran Reformation

BY

R O B E R T   K O L B

ISBN 0-86554-270-8

Library of Congress Cataloging-in-Publication Data
Kolb, Robert.
For all the saints.

Bibliography: p. 165
1. Christian saints—Cult—Europe, Northern—History
of doctrines—16th century. 2. Martyrdom (Christianity)—
History of doctrines—16th century. 3. Lutheran Church—
Doctrines—History—16th century. 4. Europe, Northern—
Church history. 5. Reformation—Europe, Northern.
6. Spirituality—Lutheran Church—History of doctrines—
16th century. I. Title.
BX8074.S35K64   1987   235'.2'09031   87-7692
ISBN 0-86554-270-8 (alk. paper)

Contents

List of Illustrations

Preface

In the autumn of 1976, a seminarian came to the Center for Reformation Research with a question about a "Lutheran Martyr" of 1525 named Leonhard Kayser. Kayser had escaped my notice, and I voiced a suspicion to the student that Kayser was no martyr but rather a peasant who had gotten caught in a sweep of rebel territory by the nobles. The student had a reference from a martyrbook by a man named Ludwig Rabus, who had also escaped my notice; so I agreed to pursue the matter. To my surprise, I found the first of the Protestant martyrologies by Rabus, a student of Luther and Melanchthon and a south German reformer of some importance in the Late-Reformation period for the cities in which he served, Strassburg and Ulm. It did not assuage my curiosity to learn that few others engaged in the study of the Reformation had heard of Rabus or his martyrbook. My curiosity had been piqued: Why might a German Lutheran have composed a book of martyrs? Why had Rabus not "succeeded" in the manner of John Foxe or Jean Crespin? To answer these questions, one must address the ways in which the Reformers dealt with the medieval usage of those holy heroes, venerated in the piety of the Middle Ages, the saints.

My research began in the summer of 1978 at Concordia Seminary, Saint Louis, and the Folger Shakespeare Library, Washington, D.C., with financial support from the Aid Association for Lutherans, a fraternal benefit society in Appleton, Wisconsin, channeled through the office of my dean, David Schmiel, at Concordia College, Saint Paul. Similar support from the Aid Association for Lutherans and the college facilitated research in the archives of Strassburg and Ulm in 1979. I am grateful also to M. F. J. Fuchs and M. Ponsing of the *archives municipales* for their assistance in examining relevant documents in Strassburg. I am similarly grateful to Dr. Specker and Fräulein Mauser of the *Stadtarchiv* in Ulm for opening its resources to me, and to Lyndal Roper, whose familiarity with its collection and whose skill in interpreting sixteenth-century Ulm were of invaluable assistance during my work there.

A fellowship from the Deutscher Akademischer Austauschdienst made it possible to work intensively on this study at the Herzog August Bibliothek in Wolfenbüttel, Federal Republic of Germany, during the summer of 1981. There, in the midst of the Sodalitas Okerensis, which is both permanent and in constant flux, the shape of the book became ever clearer. The stimulation of the people gathered at that magnificent institution, under the able direction and care of Dr. Sabine Solf, breathed new insights into much of my work. Bodo Nischan of East Carolina University, Robin Barnes of Davidson College, Mary Lindemann of Lemoine College, Kurt Hendel of the Lutheran School of Theology in Chicago, and Joyce Irwin of Hamilton, New York, were there at that time and offered provocative questions and helpful suggestions. Jill Kohl of Bristol pointed my attention to literary issues that I would have otherwise missed. Benedetto Bravo of the University of Warsaw showed me how Rabus related to his classical antecedents. In addition, Erdmann Weyrauch of the Herzog August Bibliothek reinforced the lessons of his work on Strassburg and shared other insights. Oliver Olson of Marquette University and the Herzog August Bibliothek continued his role as sounding board for my study of the German Late-Reformation; and Luther Peterson of the State University of New York at Oswego began a process of criticizing the manuscript, which has continued to sharpen and improve it in the intervening years. James Kittelson of Ohio State University has shared insights and materials from his own study of Strassburg. The manuscript was read by two friends who have criticized and improved my research and writing for a decade and a half, Robert Kingdon of the University of Wisconsin and Jerome Friedman of Kent State University. For their aid I am deeply appreciative, as I am for the continuing support of my study of the sixteenth century offered by Loma Meyer, my dean of faculty, and Alan Harre, president of Concordia College, Saint Paul (Minnesota). Their support has taken many forms, including a subvention for this volume. Without the encouragement and guidance of Marvin Bergman of Mercer University Press, this volume would not have been possible; to him I am also very grateful.

This book has arisen from my family circle. Not only did they grant me time to indulge in research and writing, but also my daughter Kelley assisted with the editorial preparations of the text and my wife Pauline has once again contributed support in the archives and libraries, as well as at home, by reading, copying, summarizing, criticizing, and at times even approving. To them, above all, I am thankful.

Abbreviations

Printed Sources

Bks   *Die Bekenntnisschriften der evangelisch-lutherischen Kirche*, 5. ed. (Göttingen: Vandenhoeck & Ruprecht, 1963).

(Martin Luther)

WA   *D. Martin Luthers Werke* (Weimar: Böhlau, 1883-)

LW   *Luther's Works* (Saint Louis: Concordia, and Philadelphia: Muhlenberg/Fortress, 1955-1973).

(Philip Melanchthon)

CR   C. G. Bretschneider, ed., *Corpus Reformatorum, Philippi Melanthonis opera quae supersunt omnia* (Halle: Schwetschke, 1834-1860).

(Ludwig Rabus)

Tomus I   *Tomvs I. de S. Dei confessoribvs, veteris. qve ecclesiae martyribus* . . . (Strassburg: Heirs of Balthasar Beck, 1552).

HdZ   *Der Heyligen ausserwoehlten Gottes Zeugen, Bekennern vnd Martyrern . . . Historien . . .* (Strassburg: Heirs of Balthasar Beck, 1552; subsequent volumes II-VIII, Strassburg: Emmel, 1554-1558).

HdM   *Historien der Martyrer . . .* , 2 vols. (Strassburg: Josias Rihel, 1571, 1572).

Manuscripts

AST　"Archives du Chapitre de Saint-Thomas," Archives municipales de Strasbourg, France.

SAU　Stadtarchiv, Ulm, Federal Republic of Germany.

TB　"Thesaurus Baumianus: Thesaurus Epistolicus Reformatorum Alsaticorum" (copied by Johann Wilhelm Baum et al.) in the Bibliothèque nationale et universitaire de Strasbourg, France (microfilm copies, Center for Reformation Research, Saint Louis, Missouri).

Introduction

GOD'S CHOSEN WITNESSES, CONFESSORS, AND MARTYRS

With the Protestant Reformation an age of martyrs came once again to Western Christendom. Not since the early church and the conversion of the European tribes had fresh tales of ultimate sacrifice and bold heroism for the sake of the faith stirred and inspired pious hearts. The Middle Ages had, indeed, seen people die for their deviant beliefs; but for the most part those martyrs had left no disciples to celebrate the spiritual triumphs of their blood and their ashes.

But in the age of the Reformation, martyrs summoned others by their bold confessions to stand up for the faith. Their stories found chroniclers who celebrated the martyrs' devotion and who continued their battle by setting their message and example before the reading public. Above all, John Foxe in England used word and woodcuts to conjure up visions of vicious torment and bold, defiant suffering. Clear and incisive critiques of medieval religion and forthright confessions of the Evangelical faith echoed through his pages. Foxe's sagas fascinated little English Christians sitting at their fathers' feet on Sunday afternoons for over three centuries and rallied them against the persecuting foe for the safety of both nation and religion.

More than exciting stories, this and other martyrologies constitute a significant part of a profound shift in the piety of Western Europe. They represent one important instrument in the transformation of practices connected with the veneration of the saints, which lay near the heart of medieval piety. Different Protestant traditions used martyrology to a greater or lesser extent, and the role of the martyrbook gives one indication of the flavor of specific national or confessional reformations. In this study I use the martyrology of Ludwig Rabus as the occasion for examining how second- and third-generation Lutheranism dealt with the new beliefs regarding the saints, who had previously functioned as purveyors of divine power on earth and as mediators between earth and heaven. The relatively limited success of Rabus's martyrbook—in comparison to the greater success of martyrologies in Calvinist and Anglican churches—points to differences in the historical and political situation and focuses on the specific dogmatic emphases of each reformation.

In celebrating the heroism of the martyr, sixteenth-century propagandists were returning to a genre which had satisfied the first Christians' need for heroic figures and for a framework in which to interpret the events—often evil—which surrounded them. In addition, it provided a model for the pious life and emphasized the importance of the Word of God for a Christian way of life. According to William C. Weinrich, in his study of the relationship of the Holy Spirit to martyrdom in early Christian literature, the earliest views of martyrdom connected the martyrs' suffering with Christ's suffering and with their witness to the Word of God. But already in the second century, this understanding of martyrdom was giving way to another perspective: "Martyrdom began to be viewed as a courageous exercise of the human will on behalf of religious truth, and as such, Christian martyrdom began to take on tragic proportions. It was the evil end of righteous men who now deserved reward and honor for their bravery and courage."[1]

Accretions to the Christian understanding of martyrdom were easily drawn from pagan religions and mixed with the ways in which believers had interpreted the role of the martyr and the necessity of martyrdom. For instance, Peter Brown points out that the relic of the saint might be revered and his or her special day be observed with appropriate ceremony and thus the sainted martyr was "associated with unambiguously good happenings;" nevertheless, "the relic itself still carried with it the dark shadows of its origin." The saint who conveyed the unalloyed mercy of God to the Christian community had died an evil death "inflicted by an evil act of power." Thus, the martyrs of the church represented more than merely triumph over physical pain, more than almost unfathomable heroism: They represented "a dialogue with and a triumph over unjust power." The martyred saints of the early church had provided its adherents with a more immediate sense of security within the divine power which had given these saints courage to face evil and ho-

---

[1]William C. Weinrich, *Spirit and Martyrdom, A Study of the Work of the Holy Spirit in Contexts of Persecution and Martyrdom in the New Testament and Early Christian Literature* (Washington DC: University Press of America, 1981) 279-80; see particularly summaries on 79 and 205.

liness to overcome it.[2]

As Christianity assumed legal and then secure cultural status in the Roman Empire during the period between Constantine and the successors of Julian the Apostate, the ever fresh supply of martyred heroes diminished and finally disappeared. The transformation of the Christian faith into the Mediterranean, and later Germanic and Celtic, cultural religion of Europe brought with it a partial loss of the biblical sense of history and the rise to dominance of certain baptized pagan, mythical attitudes. These attitudes transformed the Christian hero from a historic figure engaged in battle against historic foes bent on the destruction of the faith into a mythical figure engaged in conflict against evil forces dedicated to the harassment of everyday life and the damnation of the individual soul.[3] The saint, on the basis of his or her holiness, was thought to command the power to meet the needs of people who encountered signs of their own helplessness and impotence at every turn. Peasants and townspeople looked to cunning men, soothsayers, and witches, but above all to the saints, to provide for their physical well-being and for vengeance, love, and reassurance about death.[4] Beyond that, local patron saints also provided a glue for the community; they "personified the communal identity of their city, town, village, and nation; they cast their protective mantle across generations; they brought the faithful together

----

[2]Peter Brown,*The Cult of the Saints. Its Rise and Function in Latin Christianity* (Chicago: University of Chicago Press, 1981) 101.

[3]It is important to note, as Peter Brown does in *Cult of the Saints,* esp. 1-22, that there were also marked differences between, for instance, ancient Mediterranean beliefs in the gods and Christian veneration of the martyrs, particularly in regard to the humanity of the saints and the grave as focal point for their veneration. Brown's evidence in this book and in his article, "The Rise and Function of the Holy Man in Late Antiquity," *Society and the Holy in Late Antiquity* (Berkeley: University of California Press, 1982) 103-52, also makes clear that the saints of late-antique and early-medieval Christianity took on many of the functions of the ancient gods, not only of Mediterranean cultures but also of Germanic religious life. The relationship between pagan worship and Christian veneration of the saints was extensively discussed in the scholarship of the last century; see the differing points of view expressed by Ernst Lucius, *Die Anfänge des Heiligenkults in der christlichen Kirche,* Gustav Anrich, ed. (Tübingen: Mohr/Siebeck, 1904), and Hippolyte Delehaye, *Sanctus, Essai sur le culte des saintes dan l'antiquité* (Brussels: Société des Bollandistes, 1927) and *Les origines du culte des martyrs* (Brussels: Société des Bollandistes, 1933).

[4]Donald Weinstein and Rudolph M. Bell, *Saints & Society, the Two Worlds of Western Christendom, 1000-1700* (Chicago: University of Chicago Press, 1982) 208-209, 141-50; cf. 4-5, 37, 69, 159-60; and Keith Thomas, *Religion and the Decline of Magic* (New York: Scribner, 1971) 25-29, cf. 14-15.

in processions to commemorate past favors and implore future ones."[5]
The saints had taken their place near the very heart of the medieval faith.

Protestant reformers—and also many of their Counter-Reforma-
tion opponents—recognized the anti-biblical elements in the paganism
which had been appropriated and transformed by the under-staffed and
ill-equipped missions to various parts of Europe from the fourth through
eleventh centuries. The Protestants repudiated this dehistoricizing of the
heroic and the holy associated with these pagan accretions, and they
strove to revive the early Christian sense of history. They reclaimed providential power over daily human life for God alone, and they insisted that
mediation with him is provided by Jesus Christ alone. This meant that
holy people could no longer function as intercessors or workers of magic.

The most important medieval literary work that had embodied and
conveyed the myths regarding these intermediary sources of power, the
Golden Legend, became one focus of Protestant attack, and, as Helen C.
White has demonstrated in the case of John Foxe, was viewed as a counter-
model for his own works.[6] The reformers' theological convictions would
have forced them in any case to return to a view that the confession of
faith formed the heart of Christian piety. Focus on holy people now came
to mean a focus on those who confessed the Word and in that confession
demonstrated and advertised the power of God. That point could be effectively made, it occurred to some reformers, through a substitute for the
Golden Legend in the form of a martyrology.

Thus the story of the displacement of medieval saints in the piety
of Western Europe involves the story of the development of the history
of confessors and confessions, of martyrs and messages, of teachers and
teachings, doctors and doctrines. The sharp conflict between Protestants
and Roman Catholics in the Reformation era, by producing fresh martyrs
for the faith, aided this revival of the early Christian sense of the connection between the holy and heroic and the historic and confessional. No
Roman Catholic persecution of the rising Protestant movement made a
more dramatic impact on the Reformation than did that of Mary Tudor in
England, and no martyrologist exploited his craft more skillfully or with

---

[5]Ibid., 108-109.

[6]Helen C. White, *Tudor Books of Saints and Martyrs* (Madison: University of
Wisconsin Press, 1963) 135-41. On the medieval martyrological tradition, see
Jacques Dubois, *Les martyrologes du moyen âge latin (Typologie des sources du Moyen
Âge occidental* fasc. 26) (Turnhout, Belgium: Brepols, 1978); Henri Quentin, *Les
martyrologes historiques du Moyen Âge. Étude sur la formation du martyrologue romain*
(Paris, 1908; Aalen: Scientia, 1969); and René Aigren, *L'Hagiographie. Ses sources,
ses méthodes, son histoire* (Paris: Bloud and Gay, 1953) esp. 51-64.

greater influence than did John Foxe.

Foxe first published a Latin martyrbook on the continent, where he had fled at the outset of Mary's reign. Her government supplied him with the bulk of the subjects treated in his great martyrology, the *Acts and Monuments*. His first attempt at reciting tales of martyrs appeared in Strassburg in 1554, nine years before the publication of his master work in English. Five years later, in Basel he expanded this work into a volume which set the sufferings of John Wyclif and his Lollard successors before the Latin-reading audience on the continent.[7] When Foxe returned to England in early 1559, soon after the accession of Queen Elizabeth, his publisher, Nicholas Brylinger, cast about for someone to complete what must have been an item with a promising market and found Heinrich Pantaleone, a member of the medical faculty at the University of Basel.

Pantaleone provided a complementary volume to the one Foxe had issued in 1559 on British martyrs; the second volume, appearing in 1563, treated continental martyrs.[8] In his preface to that work Pantaleone offered his observation on Foxe's place within the development of sixteenth-century Protestant martyrology: "There have been others, of course, who have undertaken the task of describing the subject of the martyrs with great usefulness both before and after Foxe." He named two whom he considered chief among these. The second name mentioned was that of Jean Crespin, a printer in Geneva, whose martyrology had appeared in August of 1554, within weeks of the publication of Foxe's *Com-*

---

[7]*Commentarii rerum ecclesia gestarum, maximarumque per totam Europam persecutionum, a Wiclevi temporibus ad hanc usque aetatem descriptio* (Strassburg: Wendelin Rihel, 1554); *Rerum in ecclesia gestarum, quae postremis et periculosis his temporibus evenerunt, maximarumque per Europam persecutionum, ac Sanctorum Dei martyrum, ceterarumque rerum si quae insignioris exempli sint, digesti per regna et nationes commentarii* (Basel: Brylinger and Oporinus, 1559). For a brief overview of Foxe's career, see John T. McNeill, "John Foxe: Historiographer, Disciplinarian, Tolerationist," *Church History* 43 (1974): 216-29. On Foxe's long-term impact, see William Haller, "John Foxe and the Puritan Revolution," *The Seventeenth Century, Studies in the History of English Thought and Literature,* Richard Foster Jones, ed., (Stanford: Stanford University Press, 1951) 209-24. On the development of Protestant martyrology in the Reformation, see A. G. Dickens and John M. Tonkin, with Kenneth Powell, *The Reformation in Historical Thought* (Cambridge: Harvard University Press, 1985), 39-57.

[8]*Martyrum Historia, hoc est maximarumque rerum insignium, in Ecclesia Christi postremis a periculosis his temporibus gestarum, atque certo consilio per regna et nationes distributarum, commentarii. Pars secunda* (Basel: Brylinger, 1563).

mentaries in Strassburg. The first-named was Ludwig Rabus,[9] whose first effort at martyrology, *Accounts of God's Chosen Witnesses, Confessors, and Martyrs,* had also appeared in Strassburg, but in 1552—two years before Foxe published.

John Foxe, indeed, made a far greater impact on the religious and political life of England than did any other martyrologist of the Protestant Reformation in any other land. Yet, it must be admitted, Crespin and also Adriaen van Haemstede (whose Dutch martyrbook of 1559 borrowed heavily from Crespin and Rabus) did have significant impact on French and Dutch Calvinism respectively. In addition, martyr stories which circulated among the Anabaptists played an important role in rallying them to faithfulness.[10] It must also be noted that these Protestants were not alone in forging a new form of the martyrology. Roman Catholic authors in the later sixteenth century followed the examples of Rabus, Crespin, and Foxe in developing new martyrological traditions, especially where Roman Catholicism came under attack from Protestantism or from non-Christian cultures into which it was advancing.[11]

---

[9]Ibid. 3v-[4]r: "Fuerunt quidem aliqui qui ante Foxum et post illum magna utilitate res Martyrum describere aggressi sunt, inter quos D. Ludouicus Rabus & Ioannes Crispinus fuere praecipui."

[10]Crespin, *Recveil De Plvsievrs Personnes qui ont constamment enduré la mort pour le Nom de nostre Seigneur Iesus Christ depuis Iean Hus iusques a ceste anne presente M.D.L IIII* (Geneva: Crespin, 1554); Van Haemstede, *De Geschiedenisse ende den doodt der vromer Martelaren, die om ghetuyghenisse des Euangeliums Haer bloedt ghestort hebben* ([Antwerp?], 1559). On Crespin, see Arthur Piaget and Gabrielle Berthoud, *Notes sur le Livre des Martyrs de Jean Crespin* (Neuchâtel: Secretariat de l'Université, 1930), Jean François Gilmont, *Jean Crespin, un éditeur réformé du XVIe siècle* (Geneva: Droz, 1981), idem, "La genèse du martyrologue d'Adrien van Haemstede (1559)," *Revue d'histoire ecclesiastique* LXIII (1968): 379-414. See the more narrowly focused study of G. Moreau, "Contribution à l'Histoire du Livre des Martyrs," *Bulletin de la Société de l'Histoire du Protestantisme français* 103 (1957): 173-99. Phyllis Mack Crew, *Calvinist Preaching and Iconoclasm in the Netherlands, 1544-1569* (Cambridge: Cambridge University Press, 1978) 73-82, places van Haemstede's work in its historical and literary context. Tieleman Janszoon van Bracht (1625-1664), in his *Het bloedigh tooneel der doops-gesinde en weereloose Christinen* (Dordrecht: Braat, 1660), brought together much of the Anabaptist martyrological tradition.

[11]See Lorenz Surius, *De probatis sanctorum historiis . . .* (Cologne: Colinius and Quentel, 1570-1575), 6 vols., an expansion of his *Sanctorum priscorum vitae* of 1551-1558; and Georg Witzel, *Chorus sanctorum omnium . . .* (Cologne: Quentel, 1554). Even before the appearance of the Protestant martyrologies, Wolfgang Kyriander of Oettingen had used the genre as a vehicle of anti-Protestant polemic, in his *Persequutiones ecclesiae, quas secundum historicos & Chronographos . . . Collatio* (Ingolstadt: Weissenhort, 1541). On the development of Roman Catholic martyrology in the early modern period, see Weinstein and Bell, *Saints & Society* 160-61.

But the first of this band of sixteenth-century martyrologists, Ludwig Rabus, has been the least remembered of them all, even though he was a leader of moderate importance in south German Lutheranism during the period of its most severe internal struggles and even though some volumes of the first edition of his martyrbook were reprinted several times and created sufficient demand for a second edition.

In a biographical dictionary of contemporary Germans that Pantaleone published in 1566, he commented briefly on Rabus and his martyrology. In 1565 Pantaleone had visited Ulm, where Rabus was superintendent of the city's churches. He reported on the basis of this visit—in the conventions of the Renaissance biographer—that already as a child Rabus had been recognized for his outstanding ability, which had led him to the study of languages and the arts. After studying at the University of Tübingen, Rabus had heard Luther and Melanchthon and their colleagues at the University of Wittenberg for nearly a year and a half and then, after a brief interlude of service in his native Memmingen, became a pastor in Strassburg. As pastor in Strassburg his piety and erudition had been striking, Pantaleone stated, and when called to Ulm to undo the effects of the Augsburg Interim, Rabus had demonstrated great skill in "arranging all things according to God's Word" in the city's religious life. Pantaleone, of course, could not avoid calling his reader's attention to Rabus's book of martyrs: "He wrote also a very distinguished work on the Christian martyrs and divided it into eight parts by regions and time periods, . . . with this work he had commended the aptitude of his genius to posterity."[12]

In spite of Pantaleone's inflated description of Rabus, the reputation of the first Protestant compiler of martyr stories has not sustained his fame into the twentieth century. While Rabus's eighteenth-century biographer mentioned that Rabus was "among the Protestants the first to attempt an exhaustive collection of the stories of the martyrs, and indeed he did create one,"[13] and popular German works on Christian saints and martyrs mentioned Rabus on rare occasions even into the twentieth cen-

---

[12]*Prosopographiae herorum atque illustrium virorum totius Germaniae, Pars tertia* (Basel: Brylinger, 1566) 509.

[13]Johann Georg Schelhorn, "Nachricht von dem Leben D. Ludwig Rabus, eines wolverdienten Gottesgelehrten in dem 16. Jahrhundert," in Johann Bartholomaeus Riederer, ed., *Nuezliche und angeneme Abhandlungen aus der Kirchen-Buecher- und-Gelerten-Geschichte von verschiedenen Verfassern zusammengetragen* (Altdorf: Ammermueller, 1768) 217.

tury,[14] his name disappeared from some of the basic reference works of nineteenth-century German Protestantism. He has fared little better in twentieth-century scholarship.[15]

We call these works which come from Rabus's pen and others' "martyrologies," as Pantaleone did, because they were patterned after late-patristic and medieval martyrological works, and because the word "martyr" did indeed appear in Rabus's title. And yet, Rabus's work might

---

[14]Rabus made an impact on the German Lutheranism of the American frontier: C. J. Fick, educated in Göttingen, pastor in Missouri, used Rabus in *Die Märtyrer der Evangelisch-Lutherischen Kirche, Bd. 1* (St. Louis: Niedner, 1854), VI-VIII. Cf. also Ferdinand Piper, *Die Zeugen der Wahrheit, Lebensbilder zum evangelischen Kalender* (Leipzig: Tauchnitz, 1874), III:590; and Otto Michaelis, *Protestantisches Märtyrbuch* (Stuttgart: Steinkopf, 1917) 7.

[15]Rabus is covered in a brief article by Wagenmann in *Allgemeine Deutsche Biographie* (Leipzig: Duncker & Humblot, 1898) 27:97-99; but he is mentioned neither in *Die Religion in Geschichte und Gegenwart*, Hermann Gunkel et al., eds., 4 (Tübingen: Mohr [Siebeck], 1913) nor its subsequent editions, nor in *Realencyklopädie für protestantische Theologie und Kirche*, 3. ed., Albert Hauck, ed., 17 (Leipzig: Hinrich, 1905). Leon E. Halkin ignored Rabus completely in his "Hagiographie Protestante," *Analecta Bollianda* 68 (1950): 153-63. Donald R. Kelley, "Martyrs, Myths, and the Massacre: The Background of St. Bartholomew," in Alfred Soman, ed., *The Massacre of St. Bartholomew. Reappraisals and Documents* (The Hague: Nijhoff, 1974) 183, mentions Rabus but gives him little space. Johannes Moritzen, *Die Heiligen in der nachreformatorischen Zeit, I* (Flensburg: Wolf, 1971) 20-21, seems to have found only the first volume of the second edition. A. G. Dickens, *Contemporary Historians of the German Reformation* (London: Institute of Germanic Studies, University of London, 1978) 15-16, provides a very brief overview of Rabus's martyrology but notes that "the influence of Rabus can hardly be compared with that of the other three," that is, Foxe, Crespin, and van Haemstede. Dickens and Tonkin say more in *The Reformation in Historical Thought*, 41, 51-52. However, they incorrectly date both editions, imply a much more extensive use of John Bale's work than was actually the case, and imply that the work is more of a broad treatment of the history of the church than it actually is. More positive is the appreciation of Rabus's work in the *Bibliographie des martyrologes protestants Néerlandais*, Ferdinand van der Haeghen, ed. (LaHaye: Nyhoff, 1890) II:581, and in the estimate of C. Sepp, *Geschiedkundige nasporingen* (Leiden, 1873) 60, who calls Rabus's work a "bibliography of martyrologies." See also Annemarie and Wolfgang Brückner, "Zeugen des Glaubens und ihre Literatur, Altväterbeispiele, Kalenderheilige, protestantische Märtyrer und evangelische Lebenszeugnisse," in Wolfgang Brückner, ed., *Volkserzählung und Reformation* (Berlin: Schmidt, 1974) 523; Gerhard Dedeke, "Die protestantischen Märtyrerbücher von Ludwig Rabus, Jean Crespin und Adriaen van Haemstede und ihr gegenseitigen Verhältnis" (licentiate dissertation, University of Halle-Wittenberg, 1924) passim; and Wolfgang Hieber, "Legende, protestantische Bekennerhistorie, Legendenhistorie, Studien zur literarischen Gestaltung der Heiligenthematik im Zeitalter der Glaubenskämpfe" (doctoral dissertation, University of Würzburg) 1970, esp. 138-60.

better be labeled a "book of confessors." Following the model of the most ancient historians of the church, such as Eusebius, Rabus focused primarily on Christian witness in general, rather than specifically on witness unto death. For Rabus, confessing the faith was more important than dying for the faith. Most specifically, he emphasized the content of Christian confession. Like his mentors, Luther and Melanchthon, Rabus placed the Word of God at the center of his theology; that Word takes dynamic form in the proclamation and witness of Christ's followers. Thus, Rabus's "martyrbook" contained long written confessions and extensive records of oral testimony. Fewer of its pages feature exciting tales of personal sacrifice than is the case with other Protestant martyrologists. This emphasis on bold confession of the Word of God became to a large extent *the* saintly activity of the Lutheran Reformation. Although the Reformers recognized the holiness of secular callings, they emphasized the proclamation and confession of the gospel of Jesus Christ as the most eternally significant of God's assignments to his human creatures. Thus, Rabus's martyrology indicated the Lutheran substitution of a new kind of piety in place of the medieval veneration of the saints. Rabus's piety centered in God's Word, which, as a Lutheran, he regarded as God's active and powerful instrument for accomplishing his will in the world.

Foxe's *Acts and Monuments* could provide a focus for the study of the displacement or replacement of the medieval saints and for the study of the theological or ideological approach of English Puritanism to the holy and to history, as twentieth-century studies have shown.[16] But the investigation of the ways in which German Lutherans sought to deal with saints and martyrs cannot be focused on a single work or a single author, certainly not on the first Protestant martyrologist. In this volume, I survey and analyze Rabus's work along with other approaches and materials which shed light on how Lutherans digested and transformed this vital element of Christian life and thought, theology and piety. Although the Lutheran churches retained some elements of the medieval way of remembering the saints in liturgy and art, and although Martin Luther himself assumed a position as Christian hero at least vaguely reminiscent of that of the medieval saint, Lutherans abandoned the veneration of the saints apparently with relative ease. Perhaps northern Germans had never had so strong an allegiance to the saints as did Christians in other parts of Christendom. The absence of widespread, severe persecution in Ger-

---

[16]See White, *Tudor Books;* and J. F. Mozley, *John Foxe and His Book* (London: SPCK, 1940); William Haller, *The Elect Nation, The Meaning and Relevance of Foxe's Book of Martyrs* (New York: Harper, 1963); and V. Norskov Olson, *John Foxe and the Elizabethan Church* (Berkeley: University of California Press, 1973).

many prevented Lutherans from becoming heroic martyrs for their faith. Lutheran authors tended to treat the history of the faith in other than biographical genres, even though some had attempted early on to provide substitutes for the lives of the saints. But finally, Luther's insistence that all believers are saints, and that no believers could retain the trappings of providential power and salvific intervention, undercut the practice of the veneration of the saints. God provides for all human needs, Luther taught, and Christ alone can intercede for human salvation. Saints had been torn from their superhuman position and had become servants of God under his Word in every station of life.

CHAPTER ONE

Saints
and Martyrs
at Wittenberg

LUTHER AND MELANCHTHON
ON THE VENERATION OF THE SAINTS

IN 1552 LUDWIG RABUS informed his German readers at the beginning
of his book of martyrs:

> Precisely for these purposes [for our encouragement, comfort and
> instruction] there arose in the holy Christian church the ancient
> custom, long in use, that the stories of certain outstanding confes-
> sors and martyrs of Christ, whose faith and confession were cer-
> tain and above suspicion, would be presented each year, on a
> designated day, to the people. Sermons were delivered on their
> faith, patience, confession, and constancy, so that the simple folk
> might be improved through their example and learn to follow this
> example as the confessors and martyrs followed Christ's example.

But Rabus was well aware that he faced a much more complicated problem in dealing with the lives and examples of holy people.

> Unfortunately this custom, like so many other good things, fell into
> a great and ruinous abuse through false, deceiving doctrine. For
> these *legenda* (as they are called) were falsified and ruined with silly
> fables and patent lies for the most part, particularly in the German
> language, so that a person cannot follow their example if he wants

to, and should not follow them if indeed he really could. In addition, they were presented to the people as mediators and intercessors between God and the human creatures, through whose merit and intercession grace must be won for the poor sinners.[1]

Rabus viewed this as "in error and idolatrous, subject to censure and condemnation."

Rabus's words reflected the convictions of his Wittenberg instructors. Despite his love for favorite saints and his delight in stories about them, Luther—even before posting the Ninety-Five Theses—had expressed reservations regarding the popular medieval ascription of power to the saints, in sermons on the Decalog in 1516.[2] In his program of reformation set forth in his four great tracts of 1520, Luther's antipathy toward the whole range of beliefs and practices associated with the veneration of the saints was made clear. In discussing abuses of the confessional, he criticized teaching "things which are against the service of God, against faith and the chief commandments—such as their running about on pilgrimages, the perverse worship of the saints, the lying saints' legends, the various ways of trusting in works and ceremonies and practicing them."[3] Pilgrimages to holy places, veneration of holy people, and celebration of holy times, Luther was convinced, all offend God and undermine Christian piety: Calling upon the saints for heavenly intercession and for earthly exercise of magical powers takes glory away from God; travel to their shrines caused people to abandon the responsibilities of their callings in their own villages and to place their trust in personal perfor-

---

[1] HdZ, I:☞iij/r-☞iiij.

[2] "The Ten Commandments, Preached to the People of Wittenberg," 1516-1517, published 1518, WA 2:412-417. See Otto Clemens, *Luther und die Volksfrömmigkeit seiner Zeit* (Dresden: Ungelenk, 1938) 17. On Luther's view of the saints, see Lennart Pinomaa, *Die Heiligen bei Luther* (Helsinki: Luther-Agricola Gesellschaft, 1977), and Robert Lansemann, *Die Heiligentage, besonders die Marien-, Apostel-, und Engeltage in der Reformationszeit, betrachtet im Zusammenhang der reformatorischen Anschauung von den Zeremonien, von den Festen, von den Heiligen, und von den Engeln* (Göttingen: Vandenhoeck & Ruprecht, 1939) 9-39; unfortunately, the critical apparatus of the book was not published because of its author's imprisonment under the Third Reich. See also Walter Delius, "Luther und die Marienverehrung," *Theologische Literaturzeitung* 79 (1954): 410-14. Treatments of the topic by Max Lackmann (e.g., *Verehrung der Heiligen: Versuch einer lutherischen Lehre von den Heiligen* [Stuttgart: Schwabenverlag, 1958]) and Peter Manns ("Luther und die Heiligen," in Remigius Bäumer, ed., *Reformatio Ecclesiae . . . Festgabe für Erwin Iserloh* [Paderborn: Schöningh, 1980]) pursue contemporary ecumenical agendas which interfere with their historical analysis.

[3] "The Babylonian Captivity of the Church," 1520, WA 6:546; LW 36:87.

mance of religious actions and in the magical powers of the saints; festival celebrations are occasions for sinful excesses of various kinds.[4] In the Smalcald Articles Luther stated in his straightforward manner, "The invocation of the saints is one of these antichristian abuses. It conflicts with the chief article of the faith [justification through faith in the merits of Christ] and blots out the recognition of Christ. It is neither commanded nor suggested in Scripture and has no basis there at all."[5]

Luther condemned as idolatrous any adoration, invocation, or sacrifice to the saints, above all in the context of the mass. These themes were repeated in Luther's lectures on Genesis during the period in which he was addressing Rabus and others who carried on his critique of medieval practice and sought to build a new Evangelical piety during the second half of the sixteenth century. In the last decade of his life, Luther was still reacting in horror against the veneration of the saints that denied God's full exercise of saving and providential care over the lives of his people. The patriarchs, he told his students, had "regarded the promise and the works of God as sacrosanct and fully worthy of reverence and adoration." In contrast to the patriarchs' adoration of "God and God's promises and their signs" the papacy fostered "worship [of] the relics of the saints . . . the bones or the clothing of the dead."[6] Luther compared such practices to the idolatry of pagan Palestine: "People used to spurn parishes and the ministry of the Word and run to groves and the relics of the saints. And even to this day, the papists persecute the doctrine of the Word and run from the Gospel and their domestic calling to Saint James, to Mary, etc."[7] "The canonization of the saints, and the statues set up in special places for the sake of gain" were all the work of Satan and "his servants, the pope and with his entire church," who were intent on diverting believers from the forms of worship which God had ordained and centered in his Word.[8] Luther convinced his students that veneration of the saints was not only contrary to God's Word but also that it directly conflicted with God's working through his chosen instrument, that Word, in the world.

---

[4]"Open Letter to the German Nobility," 1520, WA 6:449-50, cf. 447-48; LW 44:187-88, cf. 184. "On Good Works," 1520, WA 6:229-30; LW 44:55.

[5]Bks 414.

[6]WA 44:684; LW 8:144.

[7]WA 44:521; LW 7:299.

[8]WA 42:625-26; LW 3:109.

Not only did this veneration deny God's saving power; it also debilitated pious attention to, and faith in, God's daily providence of his people. Referring to the idolatry depicted in Judges and Kings, Luther told his students that the papacy, "in a far more flagrant manner, filled everything with the idolatrous worship of the saints. One man worshiped Erasmus in order that this saint might bestow wealth. Another person worshiped Margaret in order that she might bring help to women in childbirth. And Mary was worshiped by all as a mediatrix and helper in all necessities. No one wanted to hope for or expect liberation from God."[9] Both Luther's concern for reliance solely on God and his revulsion against trust in the saints were clearly expressed in an earlier exclamation; it also made clear his rejection of the medieval concept of a holiness which lies in religious activities rather than the everyday activities of mutual human care in family life and community, which, Luther maintained, were God's way of caring for his human creatures:

> In the papacy there is a book containing the legends or accounts of the saints [Jacob of Voragine's *Golden Legend*]. I hate it intensely, solely for the reason that it tells of revolting forms of worship and silly miracles performed by idle people. These legends and accounts actually accomplish only one thing: They increase contempt of the government and of the household, yes even almost of the church itself. Therefore such tales should be shunned and utterly rejected, for the chief thing of Christian teaching is faith.[10]

In addition, it must be noted that Luther transformed the meaning of the term "saint" or "holy person" as a result of the general framework of his theology. True holiness, he believed, could not be assessed in terms of special powers for the working of superhuman feats nor in terms of heroic performances of good works. God's forgiving Word bestowed full and complete holiness on all God's chosen believers; all believers therefore were the true saints of God. Their lives were marked first of all by faith and then by prayer, love of neighbor, suffering for Christ—the practice of humanity as God had designed it in the first place. Yet all these saints were also sinners, their lives permeated by the failure to fear, love, and trust in God above all things that prevented human life on earth from enjoying the perfection of Eden. This definition of the word "saint" became Luther's primary theological definition; yet, because of its former use, he continued to use "saint" in reference to believers who had been

---

[9]*WA* 45:727; *LW* 8:203.

[10]*WA* 43:108-109; *LW* 3:325.

historically noteworthy. He did, however, change the definition of what would make a believer particularly noteworthy—not the power to mediate or provide for daily needs, but rather the assignment to confess the faith boldly.[11]

Alongside Luther on the faculty of the University of Wittenberg stood Philip Melanchthon. Melanchthon believed that the veneration of the saints had developed out of pre-Christian German pagan practices.[12] Like Luther, Melanchthon was eager to set aside practices that had afflicted the church from at least the time of Pope Gregory the Great at the turn of the seventh century, and he therefore set down the Wittenbergers' understanding of the proper Christian regard for heroes of the faith in Article XXI of the Augsburg Confession. He began with the fundamental thesis that Christians have only one mediator who intercedes for them before God, Jesus (1 Tim. 2:5). The Augsburg Confession and its Apology assert that adherents of the Confession give the saints a threefold honor. They give thanks to God because of his saints. They find their own faith strengthened by observing how good God has been to his people. They imitate the saints first in faith and then in the practice of virtues appropriate to their vocation.[13] The Apology's extensive comments on the subject of the invocation of the saints, in rebuttal to the papal Confutation of the Confession itself, summarize the negative and the positive elements of the Lutheran treatment of the saints in the sixteenth century. Melanchthon's sharp critique of medieval practice in regard to the saints addresses two distinct errors. First, his appeal to the sole propitiatory sacrifice and intercession of Christ himself repudiated the view that the saints exercise propitiatory power before God's throne. Second, by rejecting as fables and lies all the stories of the miracles worked by saints, their relics, and their holy places, he rejected the view that the saints exercise power to adjust life in general and to protect their devotees from evil powers of various kinds.

The former critique seemed more urgent to the sixteenth-century reformers and was worked out with greater clarity. Yet the latter concern was still present in 1551, when Melanchthon and his colleagues at Wittenberg formulated a new confession which was to be laid before the papal council at Trent. Melanchthon, anchoring his comments in the Lord's claim that he would share his glory with no other (Isa.42:8) and insisting

---

[11]Pinomaa, *Die Heiligen*, 141-58.

[12]"On the Church and the Authority of God's Word," *CR* 23:627.

[13]*Bks* 83b-83d, 316-26.

that God's people should serve God alone (Matt. 4:10), warned against the devil's attempts to pervert prayer by diverting it from God through pagan corruptions. He condemned invocation of the saints, singling out idolatrous prayers to Mary, for three reasons: It is impious to attribute omnipotence to creatures; it is wrong to invoke the saints, since God has not commanded it; there is one mediator between God and men, the man Christ Jesus, and no one comes to the Father except through Christ (1 Tim. 2:5, John 14:6).[14]

These positions rest upon fundamental convictions held by Luther and his associates regarding the nature of salvation, the nature of God's Word in history, and the relationship of the sacred and the profane in the created order. Luther's emphasis on salvation on the basis of God's grace alone, through the sacrifice, death, and resurrection of Jesus Christ, left no room for any saints to exercise power in the saving process. Christ alone could mediate God's saving will and its effects for the individual Christian. Luther's emphasis on the Word of God, active in human history, changed the definition of God's power and how it works in the world: No longer could mythical heroes displaying their own power command attention; those, rather, who had announced and pronounced God's saving power in his Word throughout Christian history became the new heroes of the faith. What was really important to Luther, however, was not the hero but the Word as it brought God's power to bear on human life. The "living voice of the gospel" in use, in application to people's lives, sustained God's world.[15] Those who heard that Word, in Luther's view, were not left to fend for themselves; for God provides. This left no room for special saints who could provide more immediate access to supernatural power in daily life.

Furthermore, Luther's special emphasis on the unity of the human and divine in Jesus helped bridge the gap which medieval Christians had often perceived between the distant and aweful Creator Judge and themselves. Popular medieval belief had embraced a double perception of Christ, as the judge sitting on the rainbow in all his divine majesty and power, and as the broken Man of Sorrows, who in the depths of humanity had suffered with his fellow human creatures. Luther endeavored to bring his followers to understand that the divine Christ had suffered and

---

[14]"Repetitio Confessionis Augustanae," CR 28:445-51 (Latin), 554-60 (German).

[15]See Gerhard Ebeling, Luther, an Introduction to his Thought, R. A. Wilson, trans. (Philadelphia: Fortress, 1970) 119-20, and Paul Althaus, The Theology of Martin Luther, Robert C. Schultz, trans. (Philadelphia: Fortress, 1966) 35-42.

died for them and that the human Christ exercises full divine majesty and power at the right hand of God the Father.[16] Thus, whether the stated topic focused on the role of the saints in the lives of believers or not, that subject was implicitly addressed every time the central elements of Luther's call for the reform of the church's teaching was proclaimed orally or in print, by Luther himself or any of his followers.

The proclamation of justification by grace through faith in Christ alone undoubtedly worked more effectively than did another relevant element of Luther's theological framework, namely his distinction between the sacred and the profane, for justification was relatively better understood and was perhaps more easily explained than this distinction. Luther overthrew the medieval understanding of the distinction between the sacred and the profane, as he had inherited it from popular belief and practice. He insisted that many of the sacred practices of his parents' faith, such as pilgrimages, monasticism, and veneration of relics and saints, were ungodly rather than the height of godliness, for three reasons. They were responses to the commandments of men, not of God. They did not give glory to God but served rather as devices which human creatures could use to exalt themselves before God. They distracted people from the proper performance of the callings to which God had assigned them in daily life, where, Luther believed, proper service to the Creator and Redeemer could be rendered according to God's design. God had decided to reflect his own image through the concern and care which his human creatures show for one another. They could do this by carrying out the responsibilities or offices of the three estates or situations in which God had placed them—domestic life, political life, and religious life. In these offices, which believers recognized as callings from God, God worked as if behind a mask, using his creatures to mask his presence, as he cared for creation.[17]

The Evangelical struggle against the adoration of the saints must be understood against the background of Luther's rejection of the popular medieval view that the sacred realm is the arena in which the best of human works can be performed. The Wittenbergers desired to restore the remembrance of the saints to what they believed had been its original

---

[16]Ian D. Kingston Siggins, *Martin Luther's Doctrine of Christ* (New Haven: Yale University Press, 1970); Marc Lienhart, *Luther: Witness to Jesus Christ. Stages and Themes of the Reformer's Christology,* Edwin H. Robertson, trans. (Minneapolis: Augsburg, 1982).

[17]Gustaf Wingren, *Luther on Vocation,* Carl C. Rasmussen, trans. (Philadelphia: Muhlenberg, 1957) provides the best introduction to this complex of ideas.

function. This imposed upon them, in their view, the necessity of assaulting the belief that the saints could provide supernatural power to change a person's relationship with God or mollify the afflictions of this life. The reformers thus engaged that amalgam of early Christian celebration of the martyr's confession of faith with the remnants of earlier Mediterranean and European religious practices, acccording to which devotees once had looked to gods and now looked to saints as sources of divine power for specific human needs through the manipulation of special times, special places, and special things.[18] Although other medieval theologians had criticized aspects of this non-biblical view of reality, it was not until the Reformation that a formidable attack on it could be launched—and then because Luther offered a reformulation of the framework in which the saints should be viewed, a rethinking of the relationship between the sacred and the profane. His success in bringing other Western European Christians to share this view was mixed at best, even among his own followers, who did not always grasp fully the implications of his attack on the popular adoration of the saints or the use of the power that, at least in the popular mind, was attributed to them.

Luther, Melanchthon, and their students combatted this false belief directly; but because the saints, through their intervention in daily life with their magical powers, had played such a great role in the preservation or restoration of the good in the lives of the common people, the task of refocusing pious attention toward the provident Creator, revealed in Jesus Christ, posed some difficulties. Throughout the sixteenth century and into the seventeenth, the treatment of the saints in any form always carried with it the danger of arousing old associations. Thus, the displacement of medieval beliefs regarding the saints required more than the positive enunciation of Luther's understanding of God's saving work in Jesus Christ and his daily providence. It also required engaging the saints on their own territory, so that old associations with their names and places and days would be defused. When the pious peasant confronted a crisis and turned not only to his Savior and Lord, Jesus Christ, of whom his pastor spoke at every worship service, but also to the village patron saint or the appropriate auxiliary saint, of whom his grandmother had always spoken so fondly, the battle had to be fought again. The reformers did battle against such temptations for their people in postils and explanations of the catechism, in occasional treatises and biblical commentaries, in devotional tracts and confessional documents, in the works that traced the history of God's people, and in popular biographies.

---

[18]On medieval practice, see material cited in the introduction, notes 2-5.

LUTHER AND MELANCHTHON
ON THE HISTORY OF GOD'S PEOPLE

Because the Wittenbergers presupposed that the mythical magicians of the *Golden Legend* were imported remnants of paganism, and because they were convinced that God had actually worked historically to save his people, when the reformers looked for human heroes of the faith, they focused on historical figures who had confessed the Word of God. Early in his public career Luther hailed contemporary confessors and martyrs of the recent past as this kind of hero, but he saw them in the context of a long history of heirs of Christ's suffering, who had confessed his Word through the sacrifice of their lives.

Luther's understanding of history arose from the pages of Scripture, where he found that God's Word, either as judgment or mercy, propelled the events of human life at all times. Whether in the good which he willed for his creation or in the evil which aroused his wrath, God had been in control and he had guided human history with his providential care to arrive at his purposes.[19] "God's Word was history, and God's Word created history."[20]

Human history, Luther believed, stretches from creation to the Last Day. Its climax had already come in the most dramatic intervention of God's Word in human life, in human flesh as Jesus of Nazareth. But God was continually intervening in the midst of this world's developments as he did battle with Satan and all the evils which the archfiend fashioned to oppose the Word and the people of God. At the center of Luther's interpretation of world events stood his conviction that God and Satan continuously engage in conflict. Thus, the people of God were always suffering attacks from the devil and his legions, including his human cohorts.[21]

This struggle between the church, God's faithful sheep who hear the voice of the Shepherd, and Satan's minions was always taking place on the field of "doctrine," that is, the faithful and effective proclamation and application of God's Word as revealed in Scripture. This proclamation meant, for Luther and Melanchthon, the effective delivery of the content of that Word to people, that is, the turning of sinners to repen-

---

[19]John M. Headley, *Luther's View of Church History* (New Haven: Yale University Press, 1963) 1-19, 42-55, Martin Schmidt, "Luthers Schau der Geschichte," *Lutherjahrbuch* 30 (1963): 33-34.

[20]Ibid., 59.

[21]Ibid., 34-51, 57-63; Headley, *Church History*, 19-41, 59-69.

tance under God's law and the creation of trust in God, which transforms their lives through God's gospel.[22] The devil, the father of lies (John 8:44), triumphs whenever he perverts the biblical proclamation, Luther was certain. Thus, human history consists of one attempt after another by the devil and his human liars to lead people away from the biblical truth regarding God's love for his people in Christ.

A second presupposition informing Luther's understanding of history was his belief that God works in contraries—that the wisdom of God is foolishness to this world and that his power exhibits itself in what the world considers weakness (1 Cor. 1:18-2:4).[23] Following Paul, Luther taught that God had succeeded in his battle against the devil and his lies by submitting himself to the foolishness and weakness of death on the cross. God's people cannot expect anything different; the cross, or persecution, is a mark of the church, Luther insisted in 1539.[24] At roughly the same time, commenting to his students on Genesis 29:1, he noted that life in the Word reflects Christ's own suffering. "In our life, when we are exercised by the Word in the church and use the sacraments, we are also plagued by various trials, and our faith is tested like gold in a furnace. This is the true saintliness, because of which we are called and are saints. For the Holy Spirit sanctifies through the Word taken hold of through faith, and he mortifies the flesh by means of sufferings and troubles, in order that the saints may be quickened and may present their bodies 'as a living sacrifice.' "[25]

Both his understanding of the perpetual conflict between God's Word and Satan's lies in human history and his sense that God works through suffering and sacrifice predisposed Luther to pay at least some attention to the struggles and confessions of contemporary martyrs.

Luther was profoundly affected by the martyrdom of those who had died because they were proclaiming his message. The first hymn which he himself composed celebrated the witness of two members of his

---

[22]On Melanchthon's concept of doctrine, which Luther shared, see Peter Fraenkel, "Revelation and Tradition. Notes on Some Aspects of Doctrinal Continuity in the Theology of Philip Melanchthon," *Studia Theologica* 13 (1959): 97-133, esp. 117-18.

[23]On this complex of ideas in Luther's thought, usually labeled his "theology of the cross," see Alister E. McGrath, *Luther's Theology of the Cross* (Oxford: Basil Blackwell, 1985).

[24]"On the Councils and the Church," *WA* 50:641-42; *LW* 41:164-65. See Schmidt, "Luthers Schau," 51-54; Headley, *Church History*, 40-41, 11-13.

[25]*WA* 43:612; *LW* 5:266.

own Augustinian Order, who were burned on 1 July 1523, for espousing Luther's teachings. Heinrich Voes and Johannes Esch, it had been said, recanted when faced with the flames; but Luther rejected that rumor. "The boys, they stood firm as a tower / And mocked the sophists' trouble." With patience—Luther's poetic description continued—his two followers had faced their end, gave thanks to God for their rescue from Satan, and received from God the ability to offer themselves to him. Luther's hymn particularly emphasized the evil nature of those servants of the "arch-fiend and ancient foe," "the Sophists from Louvain," who hated the Augustinians for confessing "In God we should trust solely / For man is always full of lies / We should distrust him wholly." These enemies of God's truth had tried but failed to get Voes and Esch to renounce God's Word.[26] Luther had learned how the church has always sketched the story of its martyrs.

The same traditional elements of the martyrs' story—their boldness, their confession of faith, their defiance of the enemies of God's Word, who cruelly sacrificed them on the pyre or the gibbet—occur in a number of other treatments of martyrs for the Lutheran cause which Luther penned, in one form or another, over the next two decades.[27] To console the colleagues of Heinrich von Zutphen, who had been burned in Ditmarschen in December 1524, Luther wrote a commentary on Psalm 9, along with a brief preface and a narrative of the martyr's death. In the execution and in the confession of Brother Heinrich, Luther sensed "the presence of the Spirit of God;" in Heinrich's ministry of the Word contemporaries could, wrote Luther:

> . . . experience how the Spirit demonstrates and confirms his Word with great and mighty deeds, as has been his custom from the beginning. Above all, he has given us brave and bold hearts, so that in many places both preachers and hearers are daily being added to the number of the saints. Some have shed their blood, others have suffered imprisonment, others, moreover, have been driven from their homes, but all of them endure the shame of the cross of Christ. In our day the pattern of the true Christian life has reappeared, terrible in the world's eyes, since it means suffering and persecution, but precious and priceless in God's sight.[28]

---

[26]WA 35:411-15; LW 53:214-16.

[27]E.g., his "The Burning of Brother Henry," 1525, WA 18:224-40; LW 32:265-86; "On Leonard Kayser, Burned in Bavaria for the Sake of the Gospel," 1527, WA 23:452-76; preface to "Robert Barnes' Confession of Faith," 1540, WA 51:449-51.

[28]WA 18:224; LW 32:265-266.

The martyrdom of his followers was reproducing the ancient pattern of the true Christian life, Luther believed. He displayed an extensive knowledge of and keen interest in the history of those new martyrs, as did his colleagues at Wittenberg, particularly Melanchthon. Both of them treated the history of the martyrs' confessions of faith within the general framework of their periodization of human history. The schemes for the periodization of history which Luther and Melanchthon used were coin of the common intellectual currency of their time. The development of Luther's several interpretations of the unfolding of history undoubtedly sprang from both medieval and humanist models and grew through his dialogue with Melanchthon, who lectured on history at Wittenberg, and with Melanchthon's students, such as Johann Carion, who published, in 1532, the first significant Wittenberg history, his *Chronicle* of world history. John M. Headley, however, argues that Luther developed his analysis of history before Carion arrived in Wittenberg.[29]

Luther did not always use the same periodization as he discussed history. At times, after one medieval fashion, he defined six ages of the earth, the ages of Adam, Noah, Abraham, David, Christ, and the pope. At other times he used a tripartite division of history: the eras of the patriarchs; of Abraham and the Law of Moses, which climaxed in "the final revelation in Jesus Christ [which] constitutes for Church history the central event in the light of which everything before and after must be judged;"[30] and finally of the New Testament, the era which Headley significantly entitles "The Persecutions."[31]

In treating this era of the New Testament, Luther did not lock his view tightly into sharply defined periods of the purity and adulteration of the Word of God, as might be expected. Neither of the two opposing principles of much Christian interpretation of church history, namely the idea of tradition and the idea of a fall from the purity of the Word, can be imposed unambiguously on Luther's thought. According to the idea of tradition, one claims that "the Church possesses a pure, uncontaminated, divine substance, which it bears in its succession down through time,"[32] in a chain of witnesses unbroken, even though it may become weak and thin. Melanchthon and the students of the two great Witten-

---

[29]Headley, *Church History*, 110.

[30]Ibid., 142.

[31]Ibid., 143.

[32]Ibid., 156.

bergers held this view, as we shall see; but Luther did not. "The whole idea was quite antithetical to his understanding of the relation between [the] Church and the Word. The source and continuity of the Church exist in the Word of God."[33] The idea of a fall "conceives of Church history as a progressive decline of the Church through a deprivation of revelation beginning in a fall, defection, or apostasy."[34] Headley carefully refines the significance of Luther's concept of apostasy in the church: The "fall" of the church is not merely a decline from an earlier pristine state, but it is above all disobedience to God's command, a phenomenon found to one degree or another in every age of the church. As Headley says:

> . . . For Luther no period, not even the age of the patriarchs, is normative; legitimacy does not exist in a community's congruence with a past period of the Church but in its obedience to the ever-present and active Word of God. . . . the idea [of a fall] emphasized discipleship rather than faith as the true mark of the Church. But Luther, despite all his eloquence concerning the period of martyrs, is too conscious of the doctrinal foundations of the Church's life to be misled by its outer appearance. Faith, not blood, constitutes the Church.[35]

The church's history did not record a simple dramatic fall but rather an ebb and flow of the faithful teaching of the Word. "Luther allows for a fall of a church, but it is a particular, territorial church—the Roman church—which at one time had demonstrated by its martyrs such great vitality but has now declined from its earlier existence."[36] The apostasy of the bishop of Rome, the rise of the Antichrist, formed the focal point of Luther's concern with the history of the world since Christ's time.

Luther's biblical realism did not permit him to look back to the early church as a norm of pristine purity for contemporary ecclesiastical life. However, he did frequently praise one group of believers in the patristic period—the martyrs. He claimed that the church flourished most fully during the period in which believers had been laying down their lives in the confession of the faith. Even though error and apostasy had existed alongside that confession, the papacy, the epitome of error and apostasy, had not yet made its appearance.

---

[33]Ibid., 101.

[34]Ibid., 156.

[35]Ibid., 160-61.

[36]Ibid., 159.

Luther scoured the records of the early church for evidence that the bishop of Rome had not always claimed, nor had been accorded, primacy in the church catholic. He identified the papacy as the Antichrist, because it had violated both the spiritual and temporal spheres by appropriating responsibilities from the temporal to itself and by abusing its God-given responsibilities in the spiritual. But Luther did not suggest that only the papacy had persecuted the people of Christ. Early in his career he had defined three periods of the persecution of the gospel: The first came in the violence and tribulation of the time of the ancient martyrs; the second came in the sects and heresies in the early middle ages; the third had arrived in the papal establishment of a "peace and security" for the church which embraced both heresy and persecution.[37]

Current events forced Luther to focus most often on this third period. He believed that throughout the period of papal domination of the church, the gospel had found its voice in various spokesmen, among whom Luther could number particularly Bernard of Clairvaux, and more recently the Florentine reformer of the fifteenth century, Girolamo Savonarola.[38] But the end of papal tyranny had been announced, Luther was convinced, by John Hus. The Bohemian reformer had suffered martyrdom, along with Jerome of Prague, at the Council of Constance in 1415. Luther wrote in 1525 that Hus deserved canonization, a suggestion which German sympathizers of the Bohemian had made in the 1450s. In 1536 Luther praised Hus's Christian writings and teaching, his heroic struggle with the *Anfechtungen* of death, his patient and humble sufferings, and his willingness to accept shameful death for the sake of the truth—all because he opposed the pope. Although Luther recognized differences between his teaching and that of Hus, he saw that they had a common calling to issue a prophetic call to repentance to the church; and warning against the papacy's deceit had involved them in common fate as victims of the papacy's persecution.[39] In the popular propaganda of the 1530s, Luther

[37]*WA* 2:136; 45; 3:410, 443. See Headley, *Church History* 195-223; Heinz Zahrnt, *Luther Deutet Geschichte, Erfolg und Misserfolg im Licht des Evangeliums* (Munich: Mueller, 1952) 57; and Hans Preuss, *Die Vorstellungen vom Antichrist im späteren Mittelalter, bei Luther, und in der konfessionellen Polemik* (Leipzig: Hinrich, 1906) 86-89.

[38]*WA* 12:248; Headley, *Church History*, 211-12.

[39]Ibid. 224-40; Jaroslav Pelikan, "Luther's Attitude Toward John Hus," *Concordia Theological Monthly* 19 (1948): 747-63; and Siegfried Hoyer, "Jan Hus und der Hussitismus in den Flugschriften des ersten Jahrzehnts der Reformation," Hans-Joachim Köhler, ed., *Flugschriften als Massenmedium der Reformationszeit* (Stuttgart: Klett, 1981) 291-308. In 1458 Matthau Hagen was burned at Stettin for acclaiming John Wyclif, along with John Hus and Jerome of Prague, as saints, among other charges; see *Quellen zur Ketzergeschichte Brandenburgs und Pommerns* (Berlin: de Gruyter, 1975) 300.

and Hus were placed together: In a broadsheet the two of them were depicted reading the Scriptures to a herd of sheep gathered at the foot of the cross, both of them faithful prophets to the company of God's people.[40]

Luther did view his own role in the history of the church as prophetically significant, not because of himself but because God was bringing the world to an end through a proclamation of the gospel that was unfolding in his career and the associated movement that had arisen in Wittenberg.

Luther's understanding of history did benefit, of course, from the stimulation that Melanchthon provided, and not least through Philip's abiding interest in history. In his inaugural lecture at Wittenberg in 1518,[41] Melanchthon defined history as the key to all human knowledge, especially to theology. His historical interests grew out of his training in the most significant academic intellectual movement of the period, biblical humanism. These interests were instrumental in introducing history as a subject of formal lectures in the Wittenberg academic schedule. But his contributions to the development of the discipline of history lay not only in his lectures or in his editing of the chronicle of world events composed by his student, Johann Carion, who died before completing this work.[42] His significance for the development of the discipline of history also lay, as Gerald Strauss argues, in his showing the way for his students by framing a reinterpretation and reassessment of European history, particularly the history of Germany. This interpretation centered on the conflict between papacy and empire. Its depiction of Germany as a martyred land, "besieged, despoiled, violated, her guileless and trusting people defrauded by sly foreigners—is not a pretty picture, but as a tool of pro-

---

[40]Reproduced and discussed in R. W. Scribner, *For the Sake of Simple Folk, Popular Propaganda for the German Reformation* (Cambridge: Cambridge University Press, 1981) 27, 28. It also appears in Walter L. Strauss, *The German Single-leaf Woodcut, 1550-1600* (New York: Abaris, 1975) 1291, attributed to the anonymous "MS," active in Nuremberg and Wittenberg.

[41]*CR* 11:18. On the humanist influence on Luther's use of history, see Zahrnt, *Luther deutet Geschichte* 14-19 and Hanns Lilje, *Luthers Geschichtsanschauung* (Berlin: Furche, 1932) 16-19. On Melanchthon as historian, see Wilhelm Maurer, *Der junge Melanchthon, 1. Der Humanist* (Göttingen: Vandenhoeck & Ruprecht, 1967) 99-128, and Peter Fraenkel, *Testimonia Patrum, The Function of the Patristic Argument in the Theology of Philip Melanchthon* (Geneva: Droz, 1961) 52-60, 326-29.

[42]*Chronica durch Magistrum Johan Carion vleissig zusamen gezogen* (Wittenberg: Rhau, 1532). See Gerald Strauss, "The Course of German History: The Lutheran Interpretation," *Renaissance Studies in Honor of Hans Baron*, Anthony Molho and John A. Tedeschi, eds. (DeKalb: Northern Illinois University Press, 1971) 678-86.

paganda it had great power, negatively as a means of identifying the enemy, positively as an instrument for rallying popular support."[43] This reinterpretation of German history arose within the context of Melanchthon's understanding of the whole history of God's people, an interpretation which the Wittenbergers developed in concert. The Wittenberg school of historical interpretation arose out of the interchange between humanist and theologian, or perhaps more accurately, out of the theological and humanistic points of view shared by Luther, Melanchthon, and their students.

Melanchthon, with Luther, believed that all history takes place under God's providing and guiding hand. They did not separate sacred and secular history but viewed both as played out on the field that God has laid out for his human creatures between creation and eschaton.[44] Melanchthon viewed God's Word as the instrument of his critical intervention into human history and found its saving power present in the teaching and tradition of the church, which are based upon, proceed from, and convey the power of the Holy Scriptures. Thus, Melanchthon and Luther believed those who had taught and confessed God's message before the world had played a special role in the history of the church and of all creation.[45]

Melanchthon, as editor of Carion's *Chronicle*, expressed his own understanding of human history. Peter Fraenkel describes the leitmotif of their joint product thus: "The whole of sacred history appears as a series of ups and downs of true doctrine."[46] Both Luther and Melanchthon read the Old Testament as a continuing story of temptations to listen to the devil's lies in various kinds of idolatry and apostasy and of prophetic calls to return to the Word of the God of Israel. In that struggle, the prophets who had proclaimed the word often had to suffer. The story of the New Testament church was no different, for it had always suffered from Satanic persecution from within and without. But, Melanchthon repeatedly insisted, God had always kept his Word alive in his church, however dominant error might have become. He had always raised up reformers to call the church back to the the gospel. The apostles had proclaimed Christ and thus corrected the error of the time period before his coming; but almost immediately, their contemporaries had adulterated

---

[43]Ibid., 675-77.

[44]Fraenkel, *Testimonia,* 52-60.

[45]Ibid., 225-52, see also 13-14, 34-43, 61-64, 117-18, 133-61, 208-25, 340-62.

[46]Ibid., 67.

the message. The ebb and flow of purer and falser expositions of the gospel had continued for fifteen hundred years, e.g. down to the depths of Origen's Platonism and up into the heights of Augustine's exposition of grace. But within that ebb and flow a general drift could be detected. Melanchthon believed that the continuity of the chain of witnesses had always kept the Word of God alive, but he also believed that the Roman Antichrist had gradually obscured the gospel ever more seriously. Melanchthon traced the origin of the antichristian nature of the papacy to a variety of seeds sown by Gregory the Great and his contemporaries, and he believed that the Wittenberg movement was playing the decisive role in bringing Christ's church back to the gospel, in preparation for the End-time.[47]

Luther and Melanchthon agreed that their own mission and the responsibility of their students and followers was the fearless and faithful confession of the gospel against all its foes. What Luther called "the living voice of the gospel" and what Melanchthon meant by the term "pure doctrine" was simply the preaching and teaching and even the "mutual conversation and consolation" of Christians with each other, so that the resources and aid of the gospel might be brought to bear in a critical and decisive manner on the lives of people.[48] As students of the Word and of human history, Luther and Melanchthon were convinced that the course which God had laid before the Wittenberg movement—a course which centered on the call to the bold and clear confession of the faith—would demand heroic courage in confrontation with the enemies of the Word; and they were convinced that only in a confession like this could they live out the holy life to which God had called them.

Luther and Melanchthon recognized at least two fronts on which their use of history would combat misperceptions of the holy in late-medieval religion as they knew it—in the way in which the people viewed time and in the way in which people viewed the saints of the past.

THE WITTENBERG CHRONICLES AND CALENDARS

As part of its function of providing a sense of security for its adherents, a religion must in some fashion supply a framework for the understanding of the movement of time, which engulfs the life of all creatures. Luther reflected the biblical writers' understanding that God is

---

[47]Ibid., 162-78, 64-109, esp. 96-100, 104-107.

[48]Smalcald Articles III:IV, *Bks* 449. See Friedrich Wilhelm Kantzenbach, "Aspekte zum Bekenntnisproblem in der Theologie Luthers," *Lutherjahrbuch* 30 (1963): 70-96.

drawing human history in linear fashion from creation to eschaton and that he is taking care of his people through his intervention in human history through his incarnation in Jesus Christ and through the proclamation of his Word.

Popular medieval religion had often suggested that time proceeds in secure and orderly fashion by making the circle of the year, seed-time and harvest. Pious peasants and artisans of the time, in connection with their confidence in the power of the saints, had taken assurance from knowing that the calendar would bring back the festivals of the saints, on which occasions special powers were available for those who invoked the saint whose day was being celebrated in the proper way.[49] The reformers did not make a special point of attacking this trust in the propitious day of the saint, perhaps because they had not thoroughly thought through the significance of the medieval concept of the holy day, perhaps because they believed that this aspect of the adoration of the saints was sufficiently addressed in their attacks on the ability of the saints in general to mediate divine power. It must be said, however, that some of Luther's students did not perceive any danger in the use of a calendar of saints but believed, instead, that their people needed that kind of support and structure for their lives.

Among the lessons to be learned from history was the proper appreciation of time and of God's role in its passing. Although the Wittenbergers did not directly assault the use of holy days as settings for the ritual actions which would insure the world's continuance, their works of history did address indirectly that part of the medieval use of the realm of the holy.

Historical writing in Wittenberg had at least minimal homiletical functions from the beginning. This can be seen in Carion's *Chronicle*, which remained not only the pioneer effort but one of the standards of Wittenberg historical writing. After Carion's untimely death in 1537, Melanchthon edited and revised the volume; his son-in-law, Caspar Peucer, carried on with its updating thereafter, as did others.[50] Melanchthon's new preface for the work in 1558 reveals his purposes in teaching and writing history—to bring the lessons of the ancients, both pagan and Christian, to the young of his own age, so that they might see what sin has always wrought upon its perpetrators and what God has done for his people

---

[49]See Keith Thomas, *Religion and the Decline of Magic* (New York: Scribner, 1971) 615-23. On the importance of the calendar in general for folk culture, see Ludwig Rohner, *Kalendargeschichte und Kalendar* (Wiesbaden: Athenaion, 1978) 69-76.

[50]See Maurer, *Melanchthon*, 99-128.

throughout the ages. Melanchthon's humanistic point of view led him to define the most ancient as the truest, as Tertullian had done.

In 1541 Luther himself prepared an extensive tabular outline of the history of God's people, his *Calculation of the Years of This Earth*.[51] He did not intend to present a chronicle or history, he informed his readers, but desired merely to provide them with a tool that would aid their reading of biblical and secular history by providing an orientation within the framework of the six ages of human history.

In the troubled years of the next two decades, as the Lutherans faced both the armed assault of Roman Catholic armies and internal strife, several of Luther's followers published their own chronicles and the related genre, historical calendars. Both types of "historical" literature served two purposes—to trace God's hand in the past and to reveal the temporal order of God's creation. Thereby they demonstrated the security that God's preserving hand provides; for both genres present the reader reassuring material indicating God's control of the times and seasons of human life. On the eve of the Smalcald War, when Emperor Charles V was intent on the armed suppression of the Lutheran faith, Johann Funck (1518-1566), a young pastor near Nuremberg, issued an extensive chronology;[52] and Johann Aurifaber of Breslau (1517-1568) reissued in German Luther's *Calculation* in 1550,[53] in the midst of that period after the Smalcald War when God no longer seemed to be controlling history, at least not to the advantage of the German Evangelicals.

At this time, in 1550, the production of Lutheran calendars also began with the appearance of the *Historical Calendar* of Paul Eber (1511-1569), who had studied at Wittenberg in the 1540s and remained there as an instructor.[54] During the 1550s, three more historical calendars were issued by adherents of the Wittenberg Reformation, two edited by Kaspar Goltwurm, the court chaplain of Count Philip of Hanau, who had studied at Wittenberg about 1540. His *New, Attractive Historical Calendar* appeared in 1553, and in 1559 he published an ecclesiastical calendar. Also the author of a collection of miracle stories, Goltwurm emphasized the miraculous as evidence of God's providence. He supplied very brief accounts of the

[51]"Supputatio annorum mundi," *WA* 53:1-182.

[52]*Chronologia, hoc est, omnivm temporvm et annorvm ab initio mvndi vsque ad resvrrectionem Domini nostri Iesv Christi computatio* (Nuremberg: Wachter, 1545).

[53]*Chronica des Ehrwirdigen Herrn D. Mart. Luth. Deudsch* (Wittenberg: Lufft, 1550, reissued by Lufft, 1559).

[54]*Calendarivm historicvm conscriptvm* (Wittenberg: Rhau, 1550). See Rohner, *Kalendargeschichte*, 97.

lives of saints, both ancient and contemporary, on the page or section assigned to each saint's day of the year. The popularity of Goltwurm's *Historical Calendar* is indicated by the size of the printings: the first edition of 1,500 copies was followed by a second of 3,000. His ecclesiastical calendar appeared in nine editions.[55]

Apparently less popular was the *Historical Calendar, Diary* of Michael Beuther (1522-1587), another former Wittenberg student, who assigned each day a half page and who concentrated on secular history rather than on ecclesiastical figures, perhaps to provide a calendaric reference without abetting old habits connected with the veneration of the saints.[56] More similar to Goltwurm's work in its focus on Christian heroes was the 1582 *Historical Diary* of the Marburg bureaucrat Abraham Saur (1545-1593).[57] It did not command the market for Evangelical saints' calendars, because Goltwurm's and that of Andreas Hohndorf had established themselves so firmly that they must have all but excluded competition.

Hohndorf's *Historical Calendar* appeared in 1575, three years after the death of the compiler. Vincent Sturm, an associate, completed it. Sturm also died at a young age, and his father directed the further production of the work, which was made available in eleven editions over a thirty-five year period. The Hohndorf/Sturm calendar resembled Goltwurm's in format: It offered its readers introductions to each month, with an illustration of village life appropriate to the month; general information regarding the name of the month and its Hebrew equivalent; and the "Cisio Janus" verses, poetry which had supplied medieval Christians with a handy guide to the saints' days of each month. Hohndorf and Sturm

---

[55]*Ein Newes lustig Historisch Calendarium, darinn nicht alleyn die Monat, Tag vnnd Fest des Jars, sonder auch darneben merckliche vnnd lustige Historien angezeygt vnnd verzeichnet werden* (n.p., 1553). *Kirchen Calendar. Ein Christlich vnd nutzlich Buch In welchem nach Ordnung gemeiner Calender die Monat, Tag vnd die fürnembsten Fest des gantzen jars, mit jrem gebrauch Auch der Heiligen Apostel, vnd Christlichen Bischoff, Leerer, vnd Martyrer, Glaub Leben, vnd bestendige bekantnuss . . . kürztlich verfasset . . .* (Frankfurt am Main: Egenolff, 1559). See Bernward Deneke, "Kaspar Goltwurm, Ein lutherischer Kompilator zwischen Überlieferung und Glaube," in Wolfgang Brückner, ed., *Volkserzählung und Reformation* (Berlin: Schmidt, 1974) 125-77; Johannes Moritzen, *Die Heiligen in der nachreformatorischen Zeit, I* (Flensburg: Wolf, 1971) 41-58, and Rohner, *Kalendargeschichte*, 98.

[56]*Calendarium Historicum. Tagebuch Allerley Fuernehmer, Namhafftiger vnnd mercklicher Historien . . .* (Frankfurt am Main: Zephel, 1557).

[57]*Diarivm historicvm. Das ist, Ein besondere tagliche Hauss und Kirchen Chronica . . .* (Frankfurt am Main: Bassaeus, 1582).

informed their readers of the important historical events that had occurred on each day; but they emphasized the festivals of biblical and ancient martyrs and saints and the days on which, they suggested, the confession and sacrifice of contemporary martyrs and confessors should be remembered.[58] Both Goltwurm and Hohndorf provided a substitute for the medieval lives of saints in so far as their pious readers could find in these works an Evangelical framework for the passing of the days through the annual cycle. They found no theological critique of the implicit suggestion that the observation of these signposts of the year might insure order in their world. The users of these works found little theological guidance on the leaves of the calendars at all, beyond the prefatory remarks of Goltwurm, Sturm, Hohndorf—and other compilers of similar works—which stressed the benefits of recalling historical events and heroic individuals. These benefits lay, as Melanchthon had stated, in the admonition and encouragement which history gives to those who listen to its lessons.

Only Beuther gave some indication that the rhythm of the calendar which he was setting before his audience had relevance for the general course of society;[59] and his allusion to the importance of the cyclical course of time for religious observances echoed the opinion of Eber and of Mathaeus Dresser.[60] In his treatise on festivals and important parts of the year, Dresser noted that God had instituted the sabbath as an occasion to praise him for his creation and that he had later instituted other festivals, such as passover, pentecost, and the feast of tabernacles. The church had established other festivals as occasions for glorifying God and remembering his benefits. The papal abuse of these festivals fell under Dresser's harsh criticism. In his book he endeavored to support the continuing Evangelical efforts to rid the people of their superstitious practices in connection with the old festivals of the medieval church.

---

[58]*Calendarivm historicvm. Oder, Der Heiligen Marterer Historien* . . . (Frankfurt am Main: Feyerabendt, 1575); reissued as *Calendarivm Sanctorum et Historiarum, In welchem nach Ordnung gemeiner Calender durchs gantze Jar, aller heiligen Lehrer vnd Maertyrer Leben, Bekentnis vnd Leiden beschrieben* . . . (Leipzig: Berwaldt, 1579 and subsequent editions), see Heidemarie Schade, "Andreas Hohndorf's Promptuarium Exemplorum," *Volkserzählung und Reformation* 701-703, and Ernst Heinrich Rehermann, "Die Protestantischen Exempelsammlungen des 16. and 17. Jahrhunderts," ibid. 604.

[59]Beuther, *Calendarivm* Aij.

[60]Eber, 1:7; Dresser, *De festis et praecipvis anni partibvs Liber, non solvm nomina & historias, sed vsum etiam Exercitationibus scholasticis indicans* (Erfurt: Mechler, 1584) (A8)v-B4r.

Eber saw in the study of history the key to God's revelation. He wanted people to cultivate a detailed knowledge of the history of the church and the world, so that they might understand the way God works with his people. The memory of the events and individuals through which God had worked his will on earth could be cultivated by the observance of these festivals, Eber stated. But he gave no sign that he was aware of a deeper level of significance which those festivals held for people who believed that the power of the saint was particularly strong on his or her own day. And Eber believed that the order of the sun and the moon confirms God's grace; but he did not polemicize against the magical notion that the devout Christian's repetition of the festival had been thought to confirm the order and the security of a world kept in place more by the power of time than by the power of God. Instead, he may have hoped that his readers would assimilate his understanding of the significance of the cycle of the months and seasons without his having to develop a specific polemic against a magical view of time.

The authors of each of these Lutheran historical calendars intended, according to their prefaces, to present their readers with worthy examples for Christian living, even though the very brief descriptions of the lives of their subjects, fitted snuggly into the tight dimensions of a page or a half-page, left a good deal to the reader's previous knowledge or imagination. This fact raises the question whether the calendar provided a genre that could effectively serve the stated purpose of its authors in presenting an Evangelically coherent pattern for Christian decision-making about time and events. The works of Hohndorf, Goltwurm, and others combine the Evangelical understanding of the function of recalling the saints' confessions and actions with the form of the medieval observation of festivals.

Perhaps precisely this lack of focus contributed to the failure of the calendars—in spite of their relatively wide distribution at the popular level—to make a greater impact on the intellectual life of the German Lutheran churches. The calendar genre is, of course, not well-suited for intellectual impact. Its popularity rested on the need that it fulfilled among the populace to provide a framework for the pious Christian's perception of days, of the year, of time. Hohndorf may never have thought through the implications within the calendric system in the same way in which Ludwig Rabus did, who omitted any calendric system from his martyrbook, where it traditionally would have been found. Hohndorf's and Goltwurm's attacks on medieval superstitions regarding the saints were not reinforced with attacks against belief in the propitious days of the holy people or against the feeling that certain times are holy in and of themselves or against the inclination to view these times as possessing a power distinct from the loving exercise of power by a provident Creator. The displacement of medieval concepts of holy power and holy people slowly eliminated the remnant of belief in holy time that silently adhered to the Evangelical calendars. But that remnant of medieval piety also must be counted among the factors that made the calendars of Hohndorf, Goltwurm, and the others popular pieces of literature in German Lutheranism of the sixteenth century.

THE FATHERS' LIVES:
SUBSTITUTES FOR THE GOLDEN LEGEND

Even before the Smalcald War heightened the Lutheran recognition of the reality of martyrdom in the church, the ancient martyrs and their confessing contemporaries had attracted notice in Wittenberg. Not only did Luther and Melanchthon cite their deeds and their message in lectures and treatises but they also perceived that the historical accounts of ancient believers could be used to leech away some of the pious energies devoted to the saints. That faith could then be directed more easily to the providential Father, who cares for daily needs, and to his atoning Son, who makes daily intercession for the needs of his people. Luther and Melanchthon realized that the popular literature on the saints needed to be replaced with works that reflected their understanding of the lives of legitimate Christian heroes and that projected the Evangelical perception of the saints' significance.

The *Golden Legend*, compiled in the thirteenth century by Jacob de Voragine, was by far the most popular of the medieval collections of stories of the saints. It had been reissued far more often in Germany, both in Latin and in German, than it had been in England where, as Helen C. White has observed, it prepared the way for the popular reception of Foxe's martyrology.[61] Thus, Luther recognized that his movement must meet the needs of pastors and their people for reading material on heroes of the faith.

------

[61]Robert Francis Seyboldt, "Fifteenth Century Editions of the Legenda Aurea," *Speculum* 21 (1946): 327-48, has counted eighteen High German and seven Low German editions, compared with twenty French, eleven Dutch, four English, and four Italian; of the ninety-seven Latin editions which he found, 57 came from German presses. Helen C. White, *Tudor Books of Saints and Martyrs* (Madison: University of Wisconsin Press, 1963), comments on the role of the *Golden Legend* in England, 31-66; Miriam Usher Chrisman, *Lay Culture, Learned Culture, Books and Social Change in Strasbourg, 1480-1599* (New Haven: Yale University Press, 1982) 86, 115-16, comments on the publication of this work and other lives of the saints in Strassburg around 1500.

In 1539, Hermann Bonnus (1504-1548), a former student in Witten-berg (1521-1525) and superintendent of the churches of Lübeck, at-temped to meet this need with his *Farrago of Distinguished Examples from the Apostles, Martyrs, Bishops, and Holy Fathers of the Ancient Church, Of Those who Taught the Word of God and Affirmed its Truth, and Faithfully Defended the Christian Religion.*[62] Bonnus wanted to provide a replacement for the *Golden Legend* and similar works, one of which had commanded respect in Lübeck since its publication there in 1490. Bonnus's collection included biblical saints, such as John the evangelist and apostle, and patristic fig-ures, such as Athanasius and Basil the Great. He presented several Ger-man favorites, from the Magdalene to Martin and Dorothy. He clearly designed his Latin work for pastors, and he concentrated more on the statements of faith uttered by his saints than on their deeds. He did so, probably, not only because, as a Lutheran, he wanted to emphasize confession of faith but also because, as a humanistically inclined student of Melanchthon, he was demonstrating the humanist "penchant for ad-ages and for the newly recovered biographies of ancient sages by Di-ogenes Laertius."[63] Along with brief sketches of thirty-five individuals, Bonnus treated a series of themes with examples from the lives of Chris-tian heroes. Among them are "Christian liberty and superstition," "the occasion for sin and the duty of charity in bearing the infirmity of oth-ers," "presumption and security," "prayer and how it impedes Satan." Through such topical admonitions and through biographical overviews, Bonnus intended to give the Evangelical public access to the exemplary power of the saints, while at the same time avoiding an appeal to the re-ligious power popularly attributed to them. To accomplish this, Bonnus worked hard at editing his sources.[64]

---

[62]*Farrago praecipvorvm exemplorvm de Apostolis, Martyribus, Episcopis, & Sanctis Patribus ueteris Ecclesiae, qui docentes uerbum Dei, & ueritatem illius adserentes Chris-tianae religioni fideliter patrocinati sunt* (Schwäbisch Hall, 1539). Bonnus had pro-duced the first Latin translation of the *Chronicle* of Carion two years earlier; Ronald E. Diener, "The Magdeburg Centuries, A Bibliothecal and Historiographical Analysis" (Th.D. dissertation, Harvard Divinity School, 1978) 200-201. See the discussion of this work in James Michael Weiss, "Luther and His Colleagues on the Lives of the Saints," *The Harvard Library Bulletin* 33 (Spring 1985): 174-95.

[63]Ibid.

[64]See Wilbirgis Klaiber, "Zur Wirkung von Theologie auf Hagiographie—im frühesten Versuch einer reformatorischen Bearbeitung der Antoniusvita bei Her-mann Bonnus," in Klaus Welker, ed., *Heilige in Geschichte, Legende, Kult, Beiträge zur Erforschung volkstümlicher Heiligenverehrung und zur Hagiographie* (Karlsruhe: Badenia, 1979) 63-75.

Bonnus failed to set his work in context with a preface; but both Luther and his colleague Georg Major (1502-1574) wrote prefaces for Major's *Lives of the Fathers, for the Use of Ministers of the Word*, which appeared in 1544, five years after Bonnus's publication. Major complied with a request from Luther and issued an evangelically edited replacement of the *Lives of the Fathers*, attributed to Saint Jerome, a work almost as popular in medieval Europe as the *Golden Legend*. In his preface Luther noted that Satan's corruption of the stories through stupid fables and impious lies was not the least of the works of his demonic furor—though both he and Major did express concern for the adulteration of historical sources in the transmission of the lives of the saints. Worse, through Pelagian and Origenistic errors associated with the veneration of the saints and related evils such as monasticism, the gospel of the forgiveness of sins through God's grace alone had been obscured and denied. Major's preface stressed that the reading of history, both ecclesiastical and secular, teaches how to perform the good and flee the evil. Major used five topics both as guidelines for determining the true saints worthy of remembrance and as organizational principles for presenting their lives. These five were their teaching, in accord with prophetic and apostolic doctrine, of course; the testimony which God gave in the miracles wrought through them; God's providence as revealed in their lives; the practice of their calling and the pious exercise of their duties; their exercise of prayer and worship. Major offered his readers eighteen biographical sketches, most of them longer than the brief epitomes of Bonnus; and he presented also a series of topical discussions of pious attitudes and actions, which pastors might use in their preaching and teaching.[65]

In the same year, 1544, and also at Luther's urging, Georg Spalatin issued his *Magnificently Consoling Examples and Thoughts from the Lives and Sufferings of the Saints and Other Important Men*. Luther's letter to Spalatin of 8 March 1544 was published as a preface for the work, along with Spalatin's earlier letter to Luther regarding his plans to publish. In the midst of a personal crisis, Spalatin had been inspired by Bonnus's publication to turn to the consolation that the lives of the saints offered; but worthy examples of earlier Christians had been difficult to find, because they had been suppressed in favor of very deceiving stories of wonders which the saints allegedly had worked. This suppression had imprisoned people in idolatry, Spalatin complained, rather than leading them to the consolation of the Word, which heals afflicted consciences.

---

[65]*Vitae patrvm, in vsvm ministrorvm verbi, qvo ad eivs fierei potuit repurgatae* (I have used the Wittenberg, 1560, edition). See Weiss, "Luther and His Colleagues."

Luther's preface pointed out another benefit of Spalatin's venture into the study of the church fathers. His book proved for Luther that the Evangelicals were not a new heresy but rather stood in the long line of those who used God's Word to comfort the suffering and to oppose Satan. The task of his movement, Luther indicated, included the use of the analogy of faith to purge all falsehood from the stories of the saints' preaching and their activities. In some eighty brief biographical paragraphs, Spalatin then offered his readers examples of confession and consolation from the ancient church.[66]

Like the similar works of Bonnus and Major, Spalatin's book of examples appeared in Latin, apparently designed primarily for clergy use, although in Spalatin's case more for personal devotional reading than for homiletical and pedagogical preparation. Major's book was reprinted three times, in 1559/1560, 1562, and 1578; from its second edition it was printed alongside Bonnus's work. The double work was issued in German translation in 1604, along with a "catalog of the doctors of the church," which Major had published in his 1550 treatise on the Word of God. In a preface to this list of important confessors, its translator, Sebastian Schwan, a pastor in Ratzeburg, pointed to the relationship between Paul and Titus (Titus 1:4), which Paul called a relationship of father and son, as a model for the Christian's relationship with the fathers of the church. Schwan also apologized for not including material on more recent fathers and teachers; he mentioned Johann Brenz, Johann Mathesius, Johann Wigand, Aegidius Hunnius, and urged his readers to turn to the Magdeburg *Centuries* or the *History* of Lucas Osiander for details on other, older confessors of the church. Schwan also apologized for lack of examples from the other two estates, from among the political authorities and from heads of households. Both government and household offer worthy models for Christian living, Schwan observed.[67] Luther's brand of sainthood was struggling to assert itself.

Apart from the popular calendars and historical chronicles, German Lutheran literature after Rabus's martyrology restricted presentation of heroic Christians largely to examples taken from the ancient church, published in Latin for the clergy. Schwan's apologies call attention to this situation. Only after more than a half century did Major's and Bonnus's works appear in German. It is interesting to note that a similar work, by

---

[66]*Magnifice consolatoria exempla, & sententiae, ex Vitis & passionibus Sanctorum & aliorum summorum Virorum* (Wittenberg: Schlirlentz, 1544). See Weiss, "Luther and His Colleagues."

[67]*Vitae Patrum* (Lübeck: Albrecht, 1604) esp. 87, 186-88.

David Chytraeus (1530-1604), professor at the University of Rostock, a biographical dictionary of the saints of the Bible and the ancient church, including "teachers, martyrs, heretics" and materials on the synods or councils of the church, was issued first in Latin in 1557. It was designed for use in the schools to aid in teaching history to the "boys." In 1605, a year after the German translation of Major's and Bonnus's books had appeared, a German translation of Chytraeus's biographical guide was published.[68] Either printers or preachers must have perceived a need to acquaint the growing German-reading public with the lives of the saints. These volumes included more information than the calendars and chronicles did but less than the massive martyrology of Rabus.

The events issuing from the imperial triumph over the Lutheran princes in the Smalcald War of 1546-1547 and from the subsequent promulgation of the re-catholicizing "Augsburg Interim" of 1548 shifted the focus of interest in the biographies of ancient saints and doctors of the church. A group of Lutheran pastors gathered in the city of Magdeburg was dedicated to the firm and fierce defense of their faith against every threat, whether the Emperor Charles's aggressive measures against Luther's followers or the readiness of some of those followers themselves to compromise with the imperial-Roman party. Not surprisingly, it was from the Magdeburg presses that a new set of tracts came that used the ancient examples of the martyrs as models for contemporary believers. In 1549 and 1550, the printer Christian Roedinger published two excerpts from early Christian histories, edited anonymously, designed to inspire steadfast faithfulness to the gospel and resistance to its foes. The *Tripartite History*, a composite of three, fifth-century ecclesiastical histories by Sozomon, Socrates, and Theodoret and edited by Cassiodorus in the late sixth century, provided three stories of heroic martyrdom—those of Basil, a woman in Edessa, and Barlaam; from Sozomon's work, an account of the "steadfastness and suffering" of Simeon, a Persian bishop, was translated.[69]

---

[68]*Onomasticon theologicvm recente recognitvm, in qvo praeter nomina propria fere omnia quae in Biblia extant, Plerumque etiam Sanctorum, qui Calendario usitate inscribi solent, Item Doctorum Ecclesiae, Martyrum, Haereticorum, & Synodorum, nomina & historiae breuiter indicantur. A Theophilo Lebeo* (Wittenberg: Crato, 1558). An explanation for the work's pseudonymous publication is not evident. *Onomasticon Theologicum Davidis Chytraei. Erklerung aller Manns vnd Weibss Personen Namen . . .* Valentin Beyer, trans. (Eisleben: Gross, 1605).

[69]*Eine schoene Historia, vom standhaftigkeit des Heiligen Basilij, beschrieben in der Tripartitia Historia. Item, zwo andere schoene Historien. Von dem Weiblein zu Edessa, vnd von dem heiligen Barlaam, jetzt zu dieser zeit sehr troestlich vnd nuetzlich zu lesen* (Magdeburg: Roedinger, 1549), and *Ein sehr schoene historia, von der standhafftigkeit in Bekentnis vnd leiden, des heiligen manns Simeonis . . .* (Magdeburg: Roedinger, c. 1550).

In their battle against the papacy, the Magdeburgers, called "Gnesio-Lutherans" by modern scholars, were also willing to cite a wide variety of later historical supporters of reformation, among them Petrarch.[70] The Magdeburg theologians also furthered Luther's "canonization" of John Hus, whose martyrdom at the hands of the papal party in 1415 made him a classic example of precisely the heroic and holy figure needed by the Wittenberg movement. In addition to Luther's warm embrace of Hus as a comrade in confessing the faith,[71] other Wittenbergers recognized him as a fellow confessor. Already in 1525 Luther's close friend Nikolaus von Amsdorf, the "grand old man" of the Magdeburg resistance between 1547 and 1551, had heralded Hus—together with his disciple, Jerome of Prague, the most learned man in Bohemia—as a sagacious and honorable man, a faithful follower of the gospel, and a disciple of Christ. Amsdorf promoted the general opinion in Bohemia of Hus and Jerome as holy martyrs. Amsdorf's attacks against the papal enemy in the 1550s included references to Hus, who was executed for defending the distribution of the Lord's Supper in both kinds "and for no other reason." Amsdorf canonized him "Saint John Hus," even though Amsdorf was convinced that Hus had not understood the gospel exactly as Luther proclaimed it. Amsdorf's associates in the Magdeburg circle concurred; for example, Luther's student Anton Otto published a protest against papal oppression in 1552, in which he pointed out that the Antichrist was threatening the German Lutherans in exactly the same way he had threatened Hus a century earlier.[72]

In the later 1550s, this circle, led by Matthias Flacius Illyricus (1520-1575), the Italo-Croatian Wittenberg graduate who had become the spiritual and intellectual leader of the Magdeburgers, produced an edition of Hus's works including a narrative of Hus's life. Flacius's Slavic background contributed to his interest in the Bohemian reform, along with his desire to use Hus as a polemical weapon against Rome. His collaborator, the imperial councillor Caspar von Nidbruck, tried to discourage Fla-

---

[70]*Das der Bapst mit seinem Hoffe die rechte Babilon vnd Babilonische Hure sey. Durch den hochgelarten Franciscum Petrarcham einen Welsche, der fuer 250. jarn gelebt hat* (Magdeburg: Roedinger, c. 1550). Flacius wrote a brief preface for this tract.

[71]See note 39.

[72]*Grund vnd vrsach auss der Cronicke, Warumb Johannes Huss vnd Jeronimus von Prag verbrant seyn* (Magdeburg, 1525), Aij; *Vom Bapst vnd seiner Kirchen, das sie des Teufels, vnd nicht Christi vnsers lieben Herrn Kirche sey* (n.p., 1551) Aiij/v-(Aiiij)r; *Ein gut newe Jar, den grossen Herrn in dieser Welt geschanckt* (Jena: Roedinger, 1554) Ciij-(Ciiij)r.

cius's venture into publishing the Hussite material, as Ronald Diener has shown.[73] Flacius persisted, even if the result of his efforts did not display his name or contain extensive polemic from his own pen. The volume's brief preface was signed by the publisher, although its content may well have been suggested by Flacius.

The preface begins with a notice of the long-standing custom in the church of "retaining and celebrating the memory of those who have proclaimed heavenly teaching with their voice and under threat to their lives" and with the encouragement that the duty to testify to this teaching brings with it immense benefits and the promise of perpetual remembrance. God's governance of and presence in his church can be detected when he raises up teachers for his church who refute error and assert pure doctrine even though that brings upon them horrible sufferings and a death comparable to Christ's. Such teachers were John Hus and Jerome of Prague.[74] Another indication of Hus's continuing importance to Luther's followers is found in a contemporary woodcut that depicts the family of the Saxon Duke John Frederick receiving the Lord's Supper from Hus, who is distributing the host, while Luther holds the chalice.[75]

Hus and Jerome were not the only recent martyrs to the papal fury who commended themselves as heroes and saints to Luther's students. Luther's own appreciation of the Florentine ascetic reformer Jerome Savonarola (1452-1498) may have sparked the interest of Cyriakus Spangenberg (1528-1604), Luther's student, although Spangenberg's father, Johann, an early follower of Luther, had translated Savonarola's sermons on Psalm 51 and 80 in 1541.[76] In 1556, the younger Spangenberg published a *Narrative of the Life, Teaching, and Death of Jerome Savonarola, Burned at Florence in 1498,*[77] drawing on fourteen primary and secondary sources, among them correspondence from Pope Alexander VI and both Italian and German historical writers, including Philip Cominaeus, John Poggius, and

---

[73]Diener, "The Magdeburg Centuries," 52, 73-74, 87-88.

[74]*Historia Ioannis Hussi et Hieronymi Pragensis . . . Monumenta* (Nuremberg, 1558; reprint, Nuremberg: Gerlach/Montanus, 1583) a2. See Strauss, *Woodcuts,* 1288, 1299, from the 1558 for woodcuts of Hus and Jerome on the pyre.

[75]Scribner, *For the Sake of Simple Folk,* 206-207.

[76]*Der Li. Psalm Dauids Misere Mei Deus durch Hieronymum Sauonarolam . . .* (Leipzig: Wolrab, Augsburg: Ulhart, 1542; reprinted at Leipzig: Voegelin, 1561 and translated into Low German at Magdeburg: Kirchener, 1562). *Der LXXX. Psalm . . .* (Leipzig: Wolrab, 1542).

[77]*Historia. Vom Leben, Lere vnd Tode Hieronymi Sauonarole . . .* (Wittenberg: Seitz, 1556) esp. Biiij/v, Diij/r-Dv/v, Er-(Evij)v.

Johann Stumpf. Spangenberg wrote his account to encourage steadfastness in confessing the faith on the basis of God's power and mercy, as he has exhibited them in the testimony of martyrs such as Savonarola. Spangenberg's careful tracing of Savonarola's career particularly emphasized his criticism of the papacy and the licentious way of life among the clergy of Florence; but Spangenberg went further. Amsdorf was satisfied at the time to claim Hus as a saint, even if he had not shared Luther's doctrine completely; but Spangenberg went so far as to claim that Savonarola was a Lutheran "saint" because the Florentine Dominican had, according to Spangenberg's analysis, upheld the same biblical teaching which Luther had presented to his students.

To do this, Spangenberg had to exercise some discretion in quoting Savonarola. He legitimately summarized Savonarola's teaching as a concern that God be given proper honor and that the Holy Scriptures not be used as a cover for wickedness. Spangenberg quoted sections from his father's translation of Savonarola's comments on Psalm 51, wherein he found a view of God's mercy and forgiveness close to his own, from which he could infer Lutheran interpretations of a series of doctrinal topics, including freedom of the will and good works. Citing Savonarola's criticism of hypocritical sacrifice, he argued that the friar had also opposed the sacrifice of the mass. Such stretching of Savonarola to make him fit into the mold of an ideal Lutheran confessor demonstrates the importance of the proper confession of biblical teaching for Spangenberg's concept of saintliness and martyrdom.

Biographical vehicles like this one had been used by Christians for centuries, and Lutheran writers no less turned to various forms of the recitation of the lives or portions of the lives of saints as effective means of rallying and cultivating popular support. In this case, Spangenberg admitted that he had found inspiration for producing an account of Savonarola's martyrdom in the earliest volumes of the martyrology of Ludwig Rabus. In turn, Rabus reprinted his former Wittenberg colleague's account of Savonarola in the fourth volume of his own work. Rabus's martyrology became the most extensive use of biography as teaching tool, polemical instrument, and a source of edification produced by the Wittenberg Reformation.

CHAPTER TWO

Ludwig Rabus and the First Protestant Martyrology

THE MAKING OF A MARTYROLOGIST

THE THEOLOGIANS OF RABUS'S GENERATION had been born in a world in which books like the *Golden Legend* formed a vital part of the popular worldview. They grew up under the influence of a call to reform which rejected presuppositions in the *Golden Legend* regarding the holy. They were confronted with the threat of persecution early in their ministries. It seems inevitable that someone of Spangenberg's and Rabus's ilk would have composed a martyrology.

It is likely that the two men met at the University of Wittenberg, at the feet of Luther and Melanchthon, during Rabus's time there in the twenty months following his arrival in December 1541. Born in the south German town of Memmingen in the year of its conversion to the Reformation, 1524, Rabus had studied for four years at the nearby University of Tübingen, a humanist center of learning that was turning Evangelical as he arrived there. During the period in which he earned a Master of Arts degree at Wittenberg, Luther was lecturing on Genesis and Melanchthon was working through Thucydides' works, perhaps arousing his students' interest in history thereby.[1]

---

[1] Karl Hartfelder, *Philipp Melanchthon als Praeceptor Germaniae* (Berlin, 1889; Nieuwkoop: De Graaf, 1964) 561.

1. Ludwig Rabus (*HdM* I:[Bvj]v)

Rabus returned home for a year and then left Memmingen at age twenty, to assume the office of deacon on the clerical staff of the cathedral in Strassburg, a leading city in the Evangelical movement. Its pastors, under the leadership of Martin Bucer, had tried to find middle ground between Wittenberg and the Swiss Reformation and were playing a prominent role in south Germany's reformation.[2] The very popular chief pastor of the cathedral, Matthias Zell, and his wife, Catherine née Schütz, a member of a prominent Strassburg family, welcomed Rabus into their home. Rabus credited Zell with playing an important role in his development later in life, but he and Zell's wife would fall into a violent dispute over her inclinations toward the spiritualist theologian, Caspar Schwenckfeld.[3] Rabus left the Zell home to establish his own when he married on 26 January 1546. He quickly became a popular preacher among the people of the city and reluctantly bowed to popular pressure to accept the call to succeed Zell, when he died in January 1548.

Rabus did not retain his post at the Cathedral for long. The defeat of the leading Lutheran princes by Emperor Charles V in the Smalcald War the previous April had already set political and military forces in motion which were dramatically changing the political life of the city. Severe social tensions had mounted there between the leadership of the municipal government and the city's artisans: The leaders were trying to work out a compromise with the forces of the emperor, who were threatening to

---

[2]Miriam Usher Chrisman, *Strasbourg and the Reform, a Study in the Process of Change* (New Haven: Yale University Press, 1967); Lorna Jane Abray, *The People's Reformation: Magistrates, Clergy, and Commons in Strasbourg, 1500-1598* (Ithaca: Cornell University Press, 1985); James M. Kittelson, *Wolfgang Capito from Humanist to Reformer* (Leiden: Brill, 1975) (on one of Strassburg's leading reformers); Thomas A. Brady, Jr., *Ruling Class, Regime and Reformation at Strasbourg, 1520-1555* (Leiden: Brill, 1978).

[3]In his later battle to rid Strassburg of those whom he considered sectarian heretics, Rabus attacked Zell's sympathetic defense of Schwenckfeld. Zell reprinted sharply worded correspondence between the two, which did neither any credit, in *Ein Brieff an die gantze Burgerschafft der Stadt Strassburg von Katherina Zellin, dessen jetz saeligen Matthei Zellen, . . . nachgelassne Ehefraw, Betreffend Herr Ludwigen Rabus . . .* (n.p., 1557). A pseudonymous reply to Zell, *Billiche Antwort zum vorsprung, allein auff die Vorrede des schmaehbrieffes, welchen Katharina Zellin wider Doctor Rabum offentlich hat lassen aussgehn, von Erhardo Landolff, der warheit zu lieb trewlich als ein Christ gestellet. Sampt einem kurtzem bericht auff die zwey stuck, die heyligen hochwirdigen Sacramenten, die Tauff vnnd des Herren Nachtmal belangend, von Magistro Clemente Hartman geordnet, vnd allen Christen zur warnung ohne betrug vbergeben, Responsio* (n.p., 1558), may have been composed by Rabus or by fellow Lutherans, Strassburg colleagues, who were directly affected by Zell's charges against Rabus.

occupy the city and place it under the control of its Roman Catholic bishop; but the artisans wanted to oppose both emperor and pope as stoutly as ever. A shift of power within the city led to the temporary exodus of many aristocratic families after 16 September 1548, when Charles delivered an ultimatum to the city to accept his re-catholicizing program for religious settlement, the Augsburg Interim. Nonetheless, the new civic leadership did not believe that it had the liberty to subscribe to the view of the city's ministerium, led by Bucer, that the Interim must simply be rejected and defied. The new government strove to accommodate the populace, while at the same time it was working out a compromise that would preserve the city's independence from imperial domination. This difficult task was nearly impossible in view of the success that Charles's armies had brought him in the neighboring duchy of Württemberg and in more than a score of Evangelical towns not far to the east of Strassburg. On 1 March 1549, the city council decided that Bucer and his most vehement supporter against the Interim among the clergy, Paul Fagius, had to leave the city. The two journeyed to England to join Thomas Cranmer's reform effort. The final treaty between the city and its Roman Catholic bishop, concluded in November 1549, granted the bishop extensive concessions within the city but retained its Evangelical clergy and worship services as well. While five churches remained Evangelical, three were returned to Roman rites and control.[4]

Among the pastors in Strassburg who lost their positions to Bishop Erasmus's Interim priests was, of course, the pastor of the Cathedral, Ludwig Rabus. He reacted by delivering "a very vehement witness" against the Interim in his final sermon from his pulpit.[5] But the council found tasks for its displaced preachers to perform: Rabus was responsible for the Matins service at the Dominican church and by October 1552 had assumed the post of preacher and instructor in theology at the Col-

[4]Brady, *Ruling Class*, 259-90; Erdmann Weyrauch, *Konfessionelle Krise und soziale Stabilität, Das Interim in Strassburg (1548-1562)* (Tübingen: Klett-Cotta, 1978) 132-62.

[5]Johann Georg Schelhorn, "Nachricht von dem Leben D. Ludwig Rabus, eines wolverdienten Gottesgelehrten in dem 16 Jahrhundert," in Johann Bartholomaeus Riederer, ed., *Nuezliche und angeneme Abhandlungen aus der Kirchen- Buecher- und Gelehrten-Geschichte* (Altdorf: Ammermueller, 1768), II:236. The municipal council's committee for implementing the city's treaty with the bishop issued a memorandum on 4 December 1549 which stipulated that, among others, Rabus and three assistants at the Strassburg Cathedral would have to leave their posts; J. Bernays and Harry Gerber, eds., *Politische Correspondenz der Stadt Strassburg im Zeitalter der Reformation* (Heidelberg: Winter, 1933) IV,2:1265-66.

legium Wilhelmitanum.[6]

Sometime during his enforced semi-retirement, in the midst of the tensions surrounding the Augsburg Interim, Rabus must have decided to compile a collection of stories of the martyrs of the church. It is interesting that, although he included among his "martyrs, witnesses, and confessors" some contemporaries who did not suffer execution or exile for their faith, he omitted any mention of pastors from Württemberg and the towns east of Strassburg who had suffered the persecution of exile because of the enforcement of the Augsburg Interim. Yet it is impossible to imagine that the persecutions of the Interim period, including his own relatively mild harassment by dismissal, did not play a vital role in the conception of his martyrology. Thomas Brady described the situation in the late fall of 1546: "When the war in upper Germany was lost for the Smalkaldic allies, Jakob Sturm had predicted that the decision to offer up one's goods, livelihood, and life for the gospel would prove to be a very individual matter."[7] As friends from student days at Tübingen and Wittenberg fell under the shadow of the Interim, and as his native Memmingen bowed to pressure from imperial occupation forces; as his own circle in Strassburg suffered the indignity of the partial introduction of the Interim, and as he had to leave his own pulpit and parishioners, Rabus must have associated his situation with that of others throughout the history of the church who had suffered for their faith. Twenty years later, when he wrote the preface to the second volume of the second edition of his martyrology, Rabus identified the context of the beginning of his martyrological efforts as the time of the "third and last persecution, that of the Antichrist" against the Evangelical churches of the German nation.[8] He would date the beginning of that persecution to the first Roman pressure applied to Luther in 1517, but he could not help but have viewed the period following 1548 as a key part of the "last persecution." The threats to Strassburg's and his own faith during the years following 1547 aroused and were echoed in Rabus's desire to do battle with the papal party through his book of martyrs. Like so many of his contemporaries, including the Magdeburgers, whose use of martyrs in tractarian propaganda may well have caught Rabus's eye in 1550, he saw the events of these years in an eschatological light: He was certain that the triumph of the papal antichrist through this Interim heralded the approaching end

---

[6]AST. no. 69, Carton 41, 220r-221r, 226r; AST no. 482, "Diarium collegii Wilhelmitani I, 1543-1554," 26.

[7]Brady, *Ruling Class*, 290.

[8]*HdM* II:Aiiij/r.

of the world and the final judgment.

In the battle against the Interim in Strassburg, the dispute over the observance of saints' days was of special concern to the Evangelical clergy. In 1549-1550 the celebration of these festivals became an issue in the city council a number of times. This fact may also have impelled Rabus toward an attempt to contribute to the solution of the invocation of the saints through a martyrbook which would present Evangelical substitutes for the medieval heroes of the faith.[9] It may also be significant that Rabus's martyrology appeared at the time when the Evangelical clergy of Strassburg felt support for their opposition to the Interim declining among the populace. The Strassburgers were certainly not about to embrace the faith of the Interim or its practices, but they were becoming used to the presence of the bishop's clergy in the city by 1551, and their resentment over the Interim's imposition was cooling.[10] Rabus could well have envisioned his martyrbook as a means whereby he might remind his fellow Strassburgers of the danger and threat still imminent in the papal party's hopes and designs, a means whereby he might rally their steadfastness for the Evangelical cause, which seemed to be slipping slightly in the direction of indifference.

Rabus began his martyrological work by gathering from the Bible and from the ancient church fathers—particularly patristic historians such as Eusebius—one hundred twenty-eight martyr stories. He had come sufficiently far with his compilation by the summer of 1551 that he could compose a preface to Duke Christoph of Württemberg, the leading princely defender of the Lutheran confession in south Germany. The first volume of a Latin martyrology appeared in early 1552. Later printings of the initial German volume dated its preface 1554, but the testimony of the prefaces of the two volumes of the second edition confirm the statement of the second volume of the first edition, issued a second time in 1554, that the work had first appeared in print two years earlier. The printing firm of Balthasar Beck, who died in 1551, published the first volume in both Latin and German; but the firm went out of business soon after Beck's widow supervised the printing of these volumes. Rabus then entered into an agreement with Samuel Emmel, who had established his own press in Strassburg in 1551. Emmel published the remaining seven volumes of the

---

[9]AST, No. 193, "Extraits des Protocoles du Magistrat contre l'Intérim, 1547-1559," 69, 88, 106, 108v-110, 116v, 197v-198r. I am grateful to Dr. Erdmann Weyrauch for providing this information.

[10]Weyrauch, *Konfessionale Krise*, 163.

first edition of the martyrology between 1554 and 1558.[11]

The martyrology undoubtedly took shape in conversations with his fellow Strassburgers, lay people as well as pastors. Rabus and the famous Strassburg historian, Johannes Sleidan, were friends. Sleidan had arrived in the city in 1542, and the two men must have been drawn together by common friendships in Wittenberg and similar interests in the humanistic study of history. Rabus would use Sleidan's *Commentaries on the State of Religion and the Commonwealth under Emperor Charles V* in compiling certain stories of contemporary martyrs.[12] We can only speculate to what extent Rabus may have consulted Sleidan personally and profited from his counsel as he was preparing his martyrology. No more than speculation is possible, too, regarding the possibility that, as he was turning from his second to his third volume in 1554, Rabus might have conversed with a visitor in Strassburg, the martyrologist John Foxe of England, who knew Sleidan. Nor do we have evidence that the French Protestant martyrologist Jean Crespin had contact with Rabus, although Crespin did know and corresponded with Sleidan and had visited Strassburg. J. F. Gilmont conjectures, although he does not offer proof, that the organizational form of Rabus's compilation of martyr stories might have influenced Crespin.[13] Both Foxe and Crespin published their martyrbooks in 1554. It is perhaps significant that Foxe dedicated his Latin martyrology, published in Strassburg in 1554, to Duke Christoph of Württemberg, to whom Rabus had dedicated his book two years earlier. Did Rabus suggest the duke as an interested patron of the martyrbook over conversation at Sleidan's table? Or did Rabus and Foxe meet on the basis of a letter of introduction from Rabus's former colleague, Peter Martyr Vermigli, who had gone to teach at Oxford?

---

[11]On Rabus's printers, see Miriam Usher Chrisman, *Lay Culture, Learned Culture, Books and Social Change in Strasbourg, 1480-1599* (New Haven: Yale University Press, 1982).

[12]*De statu religionis et reipublicae Carolo Quinto Caesare commentarii* (Strassburg: Wendelin Rihel, 1555), used in Rabus's treatment of Bishop Hermann von Wied, *HdZ*, VIII:ccxxiiij, and of a number of French Protestant martyrs, *HdZ*, VI: cix/v, cxiiij/v, cxxvj/r. Walter Friedensburg, *Johannes Sleidanus, Der Geschichtsschreiber und die Schicksalmächte der Reformationszeit* (Leipzig: Heinsius, 1935) 80, mentions Rabus; see also Hermann Baumgarten, ed., *Sleidans Briefwechsel* (Strassburg: Trübner, 1881) 285, where Sleidan mentioned on 20 July 1555 that Rabus had brought him word from Augsburg regarding criticism of his *Comentarii*.

[13]Jean-François Gilmont, *Jean Crespin, un éditeur réformé du XVIe siècle* (Geneva: Droz, 1981) 149, 171; see J. F. Mozley, *John Foxe and His Book* (London: SPCK, 1940) 41-43.

Certainly, Rabus shared his project with his fellow pastors in the city. Caspar Hedio, the leader of the Strassburg Protestant clergy, wrote a letter of commendation to Duke Christoph regarding Rabus's forthcoming work on God's confessors and martyrs.[14] Rabus also relied on friends in other places to assist in obtaining princely support and privileges for his work.[15]

Rabus did not spend all his time on his martyrology. The Latin volume appeared while he was subsisting at the margin of official ecclesiastical life; its preface is dated 21 July 1551. The German translation was printed within the year; but then two years elapsed before the second German volume appeared, probably because he had once again assumed a leading role in the ecclesiastical activity of Strassburg when a new order began to take shape in the city's clergy. The leadership which had directed Strassburg's reformation into a middle course between Luther and Zwingli had died. The new leadership, with Johann Marbach at its head, was initiating a process—to be repeated in several south German cities—of moving from a mediating position firmly in the direction of Wittenberg. Rabus's Wittenberg background made him Marbach's natural ally in the process. Shortly before he departed the city—as he wrote the preface to the fourth volume of his martyrology in March 1556—Rabus informed the staunchly Lutheran dukes of Saxony that the Strassburg pastors held to no other teaching than that which their predecessors had formulated in the Wittenberg Concord with Luther in 1536 and that of the Smalcald Articles of 1537 (to which, Rabus failed to mention, Bucer had refused to subscribe, but which Lutherans by 1556 regarded as a key statement of their faith).[16]

In 1552 restrictions imposed by the Interim treaty with Bishop Erasmus still irritated Marbach, Rabus, and their colleagues. Even after tensions had lessened with the imperial Truce of Passau in August 1552, the preachers were keeping up an offensive against Roman practices in the city. Rabus led the campaign from his pulpit and within the clergy, the secretary of which he became on 29 December 1552. As pastor of the Dominican church after March 1553, he served not only at the Collegium Wilhelmitanum but also on the newly reconstituted municipal marriage

---

[14]SAU 8993 II (formerly X.18.1) 152, dated 1 October 1551. Rabus seems also to have used Hedio's German translation of Josephus, which appeared the next year, *Flauij Josephi . . . Alle Buecher* (Strassburg: Emmel, 1553), in *HdZ*, I:clvij/rff.

[15]See his letter to Johannes Flinner, pastor in Heidelberg, 27 January 1557, TB XXIV:6-7; AST, no. 161, Epistolae XVI. Saeculi VIII:15-18.

[16]*HdZ* IV:)(iij/r. See Abray, *People's Reformation*, 126-39, 142-62.

court. He was a zealous antagonist both of the doctrine of the Anabaptist sectarians and the immorality of the burghers within the city.[17]

Rabus received his doctorate in April 1553 at the University of Tübingen alongside his good friend, Jakob Andreae.[18] He kept in contact with Andreae and many other prominent Lutheran theologians. He received several calls to other Evangelical cities or principalities, so it should have been no surprise when he accepted the call of the city council of Ulm to become superintendent of that city's churches in late 1556. His departure did occasion something of a dispute with the city council in Strassburg, which objected to his secret negotiations with Ulm; but finally the council could do nothing to prevent him from a kind of advancement that Rabus seemed unlikely to enjoy in Strassburg. Johann Marbach, who remained Rabus's close friend and correspondent throughout his life, was securely in place as Strassburg's superintendent.[19]

As superintendent in the city of Ulm, Rabus experienced three and a half decades of a sometimes turbulent but mostly successful ministry, caring for the spiritual needs of his people and fighting off the remnants of medieval superstition, Interimistic imposition, and sectarian heresy.[20] He continued to play a larger role in south German Lutheranism as an advisor to theologians and magistrates alike. During his years at Ulm, he

---

[17]Weyrauch, *Konfessionale Krise*, 163-184, describes the city at this time. Abray, *People's Reformation* 64, 192, makes brief mention of his ministry. His activities can be traced in the Strassburg archives, e.g. his role as secretary in AST 87/43: [2]-[11]; 87/49a:61r; 45:571-76; 178:65v, 73v, 112r, 133; his appointment to the Dominican church, AST 198:28r, 40r; his appointment to the marriage court, AST 198:159v; his strong role in clergy relations, at Marbach's side, AST 198: passim; a dispute with Anabaptists, AST 103; a meeting with Peter Martyr Vermigli in October 1553, at which this Calvinist theologian's return to the city was apparently blocked, AST 198:101r, 119v.

[18]AST 198:151r, 232v.

[19]Material relating to his departure is found in SAU 8993 II (formerly X.18.1) 151-56, and F. Fritz, *Ulmische Kirchengeschichte vom Interim bis zum dreissigjährigen Krieg (1548-1612)* (Stuttgart: Scheukele, 1934) 55-57. On the continuing relationship between Marbach and Rabus, see Johannes Fecht, ed., *Historiam Ecclesiasticae . . . Supplementum . . . Epistolis ad Joannem, Erasmum et Philippum Marbachios* (Frankfurt/M and Speyer, 1684) esp. 60-62.

[20]On Rabus's ministry in Ulm, see Fritz, *Kirchengeschichte* 54-251; Julius Endriss, *Die Ulmer Kirchenvisitation der Jahre 1557-1615* (Ulm: Hohn, 1937) 7-14, Peter Lang, *Die Ulmer Katholiken im Zeitalter der Glaubenskämpfe: Lebensbedingungen einer konfessioneller Minderheit* (Frankfurt/Main: Lang, 1977) 42-44.

produced a modest literary legacy,[21] including the final three volumes of the first edition of his martyrology.[22]

In the midst of this other occasional publishing activity during his years in Ulm, the republication of his martyrology took place. Rabus had not lost contact with his Strassburg printer, Samuel Emmel. In 1568 Emmel issued Rabus's *History of Saint Abel, Protomartyr of the Church Militant in the Old Testament*.[23] The work consists largely of citations from the Scriptures and ancient authors, among them Chrysostom, Jerome, Isidore, and John of Damascus. In a preface from the printer to the reader, Emmel stated that he had published this little volume because of the great seriousness of the subject matter and because of his respect for the author, to whose previously published martyrology the printer drew attention. Rabus's correspondence suggests that he and Emmel continued their relationship following the appearance of *Saint Abel*, which may have been something of a trial balloon, with a view toward a new edition of the larger martyrology. However, Emmel's printing establishment went bankrupt in 1571 and was purchased by one of his brothers-in-law, Theodosius Rihel. It was another brother-in-law, Josias Rihel, with whom Emmel had cooperated on some previous ventures, who inherited the connection with Rabus and who produced in 1571 and 1572 the magnificent pair of folio volumes which constitute the second edition of the Rabus martyrology.

Apparently the path toward republication did not run smoothly at all points. In early 1570, Rabus complained to his Heidelberg friend Johannes Flinner that as yet he could say nothing certain regarding the martyrology; he asked for advice on how to proceed, adding his regret

---

[21]On his catechetical work, see Johann Michael Reu, *Quellen zur Geschichte des Katechismus-Unterricht* (Gütersloh: Bertelsmann, 1904) 1:301-302. His works include: *Ein kurtze vnd Christliche Predig von notwendigem vnnd einfaltigem verstand der Sechs Hauptstuck vnsers Christlichen Catechismi* (Ulm: Varnier, 1560); *Conciliationes locorum S. Scripturae in specie pugnantium. Ex Libris D. Aurelii Augustini . . ,* 2 vols. (Nuremberg: Montanus and Neuber, 1561); *Christliche Bettbüchlins Erster Theil . . .* (Frankfurt/Main, 1565, 2. vol. 1568, several subsequent editions) [on this work, see Paul Althuas, *Forschungen zur evangelischen Gebetsliteratur* (Gütersloh, 1927; Hildesheim: Olms, 1966) 109-16]; *Wider Neun fuerneme Haubtlaster . . . Ein kurtze vnd Christliche Predig* (Nuremberg: Berg, 1561); *Ein Christliche Predig, Von dem Eingesatzten H. Euangelischen Kirchendienst, Lehr vnd Predigampt* (Ulm: Ulhart, 1573); *Euangelium am XX. Sontag nach Trinitatis: Matthei am XXII. Von der Koeniglichen Hochzeyt, vnd Hochzeytlichem Kleyd* (Strassburg: Emmel, 1567).

[22]The dates of these prefaces, all written in Ulm, are, for volume VI, 4 March 1557; VII, 6 August 1557; VIII, 24 February 1558.

[23]*Historiae de S. Abele, Ecclesiae militantis in veteri Testamento Protomartyre, Ex sacris literis . . . collecta & conscripta* (Strassburg: Emmel, 1567) Aij-Aiiij.

that some were trying to impede this work that had been desired for such a long time by so many good men. These comments may simply be oblique references to the difficulties Emmel encountered because of his deteriorating financial situation or to objections raised by Strassburgers still offended by Rabus's desertion of the city fifteen years earlier.[24]

The project did proceed, however; and two handsome folio volumes appeared, the preface to the first dated 26 January 1571, dedicated to the mayor and council of Ulm; the preface to the second dated 9 January 1572, dedicated to the civic leaders of Strassburg. The former dedication was a natural action by a city official who undoubtedly felt both gratitude and obligation toward the civil leadership with which he had worked for a decade and a half. The city council responded in a decision on 20 April 1571 to accept the dedication with appreciation.[25] The latter dedication—to the city council at Strassburg—was somewhat problematic, on the other hand, even though Rabus's difficulties with that city's political authorities had receded into the past during the intervening sixteen years between Rabus's stealthy departure from their employ and the republication of the martyrology.

That Rabus still had grave concerns about that very matter is clear from a letter which he wrote to Marbach on 21 December 1571, while he was working on the preface to the second volume. He told Marbach that he had asked his publisher, Rihel, to share the draft of the dedication to the city council with Marbach, "not only for you to inspect and read but indeed to alter, so that it is acceptable. . . . If indeed I have put something down which could offend your most honorable lords, I ask and beseech you in all love to correct it."[26]

The third point in his explanation of the decision to dedicate his volume to the Strassburg council troubled Rabus the most. In print, this point is a criticism of Satan and his followers who arouse discord within the church of God.[27] Whether this published version had been revised or not is unclear; Rabus's words as printed certainly might have implied a condemnation of critics in Strassburg; but if so, Marbach apparently did not believe that Rabus need fear the impact of those implications. On 31

---

[24]See letters to Flinner of 9 January 1568, 22 June 1569, and 1 March 1570, TB XXIV:18, 25, 29. On Emmel and the Rihels, see Chrisman, *Lay Culture,* esp. 18-19.

[25]SAU Ratsprotokolle, 32:114r.

[26]TB XXIV: 39-40.

[27]*HdM* II:Av.

March 1572, the Strassburg city council discussed Rabus's work at length, accepted it with gratitude, and awarded him one hundred thaler for his work.[28]

Rabus continued his active ministry until ill health confined him to his home in 1590. He died 20 June 1592, and was hailed as a faithful and zealous teacher of pure doctrine, a pastor and caretaker of the church of Ulm, the superintendent of its church and school.[29] As vital as he had been to Ulm, his influence on wider Christian circles was not so great as to place Ludwig Rabus among those names which commanded the consciousness of German Lutherans in subsequent centuries. His fame, if any, would have to rest on his martyrology, the first of its kind in Protestant Europe. Through its composition, Rabus had placed himself among the witnesses and confessors of his faith.

THE MAKING OF THE MARTYROLOGY

Ludwig Rabus proceeded to the task of compiling his martyrology, entitled *Accounts of God's Chosen Witnesses, Confessors and Martyrs*, with significant elements of Luther's and Melanchthon's historical and theological conceptual framework well in mind. The prefaces to his volumes offer the only real insight into his own thinking; for he edited the sources which he drew into his collection of martyr stories little, if at all. For example, in 1571 he reissued his book of martyrs, he wrote, in part to demonstrate once again the continuity of his own and his colleagues' Evangelical teaching with the "correct, true, ancient, genuinely catholic—canonical in every way—Christian teaching and preaching." This doctrine and proclamation had been presented "from the beginning of the world, in the Old Testament through the patriarchs and prophets, in the New Testament through the dear holy apostles and other apostolic Christians, and it was finally confessed with their own blood." Like Melanchthon, Rabus believed that church history served the proclamation of the Evangelical message by proving that it, not the message of Rome or of the sects, was that same teaching which had guided God's people

---

[28]Strassburg Ratsprotokolle 52:293v-295. See Adolf Hauffen, *Johann Fischart, Ein Literaturbild aus der Zeit der Gegenreformation* (Berlin: de Gruyter, 1921), 1:62. The first volume was advertized in the *Catalogus Nouus ex nundinis vernalibus Francofurti ad Moenum, Anno M.D.LXXI* (Frankfurt/Main: Corvinus, 1571) E/r, under "Bücher in Historischen Haendeln."

[29]Rabus's colleague, Jodocus Preisenstein, preached his funeral sermon, *Eine Christliche Leichpredig, Bey der Leich vnd Begrebnuss des Ehrwuerdigen vnd Hochgelehrten Herrn Ludouici Rabi . . .* (Tübingen: Hock, 1593).

from the beginning.[30]

But Rabus also recognized that "the orderly recital of the most significant events in the life of the church" could also edify pious Christians;
for church history had produced the praise of God. As Luther also had
taught, it reviews the hatred, wrath, and vengeance of Satan and his followers against the church, a task particularly important for a martyrologist. Church history reveals that baptism calls believers to citizenship in
a kingdom in which there is no idleness and in which the peace and pros-
perity of this world are not to be found. Instead, baptism sets them on a
course filled with strife, in which they risk reputation, property, family,
and their own lives for the sake of Christ. Finally, church history provides encouragement for all Christians in every situation of life to remain
faithful and to rely on the power of the Holy Spirit in times of affliction,
for it reveals God's steadfast providence, even in the worst of persecutions.[31] Luther's understanding of God's Word and its role in human history and his theology of the cross reecho through Rabus's prefaces.

Rabus must have believed that his understanding of the function
of church history would be easily caught from the reading of his prefaces
or from the varied presentations of the sources which he reprinted, for
he did very little to accompany his readers into the stories which he passed
on to them or to assist in their assimilation of the message he believed
obvious there. Unlike Foxe, he had no master plan or organization through
which he could teach by association. In his first edition, he did not organize the material in a framework which would make his lessons clearer
or easier to remember. His brief introductions to individual chapters, each
on a different martyr, dropped only occasional hints to reinforce his perceptions of what could be learned there. He must simply have hoped that
the repetition of the situations in which the martyrs confessed and the
reiteration of their public witness would impress his intended message
on his readers.

That Rabus did not display more skill at communicating his message seems at least a bit surprising, since he lived at a time fraught with
significance not only for theology and church life but also for the writing
of history. Humanist historiographical interest, ideals, and methods in-

---

[30]*HdM* I:bij/r.

[31]*HdM* II:Aiij/r-Aiiij/r.

fluenced many of his associates, such as Melanchthon and Sleidan,[32] and certainly Foxe and Crespin as well. Rabus himself was not immune to humanist influence from his associates; above all, Melanchthon's interest in the ancient fathers of the church must have turned his young Swabian student to them.

Rabus's work is a florilegium of martyr stories and confessions. He borrowed material from many sources, ancient and contemporary, and he developed a form for presenting them at least in part from Eusebius (c. 290-360), the father of church history. Eusebius had also compiled written accounts, after the manner of certain philosophers who assembled citations from previous authors, rather than following the predominant method of the ancient historians, who relied first of all on oral sources.[33] Like Eusebius, Rabus transmitted narratives and confessions of Christian heroes from his sources to his readers with little or no change or comment.

Since the Evangelical attack on the medieval treatments of the saints and martyrs involved an attack on their historical accuracy, it is natural for modern scholars to pose the same question to martyrologists of the Reformation era which they posed to their medieval predecessors, albeit without expecting them to attain the standards demanded by the canons of modern historical scholarship. Gerhard Dedeke argued that to a large degree Rabus's accounts do convey what really happened. Without presenting any documentary proof that Rabus's work contains falsified material, Wolfgang Hieber challenged that conclusion, in part on the grounds that some of the stories of Evangelical confessors standing before their judges seem to follow the same form and deliver similar content. Since Rabus did not compose the stories of his work but merely copied them, he cannot be accused personally of having altered "the facts" to fit his literary purposes. Indeed, if there is a similarity in form and content among

---

[32]See Gerald Strauss, "The Course of German History: The Lutheran Interpretation," in Anthony Molho and John A. Tedeschi, eds., *Renaissance Studies in Honor of Hans Baron* (DeKalb: Northern Illinois University Press, 1971) 663-86; A. G. Dickens, *Contemporary Historians of the German Reformation* (London: Institute of Germanic Studies, University of London, 1978); Paul Joachimsen, *Geschichtsauffassung und Geschichtsschreibung in Deutschland unter dem Einfluss des Humanismus, 1. Theil* (Leipzig: Teubner, 1910) 60-75.

[33]Arnaldo Momigliano, "Historiography on Written Tradition and Historiography on Oral Tradition," *Studies in Historiography* (London: Weidenfeld and Nicolson, 1966) 216-17; and "Pagan and Christian Historiography in the Fourth Century," *Essays in Ancient and Modern Historiography* (Oxford: Blackwell, 1977) 107-26.

some of the chapters of Rabus's book, it must indicate that Western Christendom had developed a certain form for relating such incidents. But we dare not conclude that facts had to be forced to fit form in every case. As Robert Lerner has pointed out, literary forms, or intellectual expectations, determined the way in which trials of heretics were conducted in the Middle Ages.[34] The era of the inquisitors may account for such similarities in Rabus's stories; thus these similarities say nothing about his historical accuracy. He trusted his sources and reproduced them; he does not seem to have exercised a critical eye on them.

Rabus offered his readers a few hints on how he garnered new stories to reprint, as he moved from one volume to another between 1552 and 1558. He apparently received reactions from readers who gave him counsel on how to proceed with the task of compilation, and he forthrightly requested information from his readers. But he was not selfish. He urged those who found additional information to publish it themselves, if they did not want to share it with him; for the appearance in print of such reports would "certainly serve to honor God and edify all of Christendom."[35] Rabus also referred readers to other sources when, on a rare occasion, he decided not to publish an account in full himself.[36]

With but few exceptions Rabus listed the sources from which he took his material. The most significant exception is the series of stories in volume five which seems to have been borrowed from Jean Crespin. It is impossible to determine why he omitted Crespin's name, not only in his first but also in his second edition. It may be because his struggle against Calvinist tendencies in Strassburg compelled him to avoid citing so prominent a disciple of Calvin. Rabus seldom edited his sources, even when on a rare occasion they offered a doctrinal position with which he disagreed; however, in his translation of Senarcleus's account of the

---

[34]Gerhard Dedeke, "Die protestantischen Märtyrerbücher von Ludwig Rabus, Jean Crespin und Adriaen van Haemstede und ihr gegenseitigen Verhältnis" (licentiate dissertation, University of Halle-Wittenberg, 1924) 125-31; Wolfgang Hieber, "Legende, protestantische Bekennerhistorie, Legendenhistorie, Studien zur literarischen Gestaltung der Heiligenthematik im Zeitalter der Glaubenskämpfe" (doctoral dissertation, University of Würzburg, 1970) 138-70; Robert E. Lerner, *The Heresy of the Free Spirit in the Later Middle Ages* (Berkeley: University of California Press, 1972) 5-6.

[35]*HdZ*, VI:xxij/v; III:clxxx/v.

[36]In his treatment of John Hus he referred readers to the history of the Council of Constance by Johannes Stumpf, *Des grossen gemeinen Conciliums zu Costentz kurtze doch grundtlichere vnd volkommnere dann vor nie in Teütsch gesähen Beschreybung* (Zürich: Forschauer, 1541); *HdZ*, II:lxvij.

treacherous fratricide of Juan Diaz, Rabus did edit out a favorable reference to Calvin's Geneva.[37] It is more likely that this confessional bias influenced his decision to omit mention of Crespin than that he feared
Crespin's Latin martyrology as a threat to the market and sales of his own
German book of martyrs.

Rabus's German sources usually appear in his pages as he found
them in original printings. In introductory notes to his readers on chapters from Latin originals, he set his goal in translation as the production
of "most faithful and accurate" renderings. His translations are sprightly
and colloquial; he was able to bring his Latin sources into an easily readable, interest-sustaining German. He acknowledged the assistance of
friends in translating certain entries while he was ill.[38]

In general, in the few places where Rabus's own style can be ex-
amined, he displays his literary talents well, both in the finely-honed
sentence structure of the preface to the 1551 Latin volume, filled with literary devices and classical and biblical allusions, and in the more heavily
didactic German prefaces, which reveal some literary grace. But some of
his sources make for rougher reading, and the bulk of the entire work
makes it impossible to label the martyrology light reading.

For all his literary skills, Rabus did not organize his entire project
before he began. The eight-volume first edition in German seems to have
fallen into place as Rabus found more stories. The first volume is a translation of the previous Latin collection of ancient martyr stories. A glance
at it suggests that he did not set out to write a history of the church, as
Foxe finally did, or even a history of Christian martyrs. He simply intended to provide his readers with stories of individuals or groups of
martyrs. Thus, he sorted all the ancient martyrs alphabetically. That de-
vice enabled him to place Abel at the beginning of his book, but it made
for a chronological muddle thereafter—making the book a catalog, a reference tool, a collection of edifying case studies, an index to the martyrs
of the ancient church.

Two years later in 1554, Rabus continued his work, as the title page
to the first volume indicates he intended to do. It seems safe to conjecture
that he anticipated following the first volume with martyrs from a later
time, since he completed his alphabetical listing in that volume. But the
second volume actually offers an appendix to the first, for it adds nine
biblical and patristic martyrs to those of the initial volume. Then Rabus
announced that "accounts of God's confessors and martyrs in recent and

---

[37]*HdM*, II:691v.

[38]*HdZ*, V:cclxxvj/v; VII:ccxlv/r.

our present last times" would follow. The "recent" martyrs began with a lengthy account, in contrast to the brief chapters of the first volume, an extensive narrative treatment and excerpts on the martyrdom of John Hus. To it Rabus attached the details of the death of Hus's associate, Jerome of Prague, and eight chapters concerning sixteenth-century martyrs. They begin with the first martyrs for Luther's cause, Esch and Voes, and include the English Lutheran, Robert Barnes; and Juan Diaz, a Spanish Protestant. During the following four years, six more volumes appeared, all with the same lack of organization, each simply an assembly of Rabus's latest martyr stories, in chronological order within each volume.

Rabus noted in the preface to the first volume of his second edition that his work was being reissued especially to effect the "orderly expansion" of the volume.[39] Many of his chapters on the martyrs of the biblical and patristic eras had indeed been expanded, unlike nearly all those chapters on contemporary witnesses and confessors (except for the one on Luther). The great difference between the two editions in this regard lies in the chronological reordering of the chapters and in the division of the work into five periods of confession, which roughly reflect an Augustinian model of the three eras of persecution, a scheme that Rabus had used in the prefatory discussion of Christian martyrdom in the first edition. Thereby Rabus actually formulated a new Lutheran periodization for the history of the Christian era.

The first volume of the second edition contains two books. The first book presents the stories of eleven individuals or groups of martyrs from Old-Testament times. Book Two brought together 126 martyr stories from the New Testament and the next five centuries, from the slaughter of the children of Bethlehem to the Arian persecutions of Christians in the western Mediterranean world five hundred years later. Rabus did not distinguish the first-century era of the apostles from the history of the patristic period that followed.

The second folio volume of the 1571-1572 edition of Rabus's martyrology contained three books dealing with "recent and contemporary martyrs." Book Three is relatively short and presents eight fifteenth-century victims of papal oppression, Wycliffites, Hus and Jerome, Thomas of Rheden, and Savonarola.

The year 1517 introduced Rabus's fourth period of martyrdom; and his 110-leaf biography of Luther, significantly expanded in the second edition, began that edition's Book Four. The Luther chapter is the only

---

[39]*HdM*, I:bij/r.

one in Book Four that was revised to any significant degree. The same is true of Book Five. It does begin, however, with a totally new chapter that marks the beginning of Rabus's fifth period, the presentation of the Augsburg Confession. Book Four contains a chronicle of martyrs, chiefly German Lutherans, in the 1520s. Book Five begins with what Rabus must have regarded as the maturing of the Evangelical movement, with its dramatic confession before the emperor and the world at Augsburg in 1530. It includes martyrs from the empire and points beyond. Luther's career and the confession at Augsburg represent the climaxes of contemporary confession in Rabus's work. The fifth book ends with the story from the late 1540s of the Netherlanders, Franciscus and Nicholaus Thiessen, and it faces the future of the church with the inspiration of Luther at Worms and the Evangelical princes at Augsburg, summoning those who would follow by their example of superb confession and effective witness of God's truth.

RABUS'S MARTYRS

It comes as no surprise that Rabus thought of the events of his time in connection with ancient martyrs of the church; for both Luther and Melanchthon encouraged biblical and patristic studies by word and example. Rabus was but one of many Wittenberg graduates to venture into patristic compilation and study.

Story after story of death by fire, sword, water, and more inventive methods, confront the reader of volume I. Rabus heightened the impact by interspersing confessions and examples with citations from theologians such as Chrysostom, Cyprian, Augustine, Jerome, and Bernard of Clairvaux. Even though some of the accounts he copied from ancient sources suggested that heroic martyrdom can merit salvation—and Rabus let those texts stand—, he clearly wanted to focus the attention of the reader on the faithfulness, patience, and steadfast prayer that his martyrs exhibited in the face of the enemies of the faith. His own plea for stalwart confession in the sixteenth century found support in the model which Eusebius and others had depicted repeatedly in recounting the stories of those who demonstrated joy and defiance in the face of the persecutor's threats or in the praise of the martyr's virtues, which Bernard of Clairvaux had sung.

Rabus pursued some items on the Wittenberg agenda more stridently than others. In his prefaces he avoided addressing directly the question of the relationship between Christian obedience to government and defiance of government's ungodly commands; but he did offer admonitions from Augustine, Bernard, and Isidore of Seville to obey God rather than man. Particularly in his second edition, Rabus highlighted the propriety of Christian passive resistance to oppressive political authority, the necessity of Christian confession, and consolation against the Antichrist, on the basis of God's providence through the use of the Maccabean history. The martyrdom of Eleazar and the Maccabean brothers had served as models for Christian martyrs and martyrologists from the patristic period on.[40] Rabus also devoted twenty-four pages, one of the longest of his patristic accounts, to the defiance of Archbishop Ambrose of Milan (340-397) against the imperial attacks upon the church's integrity in his day.[41]

Rabus concluded his first volume in 1552 with the epistle of Cyprian (c. 210-258) to the church at Thibaris, some fifteen quarto pages of admonition that the end of the world and the time of the Antichrist were drawing near. Cyprian's call for strength against the enemies of the gospel fitted well into the call that Rabus was issuing to his fellow Germans—however suspect the ancient bishop's words might have been for Lutheran eyes since Cyprian had prepared the people of God to suffer and die for their Lord on the basis of the threat of judgment upon those who denied him and the promise of heavenly reward for those who remained faithful.[42]

The short and snappy style of Rabus's treatment of biblical martyrs in his first edition stands in sharp contrast to the ponderous and lengthy double-columned folio glosses on relevant texts in the second edition. The first edition aimed at lay hearts, as Foxe consistently did; the second must have been written for the pastor's mind. Extensive patristic comment on the biblical texts would have been valuable for the preacher of the early 1570s, but it could not move the lay people to defense of the faith, as the brief accounts composed in the early 1550s more likely did.

Thirty percent of the chapters of Rabus's first volume in the first edition was based in part or in whole on the accounts of Eusebius; no other ancient source rivaled his importance for Rabus's initial effort. Accounts of fourth-century attacks on the faithful by Julian the Apostate and a supplement by Sozomon (c. 380- c.450) to Eusebius's accounts of Arian persecutions enriched the first volume with material for nineteen of its chapters, some fifteen percent. Descriptions by Victor (fl. 485) of those who died at the hands of the Germanic Arians added another seventeen

---

[40]HdM, I:68r-86v. On the role of the Maccabees in forming Christian conceptions of martyrdom, see W. H. C. Frend, *Martyrdom and Persecution in the Early Church* (New York: New York University Press, 1967) 16-21.

[41]HdM, I:327v-338v.

[42]HdZ, I:cclxv/v-cclxxiij/r.

chapters, thirteen percent. Rabus relied on Theodoret (c. 393-c. 458) in fourteen chapters, nine more were partly or totally quotations from the Scriptures, and another nine were derived from the writings of Augustine (354-430). Ambrose, Rufinus, Jerome, and thirteen others provided materials for one or more chapters as well.

From the ancient confessors of the church, Rabus's readers were supposed to learn that the persecutions of the sixteenth century were part of the Christian's expectation in an evil world and that it was better to suffer at the hands of human forces than to deny God. Remote in time though these ancient confessors may have been, Rabus presumed their situation as witnesses to the gospel and opponents of the world to be familiar to his Evangelical German contemporaries; and their stance remained a worthy model.

Even more to the point were those few late-medieval figures who had suffered death at the hand of the very same enemy that was threatening Rabus's contemporaries, the papacy. Rabus did not list John Hus as last in a train of witnesses that had preserved the continuity of Rabus's doctrine from Adam, Seth, the patriarchs, the prophets through the Maccabees and John the Baptist to Christ and the apostles, and beyond them through the holy fathers Polycarp, Irenaeus, Gregory Nazianzus, Basil, Augustine, and Prosper to Luther.[43] However, the Bohemian reformer of the fifteenth century did serve as Rabus's demarcation point for the advent of "these last times," the third period of his history of the church. This period he defined as that in which the Antichrist linked violence and deceit in oppressing believers.[44] Actually, he began the period with an English Wycliffite, William Thorpe, who was executed a few years before Hus and Jerome of Prague were burned at Constance in 1415. But Luther's saint, John Hus, remained the key figure in Lutheran historiography, his martyrdom opening the last stage in the Antichrist's development. From his story and those of Jerome, Thorpe and other Wycliffites, a legendary French Carmelite named Thomas of Rheden, and Savonarola, Rabus wove together a tapestry that foreshadowed the papacy's persecution of Protestants in the sixteenth century. But unlike Foxe, who used Wyclif to great advantage in building a case for a specifically English complaint against the papacy, Rabus's focus lacked nationalistic appeal; it cultivated strictly religious feelings.

The confessions that Rabus cited from these men made some points in which he certainly had no interest, for instance, Thorpe's opposition

---

[43]*HdZ*, III:Aiij/v.

[44]*HdZ*, IV:iij/v-(iiij)r; *HdM*, II:109v.

to oaths. But Thorpe also defended other articles: The element in the Lord's Supper remains truly bread after consecration, images should not be worshiped, pilgrimages are wrong, the priest does not have the right or power to confiscate the tithe for personal use. John Oldcastle called for the proper use of penance, and William White attacked celibacy and relics and Rome. Such material helped emphasize some of Rabus's concerns in his own battle against the contemporary papal party.

Furthermore, in each case these fifteenth-century figures presented models of confession against papal tyranny. Rabus dwelt on the Roman party's heinous, wanton use of violence against his innocent martyrs. Thorpe, a zealous, pious man, disputed for the sake of the gospel with prelates, who condemned him—"as is their custom"—and finally had him secretly murdered in prison. The "Antichrist's gang" had Oldcastle burned; and Savonarola was murdered with spears, fire and water because he had opposed "the Antichrist's wanton power and abomination." In the margin of the account of Thomas of Rheden, the reader is reminded that "clerics are the greatest tyrants" and is informed of "the papacy's common custom against pious preachers" — persecution.[45]

Polemic against the pope stands alongside the promotion of piety as the central theme of Rabus's treatment of medieval martyrs; Hus and the other fifteenth-century subjects he presented are thus in no significant way different from his contemporary martyrs. All their stories would provide examples and encouragement for self-sacrifice and bold confession in troubled times. Rabus was urging fellow Evangelicals to maintain the faith against threats of persecution. The immediate threat to the practice of Evangelical piety came from the power and perfidy of the papal party. Both as stalwart examples to the faithful and as polemical weapons for just such a time, the medieval martyrs served as useful, even if not uniquely significant, tools for the task that Rabus was undertaking in his martyrology.

Contemporary martyrs had certainly caught the attention of Protestant propagandists, most prominently Luther himself, before Rabus began to compile what these earlier authors had written.[46] Rabus introduced his review of the "witnesses, confessors, and martyrs" of his own age with an extensive account of Luther's life and confession (see chapter IV). Excluding Luther, whose career as confessor is set before the reader

---

[45]*HdZ*, III:j/r, xxxiij/v-xxxiiij/r, IV:ccxlv/r, III:1; *HdM*, II:1r, 87r, 95r, 94v.

[46]See Hildegard Hebenstreit-Wilfert, "Märtyrerflugschriften der Reformationszeit," in Hans-Joachim Köhler, ed., *Flugschriften als Massenmedium der Reformationszeit* (Stuttgart: Klett, 1981) 397-446.

on the first 110 folio leaves of Book Four, thirty-eight Evangelical witnesses from the 1520s are presented to the reader of Rabus's second edition; Book Five adds thirty-nine more, from the 1530s and 1540s.

Of these thirty-eight chapters in Book Four, twenty-five contained narrative and/or texts from residents in the heart of the German empire, and another eleven would have appeared as "German" (nine Dutch and two from Lorraine) to the Strassburger of the 1550s. The Scot, Patrick Hamilton, and the Parisian, Louis Berquin, completed Rabus's list of martyrs from the 1520s. The national complexion of Rabus's contemporary accounts for the 1530s and 1540s changes markedly in Book Five, in which the majority of his subjects are not German. In this Book, two individual Germans and five groups of Germans are treated along with martyrs from France, Spain, Italy, Savoy, England, and Hungary. Rabus seems to have suggested that the confession of the truth was expanding out from the center of its renewal in Wittenberg, especially after the Lutheran princes had addressed their message to the whole world in the persons of the foreign ambassadors present at the Diet of Augsburg in 1530. The Germans cited came from several parts of the empire; Rabus's own area was not favored. Persecution claimed fewer lives in Charles V's Germany than in Mary's England, Valois France, or the Hapsburg Netherlands; but Lutherans were executed or punished for their faith in Saxony, Swabia, Franconia, Austria, and Bavaria, and by bishops in Salzburg, Constance, and Cologne. Rabus's German readers gained some sense that theirs was an international cause, and yet at the same time they could see that their fellow Germans had suffered for the faith. Like Foxe, Rabus was placing national experience within the context of all of Christendom as well as all of Christian history. However, in spite of a rise in German national feeling fed by early humanist tracts, the Germans did not have the same kind of political focus for that feeling which the English had; nor did Rabus focus on and exploit this national feeling in the same effective way that Foxe would.

Twenty-seven of the confessors of Book Four were ordained, but only fifteen in Book Five. Like Foxe and Crespin, Rabus made much of lay confession of the faith. Yet many of his confessors were parish pastors, and a few were members of Orders. The lay people included the Bavarian Countess Argula von Grunbach, several people of noble rank, a municipal secretary (Lazarus Spengler, whose published confession of faith appears in Book Five), two attorneys, a physician, a printer, a soldier, several artisans, and citizens from several towns. But most of the lay models for Rabus's readers came from outside the empire; German witnesses to the faith were largely clergy.

Many of Rabus's "martyrs" did not die for the sake of their confession, but were confessors only. Nineteen chapters in Book Four do not report the deaths of the confessors but only their words or acts of confession; twenty chapters present the martyr's death. In Book Five, twenty-two chapters treat the deaths of martyrs; this correlates with the shift away from Germany to France, England, Italy, and Spain. Foxe and Crespin focus relatively more on the deaths of martyrs than did Rabus, although, as Rabus moved toward the territories that were the centers of Foxe's and Crespin's narratives, he did present a higher percentage of stories of execution. But his was, first of all, a book of confessors and not only of martyrs in the strictest sense of the word. Whereas all but two of Rabus's Dutch martyrs were executed, only nine of those from Germany proper died for the faith.

Rabus included the stories of those who recanted their Evangelical faith, then returned to it, and died for that brave repentance. Such repentance Rabus regarded as a worthy pattern for those who might succumb to temptation in a moment of weakness.

Rabus also reprinted the story of Francesco Spiera, a frequently discussed incident among German Evangelicals because it provided a historical locus for analyzing the sin against the Holy Spirit. Rabus used the original version prepared by Matthaeus Gribaldi of Padua, an acquaintance of Spiera. Spiera had apostasized from his Evangelical confession of faith and then refused to reject his recantation. He ended in despair, unable to believe the gospel for himself and wishing he could commit suicide. Rabus introduced this story with the observation that Spiera had abandoned the faith "out of fear of men and of the loss of his property, possessions, and life." The martyrologist related Spiera's oral and written denial, his terrible despair and terrifying hardness of heart, as "an example of divine wrath and God's just judgment on apostasy"[47] — for all his readers to remember.

In preparing Book Four Rabus had cast his net widely and drawn in a number of sources of different kinds. Four chapters were reprinted tracts which Luther had written to defend nuns who had escaped their cloister or to encourage ladies-in-waiting or fellow pastors under persecution. Four more combined Luther's admonition and consolation for

---

[47]*HdZ*, III:ccvj/r, *HdM*, II:713r. See Friedrich Hubert, *Vergerios publizistische Thätigkeit* (Göttingen: Vandenhoeck & Ruprecht, 1893) 16-17, 264-266, on Spiera and Pietro Paulo Vergerio's treatment of this apostasy, and Philip Schaff, *Die Sünde wider den heiligen Geist und die daraus gezogenen dogmatischen und ethischen Folgerungen* (Halle: Lipper, 1841) "Historischer Anhang über das Lebensende des Francesco Spiera," 171-210.

times of persecution with documents published by others. Two accounts—on Simon Grynaeus's narrow escape from punishment and on the execution of the Thiessen brothers in the Netherlands—had come from Melanchthon's pen; another—on the death of William of Zwollen—had been published by Luther's and Melanchthon's colleague at Wittenberg, Johannes Bugenhagen. Rabus not only used material from his friend in Strassburg, the historian Johannes Sleidan, but also from another neighbor there, the humanist Spaniard Francisco de Enzinas (c. 1520-c. 1552), who had studied in Wittenberg at the time Rabus was a student there. This native of Burgos, who had lived with Melanchthon, translated the New Testament into Spanish and lived in Strassburg from 1549 to 1552, while working on other translations. In the mid-1540s, Enzinas, or Dryander as he was called, had been imprisoned for his faith by the Habsburg administration in Brussels. His own story and eight others from his *Memoirs* make exciting reading. The *Memoirs* were first published, in French, in 1558; Rabus must have worked from Enzinas's manuscript, apparently available to the compiler in Strassburg. Rabus abridged Enzinas's stories extensively, but in a sprightly and faithful style.[48]

Most of the chapters of Book Four were based upon a single tract or two or three published works, which Rabus reproduced, in every case with either no or a minimal amount of editing. Some were brief, although Matthaeus Zell's defense of the incipient reformation of Strassburg covered ninety pages. In contrast to Foxe, who did extensive personal research, Rabus only occasionally included material which he had gained first-hand from eyewitnesses and oral sources.[49] Rabus had written to Johannes Voyt for his own account of his sermon which had provoked his persecution at the hands of his brothers in a Franciscan monastery.[50] Ra-

---

[48]My comparison of Enzinas's and Rabus's texts has been based upon the edition of Enzinas's Latin manuscript, Ch. Al. Campan, ed., *Mémoires de Francisco de Enzinas, Texte Latin Inédit* (Brussels: Société de l'historie de Belgique, 1862-1863). On Enzinas, see Chrisman, *Lay Culture* 24.

[49]Chapters on Peter Spengler, *HdZ*, V:cliiij/v-clx/v, *HdM*, II:444r-446r; on Matthias Waibel, *HdZ*, II:clij/v-clj/r, *HdM*, II:446r-449v although here Rabus also used *Ain new lied von dem bewainlichen tode Mathias Waibels* (n.p., n.d.), reprinted in Philip Wackernagel, ed., *Das deutsche Kirchenlied von der ältesten Zeit bis zu Anfang des XVII. Jahrhunderts* 5 vols. (Leipzig: Teubner, 1864-1877) III:433-36; and on Johann Voyt, see note 50.

[50]*HdZ*, VI:j/r-xxij/r, *HdM*, II:317v-326r; lvs. 317v-321r appear to be narrative material which Voyt sent Rabus, including correspondence between Voyt and his superior Heinrich Marquard, dated 16 and 22 June 1523, and 321v-326r reproduce *Eyn Sermon von Newen Jare, durch Johan Voyt gepredigt zu Weymar yn Parfusser Closter, Darumb er als ein Ketzer von den selben seinen Brudern geacht vnd mit vil verfolgung veriagt* (Zwickau: Gastel, 1523).

bus listed no sources for four of the chapters in Book Four; three of them might have been borrowed from Crespin, although it is remotely possible that both Crespin and Rabus took their accounts from a common source.[51]

The level of sophistication at which the critical issues of sixteenth-century Christianity were debated between the Roman and Evangelical theologians varied greatly, a fact that is reflected in Rabus's fourth book. The "bishop" of Lochau defended rather basic Evangelical positions on communion in both kinds, clerical marriage, and the relationship of the papacy to the church of Christ in his dialogue with Dr. Ochsenfart, the representative of the bishop of Meissen. Gallus Korn got into trouble, because he had preached on the appointed epistle lesson from James 1:27 on pure and undefiled religion and in the process had attacked the monastic system and the papacy. Such material was written originally to sway pious but unlearned readers and probably had that same impact on those who encountered it in Rabus's pages. Extended and more sophisticated analyses of a series of issues—such as Zell's on fasting, clerical marriage, auricular confession, communion in both kinds, purgatory, ordination, excommunication, the Blessed Virgin, the financial practices of the church, the mercy of God and Christian freedom, the proper use of God's law, baptism, the Lord's Supper, papal and episcopal power, and the priesthood of all believers—may have given a fine overview of a solid Evangelical presentation of the faith; but such lengthy and sophisticated critiques and confessions probably did not move either the original readers or Rabus's to strong passions in defense of the faith.

Passions were aroused, rather, by the tales of executions that Rabus related, most by burning but also beheading, hanging, and drowning. The encounters between persecutors and Evangelical martyrs or confessors also enlivened the reading of Rabus's text. Rabus and reader alike must have taken delight when Jacob Probst pointed out one learned accuser's mistakes in Latin, after Jacob had volunteered to proceed with their debate in either Latin or the vernacular. The courage of the confessors and the pathos of their situations are illustrated repeatedly in scenes of confrontation with the defenders of medieval religion—for example,

---

[51]On Nikolaus of Antwerp, *HdZ*, VI:xxxvj/r-xxxviij/r, *HdM*, II:403v-404v, cf. Jean Crespin, *Actiones et Monumenta Martyrum* . . . (Geneva: Crespin, 1560) 46v-47. On Wolfgang Schuch, *HdZ*, V:cxlij/r-cliiij/r, *HdM*, II:435v-440v; Crespin, 49v-52v; see also Ath. Coquerel fils, "Vie et mort du martyr Wolfgang Schuch, brulé à Nancy, le 21 Juin 1525," *Bulletin de la Société de l'histoire du Protestantisme Française* 2 (1854):632-648. Rabus's account of the martyrdom of Louis Berquin, *HdZ*, VI:xxxvij/r-xxxviij/r, is substantially different in length and wording from *HdM*, II:487r-488v; the latter account is substantially that of Crespin, 57r-59r.

when the authorities hounded Caspar Tauber to recant during his imprisonment, when Heinrich Zutphen was grilled by his accuser, and when Johann Beck, forced by his father into the priesthood, was tried before the authorities.

As the drama of Peter Spengler unfolded before the readers, they realized that the true defenders of Luther's message were set upon not only by the Roman ecclesiastical authorities but also by the Anabaptist and spiritualist sectarians who, already in the 1550s, were being associated in the popular Lutheran mind with Romans as enemies of the gospel. In this case, the peasants who took the field in revolt during 1524 and 1525 were the enemy. Spengler, a priest in the diocese of Constance who had married, suffered at the hands of the peasants during the Peasants' Revolt. They had wanted to coerce him into their movement; but he admonished them to lay down their arms. Not long after the revolt ended, officials of the bishop cunningly entrapped and imprisoned him. Before the episcopal court, Spengler gave his confession of faith in God's care and love and refused to reject his Evangelical beliefs. Rabus printed Spengler's critique of the papacy, which had earned him his drowning.

Rabus's sources often stressed the equanimity and even enthusiasm of the martyrs on their way to their final confessions. Alongside a rather vivid, if brief, description of the fire's advance, the joy that Esch and Voes expressed with laughter and a confession of faith is sketched for the reader. Adolf Clarenbach laughed on his way to the pyre. Johann Beck cheerfully told the witnesses of his martyrdom that he preferred Christ to the world. Hoste of the Catelyne kissed his executioners and forgave them.

Nevertheless, when his sources did not supply high drama, Rabus did not invent it. He did not try to fan the flames of nationalist feelings or religious freedom in presenting the story of Hermann von Wied, the archbishop of Cologne, whose attempt at reforming his diocese collapsed under military pressure from Emperor Charles V. Instead, Rabus reproduced important documents that yield an extensive but hardly inspiring account of the course of Hermann's reform and of his death.[52]

---

[52]*HdZ*, VIII:ccxxiiij/v-ccxcvj/v, *HdM*, II:733v-762v, based on . . . *Hermans Ertzbischoffs zu Coeln . . . einfeltigs bedencken, warauff ein Christliche in dem wort Gottes gegrünte Reformation . . . anzurichten sey* (Bonn: von der Muellen, 1543) ij/r-(iiij)r; *Bestendige Verantwortung des Bedenckens vonn Christlicher Reformation das . . . Hermann Ertzbischoff zu Coelln . . . hat aussgeben . . . Anno M.D.XXXXV* (n.p., n.d) aij/ r-(cv)v; . . . *Hern Hermans . . . Appellation . . . Auss dem Lateinischen verteutscht* (Bonn: von der Muellen, 1545) Aij/r-(Bvij)v; Sleidan, *De statv religionis* 162v, 237v-238r, 266v-267r; 169v, 180r, 347v; Johann Allsdorf, *Warhaffter vnd bestendiger bericht von dem Christlichen ende . . . des Hochwirdigsten Herrn Hermans, Ertzbischoffen zu Coelln vnd Churfuersten, etc. Anno 1552 den 15. Augusti des morgens vmb die Neundte stunde* (Leipzig: Gunther, 1553).

In the most dramatic of his chapters treating contemporary martyrs, Rabus retold the story of the Spaniard Juan Diaz, on the basis of the published account by one "Claude de Senarcleus." Rabus began his somewhat abridged translation by quoting Senarcleus's letter to Martin Bucer, who had become Rabus's colleague on his arrival in Strassburg. This introduces the drama of the death of Diaz, Bucer's and Senarcleus's mutual friend, at Regensburg in 1546, at the time of the imperial diet there. Rabus quotes Diaz's confession before the imperial ecclesiastical counselors, Peter Malvenda and Peter de Soto. Juan's brother Alphonso, an imperial official at Emperor Charles's court, hired a gang of thugs to assassinate Juan because his Evangelical views were embarrassing to his brother. They succeeded in their mission, but were pursued by one Michael Heipffer all the way to Innsbruck. There he had them arrested. Then, "contrary to all justice," they were acquitted and treated as though they had done right.[53] The fact that the papal party had approved and used fratricide reinforced one of the chief contentions in Rabus's martyrology—that the foes of the Evangelical movement embodied the forces of the Antichrist.

Foxe's *Acts and Monuments* shaped its readers' minds not only through its words but also through its illustrations, which depicted the Roman Church's persecution of God's people. Rabus's printers also incorporated woodcuts and, later, engravings into the editions of the work, but in a less than systematic and organized fashion. The initial Latin volume carried no illustrations; but Balthasar Beck's heirs decorated about seventy of the nearly 270 pages of the first German volume with woodcuts, most of them probably taken from the collection which Beck had assembled during his career. The rather simple sketches were in some cases standard illustrations, such as Peter with his key, Paul with his sword, Stephan being stoned, Daniel in the lion's den—woodcuts readily at hand in his shop, no doubt. Scenes of martyrdom may have been designed specifically for the printing of Rabus's work, although they, too, could well have been part of the printer's stock. Some woodcuts were used more than once: In the first German volume, the depiction of beheading was of particular importance (figs. 2 and 3); pictures of executions in the mouths of fierce beasts provoked the reader's engagement with the text.

---

[53]*HdZ*, II:cclxxiij/v-ccclv/v, *HdM*, II:688r-708v, translates, with abridgements, *Historia vera de morte sancti uiui Ioannis Diazij Hispani, quemeius frater germanus Alphonsus Diazius, exemplum sequutus primi parricidae Cain uelut alterum Abelem, nefarie interfecit* (Basel: Oporinus, 1546), for which Bucer had written a preface. Senarcleus is probably a pseudonym for Francisco de Enzinas.

2. The Beheading of Cyprian (*HdZ* I:lxxix/v)

3. The Beheading of Crispina (*HdZ* I:lxiij/v)

When Samuel Emmel took over the printing of the first edition of Rabus's martyrology, he used Beck's woodcuts at first, but later replaced many of them, increasing their number in volume one of the German version to eighty-six. In volume two he used only thirty-three woodcuts; in volume three, forty-eight; in volume four, thirty-three; in volume five, twenty-four; in volume six, twenty-six; in volume seven, forty-seven; and in volume eight, six. He repeated some of these woodcuts, sometimes within the same chapter, and often used the same depiction of a trial or an execution for accounts of different martyrs or confessors. He employed four woodcuts for executions by fire (for example, fig. 4), the most common path to martyrdom among his contemporaries; but he also had standard depictions for confessions before judges and other means of bringing Evangelical confessors to deliver their testimony (figs. 5 and 6). One woodcut depicting John Hus in Constance, with the motto "Sancta Simplicitas" engraved on it, occurs five times in Rabus's chapter on Hus. The imprisonments of Simon Wolder and Francesco de Enzinas are called to the readers' mind with the same picture (fig. 7). The burials of Luther and Hermann von Wied also appear identical on Rabus's pages (fig. 8). A special illustration of the assassination of Juan Diaz was provided (fig. 9).

The small and rather simple woodcuts of the first edition were replaced in the second by more complex and generally larger illustrations, in keeping with the folio format. With but few exceptions the illustrations of the 1571-1572 edition were framed using four standard depictions. One frame has two figures at the stake, one to the right and one to the left of the illustration, which is designed to depict the story at hand (fig. 10). Another depicts David and Goliath on the left and Jael and Sisera on the right (fig. 11). A third presents the crucified and the victorious Christ (fig. 12). A fourth displays two swordsmen attacking the people of God (fig. 13). The frames are interchanged without apparent reference to the content of the central illustration or the story that it accompanies. In Book One of the second edition, eleven of the fourteen Old-Testament confessors are depicted in woodcuts, although those of Eleazar and the Maccabees are frameless. In Book Two, confessors and martyrs from the New Testament are presented in illustration, but those from the patristic era hardly at all. Twenty of the 113 chapters from Rabus's own period were enhanced by illustrations, three of which were used more than once.

The number of woodcuts fell significantly in volume two of the second edition. Portraits of John Hus, Jerome of Prague, Jerome Savonarola, Martin Luther, and Matthias Zell offered a new artistic genre to the reader. Among the medieval martyrs, Thorpe and Taylour were depicted in their martyrdoms. Among the nearly eighty contemporary martyrs,

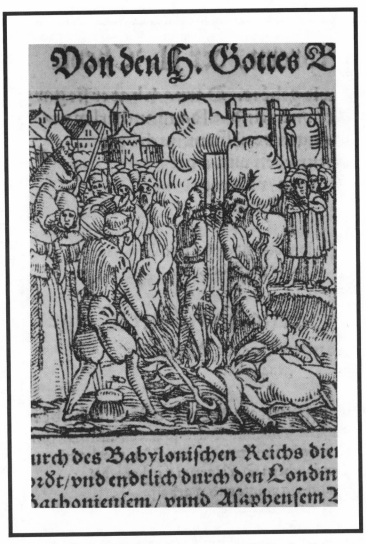

4. The Burning of Robert Barnes (*HdZ* II:cclxvj/v)

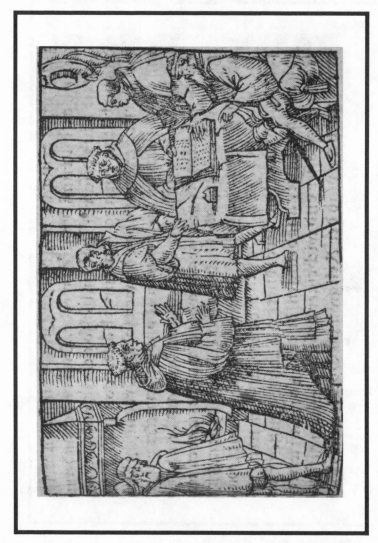

5. Persualdus before His Accusers (*HdZ* VI:lxxxix/r)

6. The Bishop of Lochau before His Accusers (*HdM* II:2llv)

7. Simon Wolder in Prison (*HdZ* VI:clxiij/r)

8. The Burial of Hermann von Wied (*HdZ* VIII:ccxcvj/r)

9. The Assassination of Juan Diaz (*HdZ* II:ccxcix/r)

10. The Martyrdom of Sanctus (*HdM* I:236r)

11. The Beheading of Cyprian (*HdM* I:201r)

12. The Burning of Nemesion (*HdM* I:252v)

13. The Beheading of Agnes (*HdM* I:271r)

only eleven chapters were illustrated (in addition to the portraits of Luther and Zell), and of those only two were unique. Four illustrations from volume one were used again, and two new woodcuts were used more than once.

Woodcuts help enliven a long book like Rabus's for the readers, and the drama of confession and death for the faith provides rich opportunities for exciting illustration. Rabus's publishers worked within the financial and technical limitations of the period. They tried to enliven his text with illustrations, but they obviously did not devote a great amount of money, imagination, or energy to making it a book of pictures. The woodcuts serve, but remain secondary to, the printed text, as is perhaps fitting in a chronicle of confessors of the Word of God.

RABUS'S READERS

Did Rabus's *Accounts of God's Chosen Witnesses, Confessors, and Martyrs* find a significant number of readers interested in the stories of the martyrs? It might be readily concluded that, since he later slipped largely from public view, Rabus was never able to engage the interest of many people with his collection of martyr stories. But the evidence suggests that this was not the case, even though German Lutherans did not demonstrate the degree of interest which Anglicans or continental Calvinists showed for other Protestant compilations of a similar sort. Indeed, Annemarie and Wolfgang Brückner speak of the "explosive initial success" of Rabus's martyrology.

His first attempt—his Latin martyrology—must have met with less than startling success; for the first volume, entitled "Volume One," was also the last. But just as John Foxe, a few years later, turned from Latin to the vernacular, so Rabus immediately translated his collection of martyr stories from biblical and patristic times into German in 1552. That volume was subsequently issued in four additional printings. The reprinting of volumes of the first edition subsided during the six-year course in which it appeared, however; volumes three, four, five and seven were reprinted once only, and volumes six and eight, not at all (see Table 1). Emmel reprinted all the earlier volumes but volume two in 1557, when volumes six and seven first appeared; so he must then have recognized a continuing market. When volume eight appeared the following year, however, the first edition's production ground to a halt.[54]

---

[54]All but the 1552 German and Latin editions of the Rabus martyrology are described in *Bibliographie des martyrologes protestants néerlandais* (La Haye: l'Université de Gand, 1890) II:533-82.

Table 1

PRINTINGS OF RABUS'S FIRST EDITION							
VOL.	YEARS PRINTED						
I	1552	1554	1554	1555		1557	
II			1554	1555	1556		1558
III				1555		1557	
IV					1556	1557	
V					1556	1557	
VI						1557	
VII						1557	1558
VIII							1558

The interest in Rabus's subject did not disappear completely. Josias Rihel, a skillful bookseller, was willing to take over the project from Emmel, his bankrupt brother-in-law, in 1571. Rihel recast and reprinted Rabus's martyrology, outfitting the compilation in a handsome folio format, with new—though fewer—finely crafted illustrations. His investment in production of the two volumes, with a total of just over 1150 folio leaves, must have rested on the conviction that the book would find a ready market in the second decade of legal Lutheranism. The demand was not so tremendous, however, that he reprinted these volumes in a third edition.

The frequency with which Rabus's work appears in the inventories of personal collections of books from the period would give some indication of its popularity. Unfortunately, relatively little is known about collections from the turn of the seventeenth century. However, in his study of the inventories of private libraries in Kitzingen (Franconia) from the period, Erdmann Weyrauch has found only one copy of the *History of Witnesses* among the 214 extant inventories.[55]

Apart from whatever general readership Rabus might have enjoyed, other church historians found him valuable. Foxe and Crespin probably could not read his German, and there is no indication that they used his volumes as a source for their works. But Adriaen van Haemstede did. The Dutch Calvinist martyrologist, who published his compi-

---

[55] I am grateful to Dr. Weyrauch for sharing this information with me. The single copy of Rabus's martyrology is found in the collection of a municipal official, Jacob Besserer (d. 1612), Stadtarchiv Kitzingen, Vormundbuch 30; fol. 1-6. Two copies of Rabus's prayerbook and one copy of another work which he edited are the only other items from his pen among the 5500 books in the Kitzingen inventories.

lation of martyr stories in 1559, extensively borrowed from both Rabus and Crespin.[56] A number of German authors who worked on various kinds of projects used Rabus's work as well.[57] The book was listed in a number of theological and historical bibliographical guides in the seventeenth and eighteenth centuries.[58]

These partial records yield at best mixed evidence regarding Rabus's durability as a popular resource for edification and historical reference. His volumes were reprinted, so they must have commanded attention and interest. That one successful printer thought the market would reward the issue of a new folio edition of the martyrology suggests that some longer-term popularity lasted into a second decade. But a third edition did not appear. Rabus had indeed produced the first Protestant martyrbook, the most extensive German Lutheran martyrology; but Rabus was not Germany's John Foxe. No one was.

---

[56]Fredrik Pijper, *Martelaarsboek* ('s-Gravenhage: Nijhoff, 1924) 47-60; J.-F. Gilmont, "La genèse du martyrologe d'Adrien van Haemstede (1559)," *Revue d'histoire ecclesiastique* LXIII (1968):402-14.

[57]For example, Heinrich Pantaleone's *Martyrum historia* (Basel: Brylinger, 1563) 6v, 66-68, 73-76, 84-96, 102-103, 146-51, 299-302, 156-57; *Prosopographiae herorvm* (Basel: Brylinger, 1566) 141-2, 179-80, 75-82 (on Hermann von Wied, Zell, and Luther); Andreas Hohndorf's and Vincent Sturm's *Calendarivm historicvm* (Frankfurt/Main: Schmid, 1575) 2, 3, 33, 37, [57], 66, 101, 106, 111, 114, 115, 151; Wolfgang Büttner's *Epitome Historiarum* (Leipzig: Apel, 1596) 1-3, 14v, 16v-17r, 75, 77, 78v, 79-84, 87, 89-90, 443v-444r. A century later Johann Conrad Goebel, *Christianus Vapulans. Oder Marter-Cronick . . .* (Mühlhausen: Eibel, 1699), cited Rabus nearly eighty times. Rabus's long treatment of Luther was mentioned by subsequent biographers, e.g. Anton Probus, *Oratio de vocatione et doctrina Martini Lutheri Doctoris Magni & Prophetae Germaniae ultimi* (Leipzig: Baerwald, 1583) C3r; Georg Gloccer, *Warhafftige Historia Vnd grundlicher Summarischer Bericht von der Lehr, Leben, Beruff, vnd seligen Abschiedt des thewren Gottes Mann Doctoris Martini Lutheri* (Strassburg: Bertram, 1586) (B6)r; Nikolaus Selnecker, *Oratio Historica de Initiis, Causis et Progressu Confessionis Augustanae et de Vita ac Laboribus D. D. Martini Lutheri* (Jena: Steinman, 1592))(3v.

[58]Johann Georg Walch, *Bibliotheca historiae ecclesiasticae* (Jena: Crocker, 1762) III:735.

• CHAPTER THREE •

The Martyrbooks
and Their Settings

THE GERMANS
AND THEIR SAINTS

REFORMATION MOVEMENTS in the sixteenth century had certain similarities which bound them together as Protestant and certain differences which distinguished them into confessional groupings. The distinctions have normally been studied and defined in doctrinal terms, which, certainly, were important. But a host of other factors also influenced the ways in which the several confessional churches of Western Europe developed both their teaching and practice.

All Western European Protestants rejected the veneration of the saints and sought to displace that pious practice from their churches' devotional life. Scholars differ on the degree to which the veneration of the saints had influenced the daily life of believers in northern European lands toward the end of the Middle Ages. On the one hand, Keith Thomas notes that "in the fifteenth century pilgrimages and hagiography were on the decline" in England.[1] On the other hand, J. J. Scarisbrick argues that in 1529 "English men and women, by and large, were profoundly addicted to the old ways. Their zest for venerating saints and relics is indisputable."[2] That zest might, of course, have been strong in fact and weaker rel-

---

[1]Keith Thomas, *Religion and the Decline of Magic* (New York: Scribner, 1971) 74.

[2]J. J. Scarisbrick, *The Reformation and the English People* (London: Basil Blackwell, 1984) 54.

ative to a century earlier.

Evidence is similarly mixed in Germany. At the turn of the six-teenth century "the veneration of saints reached its peak and at the same time took on new outward manifestations," according to Bernd Moeller's study of religious life in Germany at the eve of the Reformation.[3] It may have been precisely the fervor of that devotion, disappointed in its failure to obtain the peace it sought from the saints, that caused the people later "in some Protestant areas" to give up "their saints with alacrity."[4] Ven-eration of the saints may in fact have had a different kind of hold on the people particularly of northern Germany than it did in other parts of Christendom. In discussing the use of saint's relics Lionel Rothkrug ob-serves that in northern and eastern Germany, almost no native-born saints held the popular imagination. This is relevant for a discussion of the Ger-man receptiveness to changes in this area of religious life during the Ref-ormation.

> Prior to the 1090s virtually all European pilgrimage places were dedicated to the saints and their relics were enshrined at these holy sites. Only the non-Romanized regions of Germany possess few shrines established to saints, and relic veneration never found firm footing in these lands. For from the time of Charlemagne's mis-sionary wars against the Saxons to the campaigns of the Teutonic Knights—continuing down to the eve of the Reformation—pagan people in the north and in the lands colonized east of the Elbe were repeatedly "converted" by the sword. Unable to perceive saints either among their conquerors or among their own people, the subjugated populations founded few pilgrimage places to this type of celestial patron.[5]

Donald Weinstein and Rudolph Bell expand the significance of this observation with their suggestion that the Germans, particularly the northern Germans, had a different relationship to the saints than did, for instance, the Italians, among whom in the thirteenth century arose a cult

---

[3]Bernd Moeller, "Religious Life in Germany on the Eve of the Reformation," in Gerald Strauss, ed., *Pre-Reformation Germany* (New York: Harper & Row, 1972) 18, see 15-19, 24, 28; translated from "Frömmigkeit in Deutschland um 1500," *Ar-chiv für Reformationsgeschichte* 56 (1956):5-31.

[4]Donald Weinstein and Rudolph M. Bell, *Saints & Society, The Two Worlds of Western Christendom, 1000-1700* (Chicago: University of Chicago Press, 1982) 186.

[5]Lionel Rothkrug, "Religious Practices and Collective Perceptions: Hidden Homologies in the Renaissance and Reformation," *Historical Reflections/Réflexions historiques* 7,1 (1980):38.

of home-grown saints, to a large extent from the lower classes. In contrast, "the roster of German and Scandinavian saints had been largely completed by the end of the twelfth century and consisted of princely (39 percent in the Holy Roman Empire) and clerical power holders (54 percent) who had little in common with the later aspirations of lay piety." Weinstein and Bell note that the decline in the cult of the saints after the twelfth century was less precipitous in those southern and western areas of Germany which later remained Roman Catholic.[6] In many northern, Lutheran areas the pious had apparently never cultivated an intimate relationship with the holy departed precisely like that in most areas of Western Europe—one in which the saints and martyrs held one's allegiance because they were part of one's own tribe and social group. This coolness also made the Reformers' battle against them somewhat easier.

We may conclude that devotion to the saints was an important part of the upsurge in pious practice among the German faithful at the end of the fifteenth century and that its failure to satisfy their spiritual hunger contributed to that crisis of pastoral care which made Luther's message so appealing. If the root system of the veneration of the saints was this weak and shallow in northern Germany, then it is not surprising that the Wittenberg movement, for all its sniping against the practice, did not produce more major attacks against the saints. Luther wrote no *On the Veneration of the Saints* comparable to his *On Monastic Vows*. For the same reasons it is not surprising that Ludwig Rabus's book of martyrs did not exercise the continuing influence which contemporary martyrologies exercised in other countries. The attractiveness of desacralized heroes from Saxony or Cologne must have been limited. Because "a large majority of [medieval] British saints were martyrs,"[7] Foxe was ploughing well-cultivated ground in telling new stories of English martyrs to his readers. Crespin, too, had a more appreciative audience prepared for his work by the cultivation of medieval piety. Rabus ploughed something closer to virgin soil when he tried to plant an interest in the local heroic dead among the home-folks, at least in northern Germany.

This is not to say that foreign saints had not commanded the allegiance and fired the hopes of Germans, so that the polemic had to be carried out, particularly in South Germany. Rabus's own son, Johann Jakob, who had converted to Roman Catholicism and became a priest, took part in the early 1570s in one fierce controversy over the veneration of

---

[6]Weinstein and Bell, *Saints and Society,* 186, cf. 166-67, 176, 182.

[7]Ibid. 179.

saints with Rabus's friend and former colleague, Johann Marbach.[8]

A decade later, the battle over the saints flared up in the south German county of Oettingen. There, Abraham Nagel, a local Roman Catholic priest, precipitated conflict over the practice with his published defense of the claim that the Blessed Virgin had healed an epileptic at the pilgrimage church at Flochburg. Oettingen had been a confessionally divided principality since the Religious Peace of Augsburg; different sides of the family of the counts had opted for Rome or for the Augsburg Confession. The tension between Roman Catholics and Lutherans ran high. The Roman clergy, typified by Father Nagel, was particularly sensitive to the need to defend the medieval view of the role and power of their holy heroes. The Lutherans replied out of an equal sense of threat, undoubtedly because they realized that the ancestral interaction with patron saints still held some attraction for at least some of their people.[9]

These two polemical exchanges were not unique; neither were they so common as the continued polemic over the mass or communion in both kinds or a dozen other issues. The veneration of the saints remained a significant but subsidiary issue in inter-confessional controversy in the late-sixteenth century in Germany. This may well have contributed to the fact that German Lutherans did not lean heavily on Ludwig Rabus's massive substitute for the medieval books of saints, even though those books had been relatively popular among their ancestors.

AN ABSENCE OF MARTYRS DIMINISHES THE MARKET

John Foxe fired the imagination of the English and kept attracting new readers because his pages spoke to their fears of renewed violence against their faith and to their burning indignation over the injustice which had been wrought against their nation and its people by the adherents of the papacy. Foxe's vernacular martyrology appeared at a time at which English people lived in apprehension of a renewed effort to coerce them into the papal obedience—a Spanish invasion. Crespin wrote for Huguenots caught up in the Wars of Religion in France, and van Haem-

---

[8]Marbach replied to the younger Rabus and others in *Von Mirackeln vnd Wunderzeichen. Wie man sie auss vnnd nach Gottes Wort fuer waar oder falsch erkennen soll* . . . (Strassburg, 1571). See Rudolph Schenda, "Die protestantisch-katholische Legendenpolemik," *Archiv für Kulturgeschichte* 52 (1970):41-43. See also Adolf Hauffen, *Johann Fischart, Ein Literaturbild aus der Zeit der Gegenreformation* (Berlin: de Gruyter, 1921) 1:95-133, and Schenda, "Hieronymus Rauscher und die Protestantisch-Katholische Legendenpolemik," in Wolfgang Brückner, ed., *Volkserzählung und Reformation* (Berlin: Schmidt, 1974) 179-258.

[9]Schenda, "Die protestantisch-katholische Legendenpolemik," 28-31.

stede's pages were initially read against the background of the Spanish Inquisition's work in the Netherlands, under the shadow of Spanish occupation and civil war.

In 1551 Rabus embarked on his martyrological project because persecution threatened the Evangelical churches, the Wittenberg movement, and the proclamation of the gospel; Rabus did not, however, in contrast to Foxe and van Haemstede, sense a threat to his nation. Rabus wrote to people who, he presumed, felt as personally and confessionally threatened as he did after his dismissal from office through the introduction of the Augsburg Interim compromise in Strassburg; however, the political experience of the majority of Germans caught up in the Wittenberg movement had not prepared them for an interest in martyrology in the same way that Mary Tudor's more formidable, if not genuinely systematic, persecution had cultivated the ground upon which Foxe's sowing flourished. Furthermore, Germans had only a vague sense of nationhood, and their personal well-being was not connected with the prince—much less the state—in the way in which contemporary English, French, and even Dutch people found their lives framed by national consciousness.

Mary Tudor's father, Henry VIII, had executed English heretics in the same sporadic way that Emperor Charles V had pursued Protestants in his domains. However, the areas where Charles was able to exercise that kind of jurisdiction in the 1520s, 1530s, and 1540s, were limited to the Habsburg ancestral lands in Austria and Swabia and to his Burgundian inheritance. To be sure, disciples of Luther were executed for their faith, particularly in the Netherlands, as in the case of Johann Esch and Heinrich Voes, and also in some areas of Germany.

But A. G. Dickens was largely correct when he noted:

> In regard to Rabus it should not be forgotten that the Germans, as distinct from the Swiss and the Netherlanders, managed to postpone most of the actual killing to the far more political struggles of the seventeenth century. Their Reformation had been a relatively civilized event. Despite the bitterness of controversy, the number of genuine German martyrs remained relatively small if—as Rabus's hatred of sectarians dictated—one omitted Anabaptist and other radical sufferers.[10]

Many Germans did support Luther before their princes or city councils officially introduced Lutheran reform in their lands or against the

---

[10]A. G. Dickens, *Contemporary Historians of the German Reformation* (London: Institute of Germanic Studies, University of London, [1978?]) 16.

wishes and commands of their political authorities. But few German Lutherans suffered more than exile and loss of homes and property for their faith in the sixteenth century. The sustained drama of repeated executions that English Protestants and their French and Dutch Calvinist fellow believers had witnessed had no direct German equivalent. In Rabus's *Accounts*, a majority of those whose sacrifice for the faith embraced death itself were not German. Most of his martyrs who were German were also—significantly for the popularity of his work—clergymen.

The persecution of Luther's followers ordered by the imperial mandate of Worms in 1521 took place at best sporadically and somewhat randomly. It was not until 1546, with the Smalcald War, that Charles V could effectively attempt widespread and systematic enforcement of the Edict of Worms. Thus, Germans had less inclination than the English or the continental Calvinists to find anything approaching existential relevance in a collection of martyr stories.

The situation seems to have changed markedly in 1547-1548, especially in southern Germany, where imperial forces, including Spanish troops, occupied Evangelical cities and principalities and imposed the Augsburg Interim on the Lutherans. Hundreds of pastors fled rather than comply; but none was executed. Furthermore, the example of Strassburg, which avoided occupation by formulating an agreement with its bishop and introducing partial compliance with the Interim, illustrates the ability of Evangelical lay leaders to blunt the effect of the Augsburg Interim. Nonetheless, between the defeat of the Evangelical princes at Mühlberg in April 1547 and the formulation of the Religious Truce of Passau in August 1552, Rabus and his fellow Lutherans were fully justified in viewing the situation of their faith as precarious. The imposition of a return to medieval Catholicism, even in the refined form of the Augsburg Interim, would have been but a prelude to stricter enforcement and a more stringent crackdown, had the emperor and his brother Ferdinand possessed the military might and the ecclesiastical personnel to accomplish the intent of the Edict of Worms.

Though Rabus compiled his martyrology in the midst of this situation, he did not exploit it. Foxe and Crespin centered their attention on the martyrs closest to their own time and place; Rabus ignored the pastors who were driven out of their parishes into exile and ousted from their pulpits by the imperial religious policy of 1548. He avoided heralding in all but a very brief and general way the sacrifice of Elector John Frederick of Saxony, who, with Landgraf Philip of Hesse, was imprisoned for his faith, and who certainly was heralded by others as a saint and martyr for his stubborn refusal to buy freedom from imprisonment and a sentence of death by accepting the Augsburg Interim.[11] Rabus's sharp and continuing critique of the Strassburg municipal government's partial acceptance of the Interim makes it all the more difficult to explain why he failed to record the confession of faith their opposition to the Interim elicited from the prisoners and exiles of the period. Perhaps he could freely preach against his immediate political superiors' policy because he knew he stood secure in his relationship to them; perhaps he feared producing too pointed critiques of imperial policy because he was uncertain whether the emperor's arm might still be able to reach into Strassburg, as it had in securing the dismissal of his colleagues Martin Bucer and Paul Fagius. Yet Rabus did publish the consoling missive prepared by Melanchthon and his Wittenberg colleagues in 1555 for the exiled pastors of Bohemia and Lausitz, who had run afoul of the administration of King Ferdinand's regime. For some unknown reason, Rabus bypassed the opportunity to rally his readers to his cause through the discussion of the persecution in which he, and presumably most of them, were most intimately involved—that of the Augsburg Interim.

Persecution of Lutherans did not cease in 1555 with the Religious Peace of Augsburg. That band of theologians in Magdeburg, which had withstood the threat of imperial power immediately after the Smalcald War, dispersed after the city fathers negotiated the end of the siege of the city in 1551. Wherever they went, they confessed their faith boldly, condemning false teaching and wayward living, often to the irritation of even the most zealously Lutheran of their princes or city councils. Therefore, they were often dispatched into exile. One of them, Johann Wigand, looked back on his own experiences of harrassment and exile and composed a treatise entitled *On the Persecution of the Impious, the Exiles of the Pious, the Exiles of the Hypocrites, the Martyrdoms of the Impious, Pseudomartyrs, the Flight of Ministers of the Word, Faithfulness, Apostasy, Patience.*[12] The treatise, composed in Latin, was about preachers and for preachers; it was not designed for popular consumption, nor did its message have a chance of swaying the popular mind. By 1580, Wigand had no interest in com-

---

[11]See, for instance, the hymns which were written by Petrus Waldorf, Paul von Neuenstat, Caspar Aquila, and Ambrosius Osterreicher in the Elector's praise as a confessor of God's Word during his imprisonment, in Philip Wackernagel, ed., *Das deutsche Kirchenlied von der ältesten Zeit bis zu Anfang des XVII. Jahrhunderts,* 5 vols. (Leipzig; Teubner, 1864-1877) 3:1009-1010, 1011, 1012, 1013, 1016, 1018-1023, 1025-26. John Frederick's sacrifice attracted other adulation as well.

[12]Johann Wigand, *De persecvtione impiorvm. Exiliis piorvm. Exiliis facinorsorvm. Martyriis impiorvm. Pseudomartyriis. Fvga ministrorvm verbi. Constantia. Apostasia. Patientia.* (Frankfurt/Main: Corvinus, 1580).

municating at that level.

Only three of Rabus's eight volumes of the *Accounts of God's Chosen Witnesses, Confessors, and Martyrs* had appeared before the Religious Peace of Augsburg was concluded in September 1555. Modern scholars have exaggerated the calming and stabilizing effect of the Peace on German Lutheranism. During the following decades, the Jesuit advance in Germany and the Council of Trent confirmed for Lutheran leaders that the pope remained earnestly intent upon the destruction of the Evangelical churches. Roman Catholic military or legal action against Protestants in Bavaria and Austria, in France, the Netherlands, and England, substantiated that view and heightened the nervous sense of insecurity that accompanied it.

Among the Lutheran populace, eschatological literature in various forms provided one way in which these threats might be addressed. Eschatological treatises, never a symptom of calm and stability, sometimes specifically incorporated treatments of persecution and martyrdom. For instance, the famous hymn writer, Philip Nicolai (1556-1608), a pastor in Hamburg, published his *Commentary on the Kingdom of Christ* in 1597. On the basis of Ezekiel, Daniel, and Revelation, Nicolai traced the spread of the church of Christ throughout the world, noting at the same time that it had suffered "horrible persecution" at the hands of "Jews, heathen, Turks, papists, and Calvinists." Like Rabus and other Lutheran writers of the period, Nicolai connected persecution of the true church with the doctrinal errors of its foes. His work appeared in Latin, but was translated into German during the Thirty Years War and reissued in translation in 1659.[13] Such works indicate that German Lutherans who were younger contemporaries of Ludwig Rabus did not take their safety and security for granted. They did not rule out the possibility of the renewal of persecution in their lifetime as a prelude to the end of all things.

Nonetheless, the legalization of the faith of the Augsburg Confession must have been somewhat reassuring, especially coming after the anxieties of the period of the Smalcald War and the Augsburg Interim. German followers of Luther had lived for part or all of a thirty-year period

---

[13]On the Lutheran reaction to Trent, see Robert Kolb, "German Lutheran Reactions to the Third Session of the Council of Trent," *Lutherjahrbuch* 51 (1984):63-95. On the rising tide of eschatological literature in the period, see Robin B. Barnes, "Prophecy and the Eschaton in Lutheran Germany, 1530-1630" (Ph.D. dissertation, University of Virginia, 1980), and Barnes's forthcoming book on the same subject. Philip Nicolai, *Commentariorum de regno Christi* (Frankfurt/Main: Spies, 1597); *Historia dess Reichs Christi*, Gothard Artus, trans. (Nuremberg: Endten, 1629; Jena: Hertel, 1659).

with the knowledge that their religious beliefs were illegal and, at least in theory, punishable by the imperial government. Yet due to the protection of local princes or municipal governments, most of them had never been subject to direct police action because of their faith, and few of them had witnessed the execution of a heretic who believed as they believed. The Peace of Augsburg introduced a new sense of order and security, which, however fragile, diminished the need of thinking about martyrdom, even if the Peace did not totally obliterate fears that Roman Catholic clerics might someday persuade the emperor to carry out the suppression of the Evangelical faith. By the time Rabus's second edition appeared, a decade and a half of Lutheran legality must have given prospective purchasers of Rabus's martyrology an optimistic feeling of safety that dulled the interest and the meaningfulness which those two volumes might otherwise have had for them. And those pessimists who knew that, in some form or other, the Thirty Years War was coming, turned largely to kinds of reading other than the martyrbook.

The Thirty Years War revealed not only that the different confessional groups within German Protestantism reacted in differing ways to the thought of a crusade against the papalist foe but also had differing views of the propriety and utility of military action against imperial assaults on Protestantism. Lutheran princes within the Empire, led by Saxony, resisted the call to war for the faith issued by the Calvinist Frederick V of the Palatinate. In contrast to the bold stance in the 1540s and 1550s of the Magdeburgers and their favorite princely house, the Saxon Ernstines, and in contrast to the Scandinavian Lutheran monarchs of their own time, the princes of early Lutheran Orthodoxy, with their theologians, felt no compulsion to enter the lists against the Habsburg emperor in defense of their faith. The political activism of Puritans, Huguenots, and Dutch Calvinists was both supported by the work of Foxe, Crespin, and van Haemstede and, at the same time, contributed to their significance. The absence of more virulent official political and military activity on behalf of the Wittenberg theology and the Lutheran churches within Lutheran Germany after 1580, whether reflection or cause of wider currents within that society, may have deprived Rabus's work of one strong factor that could have contributed to the development or continuance of a mentality suitable for marketing a martyrology. In this regard it is interesting to note that two German translations of Crespin's martyrology were reissued in more than a dozen printings and circulated among German Calvinists between 1590 and 1682.[14] There is no evidence that these translations sold well among Lutherans.

Martyrologies both feed on and serve to heighten a mood of militancy; but such a mood was officially discouraged and lay largely dormant among Lutherans in Germany at the end of the sixteenth and throughout the seventeenth centuries. For these reasons, the political situation of German Lutheranism in this period was not particularly conducive to the popularity of Ludwig Rabus's martyrology.

A MATTER OF STYLE AND GENRE

Alongside the political considerations affecting the degree to which Rabus's narratives of martyrs made a lasting impact lie certain literary factors. Rabus's martyrological corpus is formidable by its sheer size—an intimidation to some potential readers. However, Foxe and Crespin must have intimidated some prospective purchasers, too, by—in Foxe's case— the folio format and, undoubtedly, the resulting high price. None of the sixteenth-century martyrbooks gained their prestige through massive sales like the best-sellers of later centuries.

But for reasons other than sheer size, it was even more difficult to keep reading Rabus's work. The impact which a book makes on its intended audience depends on how well it is written and how well it is designed for a reading public. The *Accounts of God's Chosen Witnesses, Confessors, and Martyrs* was actually composed not only by Ludwig Rabus but also—and to a greater extent—by the several dozen authors whose works he directly copied and translated. They had envisioned their audiences in various ways, and that made Rabus's compilation more difficult to read.

Furthermore, it is not clear that Rabus himself was working with a sharply defined concept of his reading public. Wolfgang Hieber observed that Rabus, in the course of the first edition in the mid-1550s, seems to have refocused his prefaces away from the Evangelical laity in the direction of their pastors.[15] While it is probable that Rabus's new call for

---

[14]An excerpted version of Crespin's martyrbook was published by the printer Christoph Rab in Herborn in 1590, *Maertyrbuch Darinnen merckliche denckwuerdige Reden vnd Thaten vieler heiligen Maertyrer beschriben werden;* subsequent editions appeared in Herborn in 1591, 1595, 1603, 1608, 1617, 1641, in Siegen and Basel in 1597, and in Smalcald in 1682. The translation of Paul Coccius, *Gross Martyrbuch vnd Kirchen-Historien . . .* (Hanau: Anton, 1606) was reprinted in 1617 in Hanau and in 1682 in Bremen.

[15]Wolfgang Hieber, "Legende, protestantische Bekennerhistorie, Legendenhistorie, Studien zur literarischen Gestaltung der Heiligenthematik im Zeitalter der Glaubenskämpfe" (doctoral dissertation, University of Würzburg, 1970) 82.

struggle against false doctrine and the sects (rather than against the sword of the papalist persecutor), which asserted itself rather strongly in the prefaces composed after 1555, found a more receptive ear in the parsonage than in the the cobbler's shop or on the peasant's hearth, it may not have seemed so to Rabus. However, the treatments of the biblical martyrs in his second edition were clearly transformed into aids for preachers. The first edition's short, crisp recitals of events succinctly described in the Scriptures metamorphosed into extensive glosses on countless aspects of the texts. This suggests that between 1551 and 1571 Rabus's vision of his audience had shifted significantly, away from the laity towards the clergy.

Rabus intended to acquaint both ordained and lay readers not only with examples of stalwart bravery in defense of the faith but also with the content of Evangelical confession—with issues raised by Luther in and for the household of faith. But his failures to edit and to synthesize his source materials meant that some of his chapters focused on issues which had lost their importance by the 1570s. German Lutherans were no longer concerned about some issues and never had been interested in others which medieval or foreign witnesses to the faith had dealt with at length in their public testimonies. In so far as Rabus's book was intended to be used as a guide to reliable statements of Evangelical doctrine, it had become largely passé by the time of the Formula of Concord (1577). The most prominent disputes of the 1520s and 1530s, which Rabus's confessors addressed, remained alive in the 1570s—among them justification through faith, communion in both kinds, papal and episcopal power. But over the half-century, the Evangelical approaches to some points of dispute with Rome had changed. Nor had German Lutherans ever been interested in the giving of oaths, as William Thorpe had been; or in the reappearance of the dead, as Adolph von Clarenbach was in the testimony which Rabus recorded; or in the concept of soul-sleep, on which Matthias Devay's confession dwells at some length. By 1571 that concept was certainly foreign, if not offensive, to those who would have paused to think about it while leafing through the many pages of Rabus's second volume. Certainly his appeal was dimmed by many such sections which would have had little interest for the lay reader.

Rabus's work suffers in the contrast between its literary structure and the frameworks that Foxe and Crespin used. Rabus chose, at first, to produce an alphabetical index to biblical and patristic martyrs, continuing later with a simple compendium of pieces of several literary types. Even with the chronological ordering of the second edition, Rabus's book does not approach the much more readable, narrative review of the history of the whole Christian church, with a special focus on the "elect nation" of the English, which Foxe created. Foxe's style of carefully constructed saga presents an argument that persuades, page after page. Rabus entrusted his argument to the individual authors from whom he borrowed, depending on his own brief prefaces and sentence-long introductions to synthesize the message that he wanted the reader to find. His chapters were too diverse to allow him to unify them with so few words.

Furthermore, though Rabus did present a fairly well-constructed, clearly-expressed theology of martyrdom in his prefaces, that theology functioned—could function—as a persuasive basis only for the individual action of faithful discipleship which believers owe their Lord. It did not develop in detail a larger—national or universal—framework of meaning into which individual confesssors might place their actions. Rabus conceived that his reader would be a part of the long chain of prophetic witnesses; but he did not forge the loose links of that chain together into a coherent narrative, nor did he do more than merely point to the dramatic, eschatological conclusion that gave ultimate meaning to participation in that chain. Unlike Foxe and what he was able to do so skillfully for the English,[16] Rabus failed to weave his theology effectively into the history of the world, the church, or the German people. Rabus's readers might enjoy dramatic confrontations of ancient or contemporary confessors with learned inquisitors and evil executioners, amplified by extended written confessions of faith; however, Rabus's readers did not receive the assistance which Foxe supplied his readers in placing the examples of heroic confession and sacrifice in a larger historical and eschatological schema.

Furthermore, Rabus did not exploit the drama of his subject in the way in which other martyrologists of his age did. The popular appeal of the martyrbook rested in part on its entertainment value. Tales of gruesome horror and daring defiance titillated pious hearts, and with relative ease a good storyteller could heighten the unavoidable drama of the martyrs' confrontation with their persecutors. John Foxe was such a master storyteller. Ludwig Rabus did not even try to refashion or heighten the material which he had assembled into a sixteenth-century form of popular journalism. His chapters, borrowed from others wth varying foci and forms, could not sustain reader interest in the way Foxe's gripping narrative did.

In addition, Rabus apparently chose the wrong genre for Lutheranism. Though one cannot compare Foxe's popular martyrology with

---

[16]See the detailed argument of V. Norskov Olson, *John Foxe and the Elizabethan Church* (Berkeley: University of California Press, 1973).

the history of dogma which became the standard church history for Lutheranism, the so-called Magdeburg Centuriators sensed far better than Rabus did what form Lutheran history-writing would have to take.

The "Centuriators," so-named because their work was popularly known as the Magdeburg *Centuries*, were from that group that had defied the emperor's forces in their namesake city in the wake of the Smalcald War. The Magdeburgers published those few tracts which, in 1550, first put ancient martyr stories to use against the threat of the imperial Interim. Soon thereafter these men formulated the schema that would give German Lutheranism its interpretation of the history of the church. Whereas England found John Foxe's person- and nation-centered narrative of the unfolding of God's plan for his people a sufficient orientation for understanding church history, the followers of Luther chose another form of interpretation for understanding the history of God's people, a form closer to Luther's theology. The Magdeburgers focused on the history of the preaching and teaching of God's Word.

Under the leadership of Matthias Flacius Illyricus, a small circle of scholars organized itself in the mid-1550s to execute a plan which Flacius had formulated for writing church history, a plan to demonstrate that the followers of Luther held to the catholic faith and that the papacy was, indeed, the Antichrist. Long given credit for having written much of the work itself, Flacius, in fact, only formulated the strategy for researching and composing what became fourteen volumes, entitled *Ecclesiastical History* but dubbed the *Centuries*, because its subject matter was arranged by century.[17] He organized the team of researchers and authors, and he spearheaded the search for primary materials from which the other team members could work. But Flacius left the writing to two close friends, Johann Wigand (1523-1587) and Matthaeus Judex (1528-1564), who supervised others as they produced folio volumes that traced developments century by century through the thirteenth.

Flacius had pioneered his particular kind of work on church history writing with the publication in 1556 of his *Catalog of Witnesses of the Truth*.[18] The German translation of this Latin work was printed seventeen

---

[17]The authorship of the *Centuries* has been thoroughly explored by Ronald E. Diener, "The Magdeburg Centuries, A Bibliothecal and Historiographical Analysis" (Th.D. dissertation, Harvard Divinity School, 1978) 39-127.

[18]*Catalogus testium veritatis, qui ante nostram aetatem reclamarunt Papae* (Basel: Oporinus, 1556), translated into German as *Catalogus testium veritatis. Historia der zeugen, Bekenner vnd Marterer, so Christum vnd die Euangelische warheit biss hierher, auch etwa mitten im Reich der finsternus, warhafftig erkennet,* by Conrad Lautenbach (Frankfurt/Main, 1573). Flacius reviewed the translation.

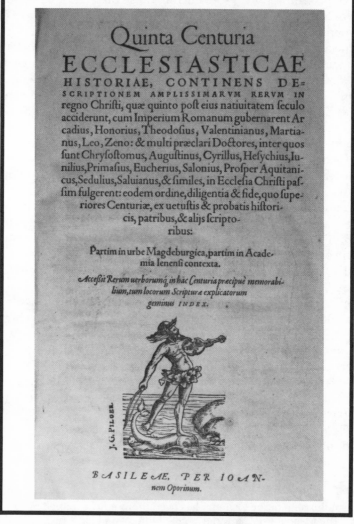

14. The Magdeburg *Centuries*, Volume V

years later; and the title of Rabus's martyrology had been incorporated into Flacius's subtitle. Flacius claimed this catalog to be a "history of the witnesses, confessors and martyrs" who had publicly given testimony to Christ; whereas Rabus had organized his material around individuals, Flacius organized his around doctrinal topics. His was not a study of the individuals who had witnessed, confessed, and been martyred for the faith; in the *Catalog* he focused exclusively on the content of their confession and witness.

Flacius developed his program for a narrative of God's governance of his people at the same critical period in which he was beginning to formulate principles for biblical interpretation and in which he was leading the attack on assaults against Luther's gospel both from the papal-imperial party of the Augsburg Interim and from the Wittenberg adherents of the Philippist compromise, the Leipzig Interim.[19] Flacius was working with a much grander and more coherent conceptual framework for writing the history of the church than Rabus was.

Flacius and Wigand had been alienated from their preceptor, Philip Melanchthon, by the divisions which the Smalcald War and the Augsburg Interim had precipitated among the Wittenbergers; but they had learned how to view the history of the church from him. Certainly, differences in emphasis and focus separated professor from students: Melanchthon, according to Massner's interpretation,[20] gave more authoritative weight to the teaching of the ancient fathers than Flacius and Wigand thought appropriate, and Melanchthon gave a measure of authority to the church that Flacius preferred to place with the Word of God in the church's mouth. Nonetheless, there was continuity between preceptor and pupils at many points. Flacius and Wigand, like Melanchthon, joyfully used the ancient fathers' writings when they witnessed to the truth of the biblical writers as gifts of God. Flacius and Wigand also

---

[19]Joachim Massner, *Kirchliche Überlieferung und Autorität im Flaciuskreis. Studien zu den Magdeburger Zenturien* (Berlin: Lutherisches Verlagshaus, 1964) 74, states that Flacius moved from biblical interpretation to the research of the history of the church; Heinz Scheible, *Die Entstehung der Magdeburger Zenturien, Ein Beitrag zur Geschichte der historischen Methode* (Gütersloh: Mohn, 1966) 14-15, disagrees. Flacius's first work on biblical interpretation, his *De vocabulo fidei et aliis quibusdam vocabulis explicatio vera et utilis, sumta ex fontibus ex Ebraica* (Wittenberg: Creutzer, 1549), appeared at the time when he was becoming deeply involved in the polemics of the period, the same period during which the incipient Magdeburg circle, Flacius included, was gathering historical ammunition against the Roman Catholics and the Philippist Lutherans. This suggests the inseparability of the three elements of polemic, biblical studies, and church history.

[20]Massner, *Kirchliche Überlieferung*, 21-28.

recognized a chain of witnesses that had kept the gospel alive through the history of the church against the concatenation of opponents to the gospel—above all against the Roman Antichrist who continued to oppose it. Both these lessons had been learned from Melanchthon.[21]

But among the themes sketched out in the Centuriator's sixteen chapters there can be no doubt as to which was the most important. It was not topic twelve, "martyrs," nor topic ten, "illustrious persons in the church (bishops and teachers),"—biography was neither the historical genre nor the focus of interest for the Magdeburgers. Above all, theirs was a history of dogma: Topic four, "on doctrine," exceeded all the other fifteen topics, providing 30.1 percent of the bulk of the fourteen volumes of final publication. The first century was covered in two volumes, in which 53.4 percent and 63.8 percent of the content was dedicated respectively to topic four. Centuries four and seven contained the shortest treatments of doctrine, at 9.7 percent and 8.7 percent respectively. The Magdeburgers' recipe for *Ecclesiastical History* was in this regard what Ronald Diener calls "a beef and hare stew."[22]

Rabus's theme of persecution was not absent from the *Centuries*. These volumes contained a separate locus on persecution in addition to the one on martyrs. In sketching the outline to be followed when treating persecutions, the Centuriators announced their intention to discuss the persecution and peace of the church under each emperor. They promised to discuss the kinds of accusations lodged against Christians and the motivations and goals of the persecutors, whether genuine hatred and misplaced zeal, or fear of sedition, or public disorder, or the antagonists' own reprehensible way of life and their various kinds of lusts. They were further interested in whether the Christians had offered their persecutors the occasion for persecution, or whether the persecutors had set themselves upon the Christians in unprovoked fury. The Centuriators promised to answer a number of questions: Who were the persecutors—the magistrate, his lieutenants, the mob, the Jews, some heretics, false brothers, apostates? How was the persecution instituted—through an edict or other means? Where did the persecution take place? What kinds of torments were employed? What kinds of appeals were heard? How did the Christians console one another; did they do so orally or in writing? Did they persevere, or did they exhibit weakness? In the case of exile, was it forced, or did the Christians leave of their own free will? How was persecution

[21]Ibid. 29-35, 41-42; cf. Peter Fraenkel, *Testimonia Patrum, The Function of the Patristic Argument in the Theology of Philip Melanchthon* (Geneva: Droz, 1961) 263-66.

[22]Diener, "The Magdeburg Centuries," 105-106.

mitigated? What sorts of defenses of the faith did the persecution produce? What prayers and miracles were associated with the persecution?
What punishments were visited upon the persecutors?[23] In their actual
treatments of each century, persecution and martyrs received little attention in most cases. Particularly in the earlier centuries, however, the narrative rehearsed the ancient sources and reproduced, in abridged form,
much of the material found in Rabus's accounts.

The *Centuries*, written in Latin and ponderous in bulk, if not in style,
had little or no appeal for lay people. But for the pastor who wanted to
use martyr stories or to trace some history of the confession of the church,
the Centuriators provided not only a systematic organization and analysis of the relevant material but also a wide overview of the history of the
church. The narrow focus on persecution and the biographical approach
which informed Rabus's work could not compete wth the Magdeburgers'
more comprehensive coverage of the history of God's people. Although
the full set of the *Centuries* cost more than most pastors could afford, its
approach dominated other attempts to summarize and interpret church
history, and its interpretation found wide acceptance among Lutherans
and other Protestants as well.

One example of a briefer, more popular version of this history-of-
dogma approach to church history which gained wide recognition and
usage among German Lutherans was the work of Lukas Osiander (1534-
1604), a Swabian theologian and ecclesiastical courtier at the court of the
dukes of Württemberg. The *Centuries* provided both an inspiration and a
model for Osiander, who extended the history into the sixteenth century.
Osiander also emphasized the struggle of the Antichrist against the proper
proclamation of the gospel and promised to pay special attention to the
persecutions that the church had suffered and to the confessions of its
martyrs. His attention focused, however, on combatting heresy and cultivating a proper understanding of the biblical message.[24]

In summary, Ludwig Rabus had used a biographical approach to
the narration of God's action among his people and had produced a massive martyrology. Through it he aimed to refocus attention away from the
mystical heroes of the medieval panoply of saints and towards the historical heroes who had provided power for believers through their recitation of the Word of God rather than through magical powers. Rabus had
brought together the Lutheran concerns for history, the Word, and the

---

[23]*Ecclesiastica Historia* (Basel, 1559-1574) I,1:3r.

[24]*Epitomes Historiae ecclesiasticae Centuria I. II. III*, 2d ed. (Tübingen: Gruppenbach, 1607) I:):(2r -):():(2r; cf. VI:):(2v.

battle against the enemies of the Word, in a form that would aid in displacing the veneration of the saints. But Rabus did not perform the task as well as he might have. He compiled other people's stories and failed to set them in a coherent and clear outline.

Moreover, the Lutheran focus on God's Word turned the writing of history in the Wittenberg movement away from Rabus's biographical approach and from his concern to do battle with the veneration of the saints through historical writing. The Magdeburg Centuriators developed a new form for writing church history—by century and by topic. They did not exclude biographical considerations from their work by any means; but biography became secondary to the history of dogma and to other concerns.

Lutherans, nevertheless, maintained an interest in biography, for they believed that God does work in human history through chosen human instruments, some of them with historic proportions. But one figure above all others absorbed most of the German Lutherans' need to have a heroic saint, and he was a hero of the Word, a man who could be called prophet and teacher, pastor and even martyr. He was Martin Luther. Whereas Luther did not directly replace the medieval panoply of saints, his image did attract much of the energy that had been devoted to earlier models of the saints, becoming himself an exemplar for the new Lutheran understanding of the holy centered on God's Word and its proclamation. The Luther of biography became a model for his followers, an inspiration above all others, and an expression of the intervention of God's grace in their world.

CHAPTER FOUR

Saint Martin of Wittenberg: Luther in the View of His Students

EARLY "BIOGRAPHIES" OF LUTHER

ON 11 NOVEMBER 1563, Cyriakus Spangenberg preached to his congregation in Mansfeld on the anniversary of Martin Luther's baptism, which had taken place on that day eighty years earlier. He observed that the ancient church had remembered outstanding teachers, martyrs, and confessors with annual festivals. These festivals, he told his congregation, had not recognized these saints as mediators, nor had the saints been offered special veneration; rather, the people of God remembered the teaching, faith, confession, and steadfastness of these holy ones on such occasions. In that spirit, Spangenberg was recalling Luther. Five years later he was still preaching an occasional sermon on Luther, and he compared the celebration of Luther's ministry in which he was leading his parish to the festivities which parents hold on the birthday of a child, food and drink aiding in the expression of their joy. The anniversary of Luther's birth and baptism gives occasion for celebration, Spangenberg stated, because he was a prophet and faithful teacher, whose teaching brought with it the very power of God, and because he could serve as an inspiring example

15. Martin Luther (*HdM* II:110v)

in times of spiritual trial.[1]

The heroic saints of the Lutherans had to be different from the intercessory wonderworkers of medieval piety. As Lutherans like Spangenberg cast about for such heroic figures, they found this one man of almost mythic proportions who could serve indirectly as a replacement for a panoply of old-style saints. The images of this new saint, "Doctor Martin Luther of blessed memory," appear in a variety of literary productions published during Luther's life and the following generation. These literary representations of Luther, the saint, reflect artistic images from as early as a report on the Diet at Worms issued in 1521, containing a woodcut of Luther as Augustinian monk with a nimbus around his head and with a dove, the Holy Spirit, above. R. W. Scribner traces the development of the depiction of Luther as saint from this and other pictures of the 1520s to material like the picture from about 1556 of Luther as patron saint, presenting his prince's family to God, and carved pulpits that add Luther to the icons of the four evangelists.[2]

Luther's image became the profile of a saint for whom his followers could give thanks, whose example could strengthen their faith, whose life could be imitated, or perhaps better, could receive attention as an exhibition of life caught up in the Word of God, a concept central to Luther's own theology and the theology of his successors.

At Luther's funeral Philip Melanchthon placed his mentor among the prophets, apostles, and fathers of the church, in the train of Isaiah, John the Baptist, Paul, and Augustine. He was one of those "most illustrious men raised up by God to gather and establish the church."[3] Both in his funeral oration and in the brief biographical sketch that he pre-

---

[1]Cyriakus Spangenberg, *Die dritte Predigte, von dem heiligen Gottes Manne, Doctore Martino Luthero, Sonderlich von seinem Prophetenampte. . . .* (Erfurt: Georg Baumann, 1564) (Avij)v-(Aviij)v; *Die Zehende Predigt, Von dem thewren Bekenner Gottes. D. MARTINI LVTHER. Das er ein rechtschaffen heiliger MARTYRER vnd Bestendiger Zeuge Jhesu Christi gewesen* (Eisleben: Petri, 1568) a/v-aij/v.

[2]For illustrations and analysis, see R. W. Scribner, *For the Sake of Simple Folk, Popular Propaganda for the German Reformation* (Cambridge: Cambridge University Press, 1981), chapter 2, "Images of Luther 1519-25" 14-36; and *Martin Luther und die Reformation in Deutschland, Ausstellung zum 500. Geburtstag Martin Luthers, Veranstaltet vom Germanischen Nationalmuseum Nürnberg, in Zusammenarbeit mit dem Verein für Reformationsgeschichte* (Frankfurt/Main: Insel, 1983) 222-223, 362. On the literature of the early period, see Andrea Körsgen-Wiedeburg, "Das Bild Martin Luthers in den Flugschriften der frühen Reformationszeit," in Horst Rabe, Hansgeorg Molitor, and Hans-Christoph Rublack, eds., *Festgabe für Ernst Walter Zeeden* (Münster: Aschendorff, 1976) 153-77.

[3]CR 11:272-78.

pared for the second volume of the Wittenberg edition of Luther's works, Melanchthon reflected some of the glory ascribed to Luther by his devoted followers. However, as James Michael Weiss has demonstrated, Melanchthon "clearly intended to distance himself from their unmitigated enthusiasm and to praise Luther in terms of Melanchthon's own ideal of reform and humanistic learning." Yet, when he turned to composing the preface for the printed sermon, Melanchthon stepped back from the somewhat muted criticism of Luther's harshness present in the funeral oration. In the preface Melanchthon tried with limited success to reshape the picture of Luther already current among his devoted students according to a model prescribed by Philip's own ideas, shifting the balance between a focus on Luther as God's instrument and a focus on Luther's great deeds in behalf of the church slightly toward the latter.[4] In both essays Melanchthon concurred, with certain qualifications, in the high appreciation for Luther accorded him by students and friends at the time of his death. Their association of Luther with the ancient spokesman of God must have come quite naturally; for during the last fifteen years of his life, Luther himself had made similar observations about the role into which God had cast him. His belief regarding this role as a spokesman for God must be understood against the background of his concept of what is called "the living voice of the gospel."

Luther taught that the biblical message does not only lie static on the page, a sign pointing passively to heavenly reality. When spoken, the words take that biblical message and apply it to contemporary lives; they do more than merely talk about God's attitude toward his human creatures and his previous actions in their behalf. Those spoken words convey what they describe as they proclaim God's wrath and his mercy. They do the work of God in condemning and, above all, forgiving and restoring to new life. Thus, one might speak of a "real presence" of God's power in that scripturally anchored proclamation of the Christian. Luther's followers saw a particularly good example of the living and active word in Luther, especially because he had a particular calling to the public ministry and to the role of reformer.[5]

With the authority of both Luther and Melanchthon behind them, it is little wonder that Luther's first biographers viewed him as a man of

---

[4]James Michael Weiss, "Erasmus at Luther's Funeral, Melanchthon's Funeral Oration for and Biography of Luther," *The Sixteenth Century Journal* XVI,1 (1985):92.

[5]See Mark U. Edwards, Jr., *Luther and the False Brethren* (Stanford: Stanford University Press, 1975) esp. 112-26 on Luther's prophetic self-appraisal; and on the concept of the living voice of the gospel, see Paul Althaus, *The Theology of Martin Luther*, Robert C. Schultz, trans. (Philadelphia: Fortress, 1966) 35-42.

God of the likes of Isaiah and Paul. They demonstrated their affection, respect, and appreciation for their German hero of God's Word in a number of literary genres, among them several forms of "biography."

Luther as Martyr and Confessor

The classic confessor in the ancient church, the basic model of the Christian saint, was the martyr. Søren Kierkegaard once remarked, "Luther really did incalculable harm by not becoming a martyr."[6] Luther's students would have disagreed; they believed that he was, in fact, a martyr. In his sermon on Luther the martyr, Cyriakus Spangenberg defined the term: a martyr is a witness "who gives a public confession of Jesus Christ with the mouth, that he alone is our righteousness and that there is no other forgiveness of sins to be found except in him." Spangenberg immediately noted that the devil and the world battle against that confession, with the result that many such confessors must die for their faith. But death is not essential to make a witness of the Word a martyr. Martyrs may fall into any one of four categories. Some were plagued by Satan but experienced no external persecution, even though they were ready to die for their faith. Some were publicly slandered and mocked but received no physical punishment. Some were imprisoned for their confession. Some died for their faith.

Spangenberg argued that Luther had been a martyr on several counts. His sermons and written works proved that he had confessed Christ in the face of opposition from popes and bishops, from the emperor and the estates of the empire, from sects and heretics. Spangenberg found Luther's bold and straightforward witness particularly in his writings; he singled out the general confession that concludes the reformer's *On the Lord's Supper, Confession* of 1528 as well as the entire document itself, along with the Schwabach Articles, the Augsburg Confession and its Apology (which, despite Melanchthon's authorship, seemed to Spangenberg to be Luther's confessions), the Smalcald Articles, and the Shorter Confession Against the Sacramentarians of 1544.

Furthermore, Spangenberg argued, his confessor had suffered for the faith both publicly and secretly. He had always been ready to die for the faith. In his own anguish he had shared the sufferings of his followers who were imprisoned or executed for the faith. His foes had publicly attacked him and made his life difficult. The crosses of family life had fallen

---

[6]Alexander Dru, ed., *The Journals of Søren Kierkegaard* (New York: Oxford University Press, 1938) #1304, cited by Ernest B. Koenker, "Søren Kierkegaard on Luther," in Jaroslav Pelikan, ed., *Interpreters of Luther, Essays in Honor of Wilhelm Pauck* (Philadelphia: Fortress, 1968) 240.

upon him, especially in the form of the sickness of his children and the death of his daughter Magdalena. Apostates, such as Johann Agricola and Andreas von Carlstadt, had plagued him, as did others who heard Luther's proclamation of the Word but did not repent. Among those who afflicted Luther with their abuse of the gospel, Spangenberg enumerated the common man, who vaunted a false religious security; the citizens of the towns, who always wanted compliant pastors; the nobles and the political authorities, who wanted to call "gospel" whatever served their purposes. In addition to all this and to slanders, lies, the papal excommunication, and the imperial declaration that he was an outlaw, Luther also suffered the devil's temptations to doubt and despair. But with the comfort and power of the gospel Luther had triumphed over all these evils through the reading of the Scriptures, prayer, the use of the sacrament, patience, a firm consciousness of his calling, and his contempt for the devil and the world. Spangenberg urged his hearers and readers to confess in the same manner as Luther had, to bear their crosses, and to confront temptations to apostasize with full confidence in the victory which Christ shares with his people.[7] In Luther's life, Spangenberg had found a pattern and model that was useful for the admonition of his parishioners and his reading audience. Most of them would not encounter all the temptations and adversities Luther had, but many of them knew the trials brought on by the illness of their children or their own doubts of God's mercy.

Spangenberg began preaching his series of sermons on Luther's life in 1562, the same year that Johann Mathesius began a similiar project. The first attempt at a lengthy study of Luther's life and thought had appeared six years earlier in the fourth volume of Ludwig Rabus's *Accounts of God's Chosen Witnesses, Confessors, and Martyrs.*

For Rabus, Martin Luther was "our dear father and the prophet of the German nation," indeed, the foremost witness, confessor, and martyr of his age. Others, Rabus admitted—above all Philip Melanchthon—had previously set forth Luther's story:

> . . . the life, death, and especially the many battles and struggles, which through God's gracious support this worthy, highly-enlightened, and true man of God, Doctor Martin Luther of blessed and holy memory, had endured with great constancy for the sake of the confession of the truth of the gospel.[8]

---

[7]Spangenberg, *Die Zehende Predigt*, passim.

[8]*HdM*, II:110r; treatment of Luther in this second edition is extensively revised from the version found in *HdZ*, IV:j/r-cccxliiij/v.

Rabus placed Luther among the biblical, patristic, late-medieval, and contemporary martyrs, from Abel through Luther's followers such as Johann Esch and Heinrich Voes, and other Protestants, such as Juan Diaz, who had died for the faith. Luther was certainly not the only con-, fessor who qualified for Rabus's consideration without having given testimony through death at the executioner's hand: Confessions from the pens of Rabus's own mentor in Strassburg, Matthaeus Zell, of the noble-woman Argula von Grunbach, of the municipal secretary Lazarus Spengler, and of many others, also appear in his book.

Martin Luther does, however, occupy a key position in the outline of Rabus's history of Christian martyrdom. In the first edition, the account of Luther's career of confession is the longest of the 223 chapters in the eight-volume work. It reveals more of Rabus's personal care and energy in its initial form than do most entries, for Rabus here broke with his usual format of simply reprinting another text, and he approached narrative description by fashioning bits and pieces of Luther's history through which to link the lengthy citations. Furthermore, Rabus's chapter on Luther is the most extensively revised section of the second edition of the martyrology. In the second edition, Luther's witness inaugurates the contemporary era of martyrdom; for even though Rabus's third great period, that of the papal oppression of the church, had begun at the time of John Hus, "the almighty eternal God had let the gracious light of his Holy Word shine on and illumine the German nation in most gracious fashion" through Luther's confession.[9]

Rabus's treatment of Luther is not strictly speaking biographical. It is a chronological overview of Luther's thought rather than of his life; and this overview contains no analysis at all. Rabus did little more than copy entire tracts and letters from edited versions of Luther's works, providing his readers with a kind of "reader's digest" of Luther's literary career, with brief appropriate commentary on intervening events from time to time. Melanchthon's biographical pieces served as Rabus's prime source for the narrative of Luther's early life in the first edition, and Mathesius's homilies on Luther's life provided Rabus with materials for expansion of these narrative sections in the second edition. The sections from Luther's writings were, for the most part, lifted from the Jena edition of his works. The publication of the first two volumes of the Jena German series in 1555 appears to have moved Rabus early in 1556 to devote 244 of the 295 quarto leaves of his fourth volume to Luther's career and message. This sugges-

---

[9] *HdZ*, IV:[*iiij]v-)(r.

tion is strengthened by Rabus's dedication of the volume to the patrons of the Jena project, the "young lords" of ducal Saxony, the sons of Elector John Frederick the Elder, who resolved to issue their own version of Luther's works, since the Wittenberg edition had slipped from their family's hands after their father's defeat in the Smalcald War.[10]

Of course, Rabus could not simply reproduce what he found in that new edition of Luther's writings. He was selective. He omitted many items which the Jena editors had compiled. Furthermore, on rare occasions, he seems to have consulted the text of another publication, perhaps an earlier printing that he had in his own library. The first two volumes of the Jena edition supported Rabus's effort only so far as the death of Frederick the Wise in May 1525. In the first edition of Rabus's biography, the Jena material and the accompanying narrative accounted for just over sixty percent of his account; the second edition added some later documents and comments and altered the balance between periods before and after 1525. Rabus took this later material from the Wittenberg edition and from other sources.

In the introductory narrative on Luther's life, before his literary career began, Rabus brought to the reader's attention Luther's early engagement with the Word of God. Upon the completion of his Master of Arts degree in 1505, Luther went into the Augustinian monastery in Erfurt, "contrary to the desire of his parents and friends, as Mathesius writes." Rabus only briefly mentioned Mathesius's tale of the thunderstorm conversion and Luther's loss of a friend through an accidental, fatal stabbing. Rabus also mentioned Luther's quarrel with his father over the son's entry into monastic life; and Rabus observed that many of Luther's friends, whom he invited to a farewell banquet, thought it was an utter shame that "so powerful a genius should lie buried in this half-dead monastic way of life;" and thus they tried to persuade him not to enter the cloister. Rabus was building the various aspects of his case for Luther's heroic status as confessor. Following Melanchthon and reflecting some of his humanistic techniques, Rabus analyzed Luther's decision to become a monk in this way: The cause of his choosing the monastic way, in which he believed he could serve God better and live more piously, was not Luther's poverty but rather his very strong drive and desire to live in a God-pleasing way. Once within the cloister, Luther devoted himself with particular diligence to the reading of Scripture, with the result that his agonies and terrors increased. From Mathesius, Rabus recounted for the readers of his second edition that Luther's fellow monks

---

[10]Ibid., ij/r,)(r-)(iij/v.

had a poor opinion of him, made him janitor, discouraged his studies, and sent him out to beg rather than study, so that the monastery could become rich. Here was a martyr in the making

Following his first mass, in 1507, Luther's monastic brothers once again took the Bible away from him, Mathesius had written, and they filled him instead with their sophistry and the teachings of the Scholastics. But Luther returned "continually and faithfully" to the cloister's library to study the Bible. At the same time, God sent him an unnamed confessor, an older brother in the monastery, who gave him the comfort he could not find in his saying of the mass. The confessor proclaimed to Luther the gracious forgiveness of sins in the Apostles' Creed. He recalled for Luther Saint Bernard's counsel, that the mercy of God had been won for him through the sacrifice and blood of his obedient Son and that this mercy is pronounced by the Holy Spirit through the words of absolution in the church. Rabus inserted this passage from Mathesius into his earlier text from Melanchthon; thus in his second edition Rabus expanded on the comfort Luther's confessor gave in proclaiming to him the forgiveness of sins. The monk remained anonymous. The final outcome of their encounter, however, was that Luther found comfort in the word of Scripture, "through faith we become righteous." Rabus followed Melanchthon in stating that this conviction had grown day by day in depth and breadth; Rabus and his contemporaries knew of no "tower experience," which had provided Luther with instantaneous insight. They believed that the root of Luther's evangelical breakthrough lay in his conversations with his brother and confessor in the Erfurt cloister.[11]

Rabus followed Melanchthon and, later, Mathesius in tracing Luther's studies and early lectures; he dated the beginning of Luther's reformation to the public controversy that broke out after Luther attacked "the blasphemous and deceptive preaching of indulgences." That date was important to Rabus, because it demonstrated that Luther had fulfilled John Hus's prophecy that a hundred years after his burning (1415) God would raise up someone to give answer to those who had executed him.[12] Rabus gave less prominence to such predictions regarding Luther

---

[11]Ibid., iij/r; *HdM*, II:116-117r. On recent debate about Luther's evangelical breakthrough, see W. D. J. Cargill Thompson, "The Problems of Luther's 'Tower Experience' and its Place in his Intellectual Development," *Religious Motivation: Biographical and Sociological Problems for the Church Historian* (Studies in Church History 15, Derek Baker, ed.; Oxford: University Press, 1975) 187-211; reprinted in W. D. J. Cargill Thompson, *Studies in the Reformation, Luther to Hooker*, E. W. Dugmore, ed. (London: Athlone, 1980) 60-80.

[12]*HdZ*, IV:vj.

than did some contemporaries, but, like them, he was convinced that Luther fitted into God's plan for his people and that Luther's place in history had been foreseen.

Even though Rabus dated the beginning of the Reformation with the indulgence controversy, he spent relatively little space on it. He ignored much documentary material which he could have picked up from the Jena edition.[13] More important to Rabus was Luther's confrontation with Cardinal Cajetan at Augsburg in 1518. Styled in the form of dialogues between the papal inquisitor and the Evangelical confessor, Rabus's report of their encounter falls into that genre much beloved by all Protestant martyrologists. He was reproducing material gathered by Georg Spalatin here; and like other Evangelical writers, Spalatin knew how to record confrontations like these in such a way as to demonstrate who was right and who was wrong, who was victim and who was persecutor.[14]

Rabus moved quickly over the Leipzig Debate and other events of 1519 and 1520 to the heart of his presentation of Luther's "martyrdom," his testimony before the emperor at Worms. Rabus began to set the scene for Luther's confession in the presence of the imperial estates with the text of his letter to Emperor Charles V of 15 January 1520. In this letter Luther had sent his best wishes to the emperor while, at the same time, pleading the cause of divine truth as he had been proclaiming it. Although the martyrologist failed to incorporate political details available in Mathesius, he did see it as important for his readers to know about Luther's initial contact with the young emperor. Following the ancient example of Saint Athanasius, who suffered exile by political authorities because he confessed truth, Luther announced to Charles the decision to appeal to his imperial majesty that Charles take the cause of divine truth under the shadow of his wings.[15] Rabus continued this with correspondence and stories related to Luther's confession at Worms. From Mathesius, for instance, he took the favorable comparison drawn between Hus and Luther, and the tale of the priest from Naumburg who had admonished Luther to be faithful to the truth, reminding him that God would be with him as he gave him a picture of Savonarola.

Rabus's readers had to notice that Luther had gone to Worms as one of a long train of witnesses, confessors, and martyrs. From the Jena

---

[13]*Der erste [-achte] teil aller Buecher vnd Schrifften . . . Doct. Mart. Lutheri* (Jena: Richtzenhan, 1555-1559) 1:114ff.

[14]*HdZ*, IV:viij-xix.

[15]Ibid., IV:xliij/v.

edition Rabus reprinted in full Luther's words before the assembled diet on both his appearances before it. At the end of his confession on the second day, his words, "Here I stand, I can do no other, God help me, Amen," were set off on a separate line in slightly larger print. The first edition of the martyrology featured a woodcut of the Wittenberg monk standing before the emperor with "Here I stand" scrawled across the print (fig 16).[16]

More than ten percent of Rabus's account of Luther's life presents material related to his confession at Worms. Several letters show the reader how "Dr. Martin Luther, or the almighty, eternal God through him, initially conducted the course of the gospel." Dramatically juxtaposed to these letters stands the announcement that the imperial majesty had issued "a public, harsh, grievous, and horrible mandate or edict against Dr. Martin Luther, his teaching, his books and writings, and all who supported his person or accepted his teaching." Had the edict not been too long, Rabus stated in a rare display of sensitivity for his readers' patience, he would have printed it in full. Instead, he offered only its concluding paragraphs, two and a half folio pages long.[17]

Rabus's story proceeds year by year, with brief biographical summaries as interludes to texts reprinted from Luther's works, and concludes with the reprinting of the published account of his death, which describes Luther's final confession of faith.[18]

In his presentation of Luther's life, Ludwig Rabus did not demonstrate masterful skill as a biographer by the humanistic standards of the day. At points, his narrative flows rather nicely and holds the reader's interest, particularly in the early pages of his recital of the young Luther's life, before the time which Rabus had printed sources to reproduce. But his total scheme and scope seems unclear and uneven. At points, particularly in his expansion of the chronology of Luther's life in the second edition, Rabus piled up titles of works that Luther had composed, even when they seem not directly related to the fundamental motif of Luther as confessor. One can hardly do better than Wolfgang Brückner's description: Rabus's sketch of Luther's career is "neither a biographical nor a mythic description of his life. On a rough scaffold he constructed a comprehensive picture of the teaching and the stuggles over the teaching of

---

[16]Ibid., IV:xlij/v-lxxxix/r.

[17]Ibid., IV:lxxix-ciij.

[18]*HdZ*, IV:ccxiiij-ccxliiij, the text of Johann Aurifaber, Justus Jonas, and Michael Coelius, *Vom christlichen Abschied aus diesem Leben des Reverendi Dr. Martini Lutheri* (Wittenberg: Lufft, 1546).

16. Luther at Worms (*HdZ* IV:lxv/v)

the reformer,"[19] whom Rabus regarded as a "worthy, highly-enlightened, and true man of God," "our dear father and the prophet of the German nation."[20]

Luther as Prophet and Doctor

If the key to Rabus's understanding of Luther's significance lies in the motif of martyrdom or confession, as it shaped his major literary work, then the theme of Luther's prophetic and apostolic role must be seen as having shaped Johann Mathesius's major work, his homiletic biography of his former professor, delivered in seventeen sermons, preached from November 1562 into 1564.[21] The first fourteen homilies chronicle Luther's career. In the first, Mathesius treated the years from 1483 to 1516; in the second, those critical years between 1516 and 1520; in the third, "how Doctor Martin Luther confessed his teaching before the emperor and the entire empire at Worms." How he was taken prisoner on the way home and led to the Wartburg and his sojourn on this Patmos formed the subject of the fourth sermon. Accounts of Luther's battle with Carlstadt, the "heavenly prophets," and the revolting peasants were rehearsed in the fifth sermon; in the sixth, Mathesius reviewed dealings with the sacramentarians in 1526 and 1527. The preacher's own recollections of life at Wittenberg lie in sermon seven alongside the events of 1529, when Luther attended the Marburg Colloquy. In sermon eight, Mathesius treated the Augsburg Confession and the events of 1531 and 1532; and in sermon nine, Mathesius expanded on Luther's treatment of Aesop, composed during the diet of Augsburg. The years 1532-1535, including Luther's conflicts with Duke George of Saxony and the Anabaptists, received treatment in sermon ten; the eleventh is a review of the late 1530s; and in the twelfth Mathesius treated life in Luther's household in the Black Cloister. Sermons thirteen and fourteen describe the end of Luther's life, his death and burial. Mathesius commemorated Luther's death with a special funeral sermon of remembrance. He concluded his series with one sermon on the University of Wittenberg and another on Luther's ac-

---

[19]"Luther als Gestalt der Sage," in Wolfgang Brückner, ed., *Volkserzählung und Reformation* (Berlin: Schmidt, 1974) 271.

[20]*HdM, II:110r.*

[21]Johann Mathesius, *Historien Von des Ehrwirdigen in Gott Seligen Thewren Manns Gottes, Doctoris Martini Luthers anfang, lehr leben vnd sterben* . . . (Nuremberg, 1566; I have used the Nuremberg: Berg, 1580 edition). On Mathesius's work, see Hans Volz, *Die Lutherpredigten des Johannes Mathesius: Kritische Untersuchung zur Geschichtsschreibung im Zeitalter der Reformation* (Halle: Waisenhaus, 1929).

counts of mining and his uses of analogies from miners' lives—appropriate for Mathesius's parishioners in Saint Joachimsthal, a mining community.

In contrast to both Spangenberg's and Rabus's, Mathesius's work comes much closer to a modern biography. As we discuss below, Spangenberg's thematic treatment discussed much more the motifs of Luther's thought and the significance of his activities; as we discussed above, Rabus depended on Luther's texts, instead of accounts of his deeds, for his "biography." Mathesius rehearsed the setting and the events of Luther's unfolding career with frequent reference, to be sure, to specific published works; but his emphasis was on actions. Mathesius also added recollections and observations from his own Wittenberg experiences, which are not to be found in Rabus. He did so with a graceful literary touch in many places. The mark of Melanchthon's humanistic training is visible in Mathesius's account.

Ernst Walter Zeeden argues that Mathesius's Luther is above all a curate of souls;[22] however, the more general theme of the "worthy, German prophet" is repeated throughout Mathesius's homilies from the preface through the closing remarks that are the climax of the fifteenth sermon. There, Mathesius assures his readers that God need not always bestow the prophetic or apostolic calling through miracles and a special grace; he can also choose prophets and apostles through ordinary means. Such a prophet and apostle was Martin Luther, one who held to the Word of God according to the Scriptures as a called servant of the church and a Christian brother.[23]

Mathesius defined Luther's prophetic persona primarily as one who proclaimed God's Word, who applied the admonition and consolation of law and Gospel to his parishioners. The heart of Luther's message, Mathesius believed, could be found in "the pure mercy of God, based alone upon the merit, blood, and intercession of the only mediator's gracious forgiving of sins and his righteousness imputed to us, not on the basis of our repentance, faith, or good conscience."[24]

But Luther was a prophet not only because he had proclaimed the Word of God but also because he had foreseen the future. Mathesius re-

---

[22]Ernst Walter Zeeden, *Martin Luther und die Reformation im Urteil des deutschen Luthertums* (Freiburg/Breisgau: Herder, 1950) 37.

[23]Mathesius, *Historien* D2r, 30r, 37r, 51, 179v. For artistic depiction of Luther in prophetic and pastoral roles, see Scribner, *For the sake of simple folk*, 204-207, 220-224, 240.

[24]Ibid., 109v; cf. 40v-41r.

flected a widely held view among Lutherans that Luther had foreseen an ever-darkening future of apostasy and affliction in judgment against desertion of the gospel—a future that had become the present for Luther's followers in the time of the Smalcald War and the Augsburg Interim. Anton Otto believed that Luther had "had the spirit of Micah in prophecying; this means that he announced nothing good but rather evil to us; and, indeed, experience shows that it was neither false hypocrisy nor a deceiving spirit that spoke through him."[25] In his parsonage in Nordhausen, this student of Luther's collected prophecies of "Doctor Martin Luther, the Third Elijah" and published them in 1552, the same year that the Hamburg pastor Johannes Amsterdam released a similar collection. Both had been engaged for four years in the battle against the Interims and the adiaphorists; and they turned Luther's often expressed concerns about the fate of his message in his successors' generation into propaganda for their cause.[26]

A quarter-century later Johannes Lappaeus, a Saxon pastor, published the "true prophecies of the faithful prophet and holy man of God, Doctor Martin Luther, of blessed memory, in which he proclaimed the current lamentable situation of the German nation, the destruction of the churches, the adulteration of teaching, the many forms of God's terrible punishment, the last day, etc. . . . as a warning to Germany and as instruction and consolation for all afflicted Christians."[27] In the preface to a new edition of Lappaeus's work published in 1592, Micheal Neander wrote that Luther had possessed the gift of prophecy and could thus foresee the future; for it was the same divine, prophetic spirit that had spoken through both the ancient prophets and through Luther. Neander

---

[25]Anton Otto, *Etliche Propheceysprueche D. Martin Lutheri, Des dritten Elias* (Magdeburg: Lotther, 1552) Aij/r.

[26]Johannes Amsterdam, *Prophetiae aliqvot vere: Et sententiae insignes reuerendi patris Domini Doctoris Martini Lutheri, Tercij Helie: De calamitatibus defectione, & Tenebris, Germaniae obuenturis, eo in Domino mortuo & perpetuo viuente* (Magdeburg: Lotther, 1552); in German as *Etliche warhafftige weissagung, vnd fuerneme spruche des Ehrwirdigen Vaters, Hern Doctor Martini Luthers, des dritten Helie . . .* (Magdeburg: Lotther, 1552).

[27]Johannes Lappaeus, *Warhafftige Prophezeiungen des thewren Propheten, vnd Heiligen Manns Gottes, D. Martini Lutheri seliger Gedechtnis, Darinnen er den jetzigen kleglichen Zustandt Deutscher Nation, die Zerstoerunge der Kirchen, Verfelschunge der Lere, vielerley grewliche Straffen Gottes, den Juengsten tag, vnd anders dergleichen mehr gar eygentlich zuuor verkuendiget hat. Dem gantzen Deutschlandt zu Warnung, vnd allen betruebten Christen zu Christlichem Vntericht vnd Trost aus allen seinen Schrifften vleissig zusamen gezogen* (Ursel: Heinrich, 1578).

stressed that Luther had always "driven Christ home;" for, "he knew nothing but how to teach faith in Christ . . . and based his teaching, preaching, consoling, chastizing, his life and death, on the wonderful chief article of our redemption through Jesus Christ, who is received and held only through faith, before and apart from all works"[28]—a view that corresponds to Mathesius's understanding of Luther's prophetic role.

Closely connected with Mathesius's definition of Luther as prophet is his description of Luther as a doctor of the holy Scriptures. Luther appears in his pages most frequently entitled "Doctor," his normal title, and occasionally as "our Doctor." In his interpretation of Genesis, "our Doctor proved himself and is there to be heard as a prophet of God and a servant of Jesus Christ, and a teacher and interpreter of the holy Scripture, from which he has brought forth for us much saving doctrine, for the cultivation of patience and comfort and steadfast hope as a wise and experienced *Pater Lector.*"[29] In his first sermon, Mathesius had noted that Luther, called as a regular Doctor of the Holy Scriptures, "took the Holy Bible of God very seriously, read it through with utmost diligence, and took the counsel of the ancient fathers and doctors of the church" in interpreting the text of the Scriptures, that he might set forth Christ according to the apostolic rule and canon.[30] Luther's contribution to the biblical understanding of the German nation also included, for Mathesius, his translation of the Scriptures. "This was one of the greatest miracles, that our God so arranged it through Doctor Martin Luther that before the end of the world he would prepare for the children of the firstborn Japheth [Noah's son, from whom the European peoples are traditionally said to have descended], whom he honored with the highest crown and scepter on earth [the Holy Roman Empire], a beautiful German Bible; and there he speaks to us, explaining what the eternal divine essence and gracious will is, in good, plain, understandable German words."[31]

Mathesius's Luther was also certainly a pastor, a *Seelsorger*, as well as a prophet and doctor. Through his preaching he consoled sinners and moved them to a life of repentance and good works. Through his example, particularly in his home and family life, he proclaimed his message and applied it to his people's lives. He carried out pastoral functions in Wittenberg as he preached repentance and the saving blood of Christ, as

---

[28]*Propheceiung* (Eisleben: Gaubisch, 1592) Ciiij/r.

[29]Mathesius, *Historien*, 160v-170r; cf. 37r.

[30]Ibid., 7v-8r; cf. 8v, 38v.

[31]Ibid., 150r; cf. 107v, 151-153.

he warned against false teachers, as he distributed the Lord's Supper.[32] For all the distance that Luther's prophetic stature might have put between him and the poor peasants who revered him, his pastoral service and above all his home life had brought him closer; and that had helped make him not only a hero but also an example for the pious—as did also his bearing of suffering. Commenting on Luther's sojourn at the Wartburg, Mathesius wrote:

> Since we do not recognize the power of God's Word apart from the holy cross, and flesh and blood cannot be extinguished and exterminated without the rod of God, God sent our hermit [Luther] all sorts of crosses, for which he heartily thanked God in writing to a good friend; for he experienced a harsh, dangerous illness, which made him despair of his life. Likewise, the devil plagued him severely with anxious thoughts and tried to drive him mad with all kinds of phantoms and foul apparitions. In such spiritual trials and temptations, God's Word and his own burning longing and heartfelt intercessions by his brothers were his staff and stay of comfort, on which he leaned and through which he endured at God's side with patience.[33]

The devil's instruments became ever more concrete; and the theme of conflict, which played a larger role in Rabus's and Spangenberg's presentations of Luther's life, surfaced in Mathesius's biography also. Conflict with papists and ravers of the spiritualist and Anabaptist variety troubled Luther throughout his career—an experience far removed from that of most of his followers. But the reformer's endurance of slander, rejection, and even the murderous designs of his enemies, whom Satan had enflamed against him,[34] could give consolation to the artisans and peasants who read Mathesius's work. This saintly victim of demonic attack, their brother and hero, stood with and therefore linked them with Moses, David, Paul, and Athanasius, so Mathesius observed. He further compared his professor to Hus, whose prophecy of Luther he had already noted, and to Savonarola, both from more recent times.[35]

That the crosses and confession of his professor had made an indelible impact on Luther's sermonic biographer is obvious thoughout the work. Mathesius was recounting his personal encounters with Luther

---

[32]Ibid., 132.

[33]Ibid., 29.

[34]Ibid., 34v-35r, 42r, 47r, 60v, 117r, 130.

[35]Ibid., 55r, 85, 4r, 187v.

when he observed that, although one's life and good example cannot improve the content of one's teaching, it is good and furthers the doctrine when the preacher leads a Christian and reasonable life and lets his light shine at the table and in the conduct of his household; this Luther had done, Mathesius himself recalled.[36] Mathesius believed strongly, as he proclaimed to his congregation at the end of his tenth sermon, that it was of utmost importance for the church to continue to listen to the admonishing and comforting words of "our dear prophet and doctor: so that it might be ready to receive the Lord on the Last Day."[37] Here was a new saint, a saint, above all, of the Word of God.

Luther as Man of the Word and of the Mines

At almost the same time as the people of Joachimsthal heard this admonition, the congregation of another mining village far to the northwest—Mansfield—was hearing the first in a series of sermons on the same topic—the life and teaching of Martin Luther. Their pastor, Cyriakus Spangenberg, interpreted Luther's role in the church in twenty-one sermons, the first thirteen of which depicted him largely in terms of his service in the proclamation of the Word. They dealt with Luther as a faithful householder, a spiritual knight, a prophet, an Elijah, an apostle, a Paul, an evangelist like John, a theologian, an angel of the Lord, a martyr, a pilgrim of God, a Jacob, and a priest. The final eight sermons compare Luther to various kinds of mine workers, a motif which made good sense in Mansfeld, the mining center in which Spangenberg ministered.[38]

Spangenberg praised Luther's virtues with few exceptions, but he did not sketch the details of his life; he relied less on biographical anecdotes than he did on quotations from Luther's works and the preacher's own comparison of his mentor with heroic figures of the Word to convey Luther's greatness to the people. To a far greater extent than Mathesius's sermons, Spangenberg's homilies adhered to a biblical text, or at least found solid introduction in one. They were more doctrinal, as well, often a lengthy exposition of Spangenberg's understanding of Luther's teaching on particular topics.

---

[36]Ibid., 132v.

[37]Ibid., 118r.

[38]The titles of the individually published sermons follow the form of that cited in note 1; between 1563 and 1574, editions were issued in Eisleben, Erfurt, Frankfurt/Main, and Mansfeld. These were drawn together in one volume, *Theander Lutherus* (Ursel, 1589). See Wolfgang Herrmann, "Die Lutherpredigten des Cyriacus Spangenberg," *Mansfelder Blätter* 39 (1934/35): 7-95.

Spangenberg's Luther certainly was in every respect a hero of the Word. He began his argument that Luther had indeed been a true prophet by demonstrating that he was not a false prophet. Luther had been given appropriate gifts and a proper call to proclaim the message of the Scriptures, which Spangenberg summarized in four points: salvation comes through Christ alone, faith in Christ produces good works, God's Word comforts troubled consciences, and sinners must be called to repentance regardless of who they are.[39] But above all, Luther had delivered the truth of the Scriptures faithfully to his people; and that faithfulness to the prophetic and apostolic message identified him without doubt as a prophet of God. God bestows the gifts of the proper interpretation of Scripture and the effective proclamation of Christ more richly on some of his servants than on others; and Luther "was the greatest and best prophet which the world has had since the time of the apostles, and he was superior to all other teachers since that time, made comparable to the Old-Testament prophets by God." Spangenberg thought Luther more like the Old-Testament spokesman of God because Luther had exercised the responsibility of criticizing the sins of temporal rulers, a task not performed by the apostles.[40]

Spangenberg agreed that Luther had been a prophet not only because he embodied the living voice of the Gospel but also because he had foreseen God's wrath coming on Germany and also because he had held forth the promise of God's continued mercy in the future. Luther had also predicted the losses which the papacy would suffer. These predictions had served Luther's proclamation of both law and gospel; Spangenberg stressed that God had designed Luther's prophecies to cultivate patience and penitence in the people and to confirm the truth of Luther's teaching.[41] In Spangenberg's eighth sermon—on Luther as theologian—the reader also learned of the prophecies that others had uttered regarding Luther's coming to free the church from papal enslavement—those of John Hus; Johann Hilton; and a Franciscan, whose prediction of Luther's appearance in 1511 had been reported by Johann von Staupitz.[42]

Among the miracles which Spangenberg associated with his new saint was none comparable to the wonderworking interference in the

---

[39]*Die dritte Predigte* Bv-C, Dij/v-Diiij/v.

[40]Ibid. Cij/r-Ciij/r.

[41]Ibid. (Dviij)r, (Evij)r.

[42]*Die Achte Predigt. Von dem werden Gottes Manne, Doctor Martin Luther, Das er der fuertrefflichst vnd groessest THEOLOGVS gewesen, von der Apostel zeit her* (Erfurt: Georg Bawman, 1566) (Bvj)v-Cij/r.

natural order so often attributed to medieval saints. Instead, he counted as miraculous the fact that a common monk from an ordinary monastery had been able to storm the Antichrist's empire without support from pope or prelate or council. In comparing Luther to Elijah, Spangenberg observed that Luther had raised people to life from the death that they were suffering as slaves of the papacy, even as Elijah had raised the widow's son. Spangenberg also counted it a miracle that Luther had overwhelmed temporal authorities and their opposition to the will of God without a sword.[43] Spangenberg did not return to the model of the medieval worker of magic, even if the desire of his audience for the miraculous in wonders and predictions of the future did influence the way in which he described Luther. Clearly Spangenberg preferred to emphasize Luther's virtues, which were, incidentally, the virtues of a supervisor of a mine: honesty, a God-fearing heart, reliability, modesty, and a good understanding of his tasks.[44] He also focused on Luther's sufferings, as noted above.[45]

Spangenberg's efforts to assist others in appreciating God's gift of Martin Luther did not end with this series of homiletic presentations. In 1569 and 1570, he edited four volumes of sermons on Luther's hymns, the *Luther's Cithara*. Spangenberg believed that:

> The Holy Spirit was no less powerful in Luther's hymns and beautiful melodies than he was in David's harp in increasing and spreading the praise of God, driving out the devil, comforting troubled consciences, overcoming death, softening hardened hearts, and converting them to God . . . So it must be recognized that among all the master singers since the apostolic time, Luther was the best and most skillful. . . . In his hymns and songs one finds not a single syllable which is unnecessary or wasted. His hymns flow and fall in the

---

[43]*Die dritte Predigt* Ciij, (Dviij)r; *Die vierde Predigt Von dem grossen Propheten Gottes, Doctore Martino Luthero, das er ein rechter Helias gewesen* (Erfurt: Georg Bawman, 1564) Ciij/r; *Die Fuenftte Predigt, Von dem Apostelampt des trefflichen Mannes, D. MARTIN. LVTHERS.* (n.p., 1565) 22v-23r.

[44]*Die sechste Predigt. Von dem werden Gottes Lerer: Doctor Martin Luther. Das er ein rechter PAVLVS gewesen.* (Erfurt: Georg Bawman, 1565) 23-25; 29v-34; *Die Neunde Predigt, Von dem heiligen Manne Gottes, D. MARTINO LVTHERO, Das er ein rechter Engel des Herrn, vnd eben der Engel, dauon Apocal. 14. geschrieben stehen, gewesen sey* (Eisleben: Petri, 1568) Diij/r-Dv/v; *Die XX. Predigt: Von Doctore Martino Luthero, wie ein getreuwer vnd erfahrner Geschworner er auff vnsers HERRN Gottes Berge gewesen* (Frankfurt/Main: Nicolaus Bassaeus, 1574) (cvij); *Die XXI. Predigt. Von D. Martin Luther, dem Werden Gottes Manne, Das er ein weiser vnd fuersichtiger Richter auff dem Berge des Herrn gewesen* (Frankfurt/Main: Nicolaus Bassaeus, 1574) C/v-Dvr.

[45]*Die Fuenffte Predigt* 29v-30v; *Die sechste Predigt* 34-48.

17. Cyriakus Spangenberg's *Cythara* (1569)

loveliest, prettiest way, full of spirit and of instruction. Every word is a sermon in itself. . . . Nothing is forced, nothing is tacked on, nothing is misplaced. The rhyme flows easily and nicely, the words are well-chosen and just right, the melodies and tunes lovely and zesty . . . . In summary, you will not find anything to compare with Luther's hymns, much less any better than his, as all pious hearts who know Luther's hymnal must recognize: God has given us through him in his hymnal something great and wonderful, for which we must be eternally grateful.[46]

When Spangenberg compared Luther favorably with David, he was not equating Luther's words with the inspired words of Scripture in reference to their origin or authority. Spangenberg's understanding that the biblical message could be conveyed by the "living voice of the gospel" in the mouths of Christ's servants enabled him to suggest that Luther's proclamation in sermon or song could accomplish all that God had designed his Word to do to free troubled consciences. Spangenberg believed that the Holy Spirit had guided Luther's utterance of the Word both orally and in writing. In the fourth volume of *Luther's Cithara*, he wrote of the hymn, "Lord, Keep Us Steadfast in Your Word," that "Luther composed his hymn for the good of Christendom on the basis of the Holy Spirit's impelling him. . . . Through this hymn great miracles have occurred and will occur." That hymn had held at bay many misfortunes and had stopped Satan in his tracks.[47]

Cyriakus Spangenberg obviously loved his Wittenberg mentor; more than that, he, like Rabus and Mathesius, recognized the action of God in Luther's life and particularly in his message. From Spangenberg's perspective—more so than for Mathesius—God's action had been not just on behalf of the German nation but for the whole Christian world.

Spangenberg's own career demonstrated that he was willing to suffer exile and harrassment in defense and propagation of his understanding of Luther's message and in order to aid others in celebrating the gift of God which had been the life of this holy man. Luther's example— Spangenberg maintained throughout his active life—could give them the assurance that God was present in their lives through the power of that Word, as Luther had conveyed it in writing, in preaching, and in song.[48]

---

[46]*Cythara Lvtheri. Die schoenen, Christlichen trostreichen Psalmen vnd Geistliche Lieder, des Hochwirdigen thewren Lerers vnd Diener Gottes D. Martini Lutheri. Der Erste Theil* (Erfurt: Georg Bawman, 1570) Aiij.

[47]*Cythara Lvtheri. Vierde Theil* (Erfurt: Georg Bawman, 1570) AAiij/v.

[48]For example, *Die Neunde Predigt* Aij.

NEW SPIRITUAL SONGS
ON THE HIGHLY GIFTED MAN, MARTIN LUTHER

Early in Luther's career, others had already wanted to celebrate his message and person in songs of their own. The importance of the use of hymns or spiritual songs and other forms of music in the spread of the Reformation cannot be overestimated; Luther became a German folkhero in part because the people could sing of his exploits.

Michael Stiefel (1487-1567), an Augustinian monk, expressed his devotion to his fellow friar's cause in a thirty-two stanza hymn published in 1522, entitled "On the Properly Grounded Teaching of Doctor Martin Luther, Faithful to Christ, a Very Beautiful and Finely-Fashioned Song." Stiefel's theology, always heavily eschatological, began by identifying Brother Martin as the angel whom John had prophecied would come "with an eternal gospel to proclaim to those who dwell on earth" (Rev. 14:6-7). In view of Stiefel's tendency towards eschatological perspectives, the theme of conflict, which pervaded Luther's life in the view of his disciples, must have come quite naturally to Stiefel in that year following Luther's excommunication by the pope and the emperor's declaration of him to be an outlaw. Stiefel began his song by noting that whereas the bishop of Rome had broken into God's barn like a wolf, Luther had inclined his heart towards God, mastered the Scriptures, and struck his opponents in Worms dumb with his testimony to the truth. Stiefel continued with a review of the Ten Commandments and their accusation against sin, followed with a summary of the promises of God for those who trust in Christ, and concluded with a prayer to "my God, Lord Jesus Christ," for protection against the devil's deceit when the Antichrist attacks. Other songs composed about this time similarly reflect these themes of conflict with the papacy and of the proclamation of the truth.[49]

Luther's death in 1546 occasioned a small outburst of hymnic activity of the same sort.[50] Two decades later, as the memory of Luther began to grow dim, he still stimulated poetic adulation. His good friend, the court musician Johann Walther (1496-1570), composed "A New Spiritual Song, on the Precious and Highly-Gifted Man, Doctor Martin Luther, Blessed of God, Germany's Prophet and Apostle" in 1564. No new themes appear: The first eight stanzas, each with eight lines, describe "The Anti-

---

[49]Philip Wackernagel, ed., *Das deutsche Kirchenlied von der ältesten Zeit bis zu Anfang des XVII. Jahrhunderts* 5 vols. (Leipzig: Teubner, 1864-1877) 3:74-75; see also songs by Jörg Graff and Konrad Kern, 3:377, 379-82, 419-22.

[50]Ibid. 3:974-77, 896-98, songs by Martin Schrot, Johann Friedrich Petsch, Erasmus Alber, and Leonhart Kettner.

christ's Epoch and Rule;" the next sixteen, "The Revelation and Over-throw of the Antichrist;" the third section of the hymn is entitled "The Gracious Visitation of God, and the Joyous Period of the Gospel, the Great Light and the Bountiful Revelation of God's Word, Together with Many Other Blessings of God, which Luther demonstrated to Germany" (twenty-six stanzas); and the conclusion (of fourteen stanzas) contained "An Admonition to Thankfulness for the Great and Many Blessings and the Gracious Visitation of God." In words reminiscent of Jeremiah 1, Walther stated that God had chosen Luther from his mother's womb to be his instrument for the destruction of the papacy. God had given him wisdom and understanding so that he might teach God's Word. Walther reviewed Luther's teaching in detail, emphasizing his proclamation of Christ as the Lamb of God but also touching on the proper distinction of law and gospel, the cleansing of the mass and the use of the sacraments, the explanation of Christian freedom from the papal oppression of Christian consciences, use of the Scriptures and the catechism. Walther gave thanks for Luther's opposition against raving sectarians and Erasmus. The author addressed his departed friend as "true prophet," "the third Elijah," "the horseman and the chariot of Israel," terms used for Luther at least since Melanchthon's parting tribute to his colleague in 1546. Walther concluded the sixty-four-stanza song by pointing out that it had been written to honor Christ and to increase the faith of believers in his blood, death and grace.[51]

Nikolaus Selnecker, shortly after he had participated in the composition of the Formula of Concord, composed a "Prayer for Pious, Faithful Teachers, who set forth God's Word Clearly and Purely, as God Brought It Forth Once Again through Doctor Luther," on the basis of Psalm 106. In this song Selnecker longed for the harmony which he thought had left the church when Luther died, before intra-Lutheran disputes broke out; he sought God's gift of teachers who would, like Luther, faithfully proclaim the Word.[52] In 1590 Valentin Hebeisen reviewed both Luther's career and teaching in sixty-three stanzas of his "Hero's Song, of Doctor Martin Luther." At the end of the century, the Prussian poet and schoolmaster Peter Hagen (1569-1620) composed a "Festival Song of Thanksgiving expressing Gratitude for the Great Work of Reformation against the Papacy which was begun and completed by the Precious Tool of God," namely, Luther.[53]

---

[51]Ibid., 3:152-57.

[52]Ibid., 4:287-88.

[53]Ibid., 5:152-59.

We ought not press too much significance from the use of the genre labeled "spiritual songs" whereby Luther's students expressed appreciation for their mentor. Particularly the earliest were propaganda songs, much more akin to medieval songs that celebrated princely figures or to ditties that conveyed political opinions of one kind or another than to hymns of praise to saints. The celebrations of Luther in song from the end of the century are, if hymns at all, dedicated as much to Luther's message as to his person, less to the prophet than to the prophet's Lord. They praise God by calling attention to the divine struggle which God's instrument, the German prophet and apostle, Martin Luther, had waged in behalf of truth and against papal deception. Nevertheless they did convey an awefilled appreciation of this instrument, acknowledging Luther minimally to be a special tool of God and a saintly inspiration, a teacher and a pastor, proclaimer of the Word and shepherd for lost and terrified consciences.

"DILIGENTLY READ THE WRITINGS
OF OUR FATHER AND PRECEPTOR"

Those who had enjoyed Luther's teaching and his pastoral care while they were his students wanted his dynamic influence to continue to make its impact in the life of the church. Hence they fostered his image as saint and hero, prophet and doctor. They believed that Luther's power lay in his expression of the Word of God, and they believed that his influence and impact would continue if only his writings could be widely read and used.

The preoccupation with Luther's words among his students began with the edition of Luther's works planned at Wittenberg before the reformer's death. In the intra-Lutheran disputes following the Smalcald War,[54] that edition elicited a rival, the Jena edition. This fascination with Luther's words was reflected further in the publication of the *Table Talks.*[55]

---

[54]*Der erste [-zwelffte] Teil der Bucher d. Mart. Luth.* (Wittenberg: Lufft, 1539-1561) and *Tomus primus [-septimus] omnivm opervm reuerendi domini Martini Lutheri* (Wittenberg: Lufft, 1545-1561); *Der erste [-achte] teil aller Buecher vnd Schrifften . . . Doct. Mart. Lutheri* (Jena: Richtzenhan, 1555-1559) and *Tomus primus [-qvartvs] omnivm opervm Reuerendi Patris D.M.L. . . .* (Jena: Rödinger, 1556-1558). On the Wittenberg edition, see Eike Wolgast, *Die Wittenberger Luther-Ausgabe, Zur Überlieferungsgeschichte der Werke Luthers im 16. Jahrhundert* (*Archiv für Geschichte des Buchwesens XI, 1-2*; Frankfurt/Main: Buchhändler-Vereinigung, 1970). On the dispute between partisans of the two editions, see Eike Wolgast, "Der Streit um die Werke Luthers im 16. Jahrhundert," *Archiv für Reformationsgeschichte* 59 (1968): 177-202.

[55]*Colloqvia oder Tischreden Doctor Martini Lutheri* (Frankfurt/Main: Schmidt, 1568).

18. The Jena Edition of Luther's Works,
German Part, Volume 1

These massive editions, however, lay beyond the financial capacity of most pastors in the late-sixteenth century. Some of Luther's followers collected selections of Luther's thought for application in specific situations,[56] as, for example, had Otto, Amsterdam and Lappaeus, when they published samplings of Luther's prophecies of divine judgment on an apostate Germany. These special collections, or florilegia, of Luther-citations first appeared about the time of his death, in answer to two specific needs for the Word, the one consolatory and the other polemical.

In the year before Luther's death, his colleague, Caspar Cruciger (1504-1548), produced a volume of selections from Luther's writings and sermons offering comfort to those who suffered from the approach of death or from spiritual anxiety. Two years later, Luther's amanuensis, Georg Rörer (1492-1557), edited expositions of Scripture passages for comforting and teaching believers primarily from Luther's writings, but including suitable selections from other Wittenbergers as well.[57] This type of florilegium continued to appear in Lutheran circles throughout the following decades and met a need that the old literature on the saints had met.[58]

Directly related to these consolatory collections were books of Luther's prayers, which became valued guides, models, and inspirations for the prayer-life of his followers. Luther had composed prayerbooks dur-

---

[56]I am deeply indebted for this material and for suggestions on many of the following points to Dr. Ernst Koch of the Theologisches Seminar, Leipzig, D.D.R., and particularly to his communication entitled "Lutherflorilegien zwischen 1550 und 1600," prepared for the seminar on Luther's successors at the Sixth International Congress on Luther Research, Erfurt, D.D.R., 14-20 August 1983.

[57]Caspar Cruciger, ed., *Etliche Trostschriften vnd Predigten für die, sie in Todes vnd ander Not vnd anfechtung sind* (Wittenberg: Creutzer, 1545); Georg Rörer, ed., *Vieler schoenen Spruche aus Goettlicher Schrifft auslegung, daraus Lere vnd Trost zu nemen, Welche der ehrnwirdige Herr Doctor Martin Luther seliger, vielen in jre Biblien geschrieben* (Wittenberg: Lufft, 1547).

[58]For example, Andreas Musculus, *Thesavrvs: Hochnutzlicher tewr Schatz vnd Guelden Kleinot . . . Aus der Buecher vnd Schrifften des heiligen Mans Gottes Lutheri, zusammenbracht* (Frankfurt/Oder: Eichorn, 1577), a revision of Musculus's earlier *Das Erste [-Vierte] Theil des Gueldenen kleinots . . .* (Frankfurt/Oder, 1561-1562); Johannes Pilicarius, *Trostspiegel der armen Suender . . . Aus den Buechern des Ehrwirdigen Herrn D. Martini seligers zusamen gezogen* (Leipzig: Berwald, 1556); Georg Walther, *Beicht vnd Bettbuechlein Darinn schoene vnd kurtze erklerung, in Frag vnd antwort, aus dem Catechismo Lutheri vnd andern Schrifften gezogen* (Frankfurt/Main: Feyerabent, 1581); Georg Walther, *Trostbuchlein, Auss der heiligen Schrifft, vnd D. Martini Lutheri Buechern, von wort zu wort gestellet* (Nuremberg: Berg and Newber, 1559).

ing his lifetime; and his prayers were published with those of other reformers in subsequent collections also. But in 1565, Anton Otto, editor also of his professor's prophecies, began the task of bringing together Luther's prayers from various printed sources into one, handy sampling. Directly or indirectly, Otto's work shaped subsequent collections of Luther's prayers. Cyriakus Spangenberg's associate in Mansfeld and fellow-exile in Strassburg, Peter Treuer, produced the largest assembly of the reformer's prayers in 1579, some five hundred in number. His former colleague, Caspar Melissander (1549-1591), reworked Treuer's collection and reduced it in size, failing—or, perhaps, refusing—to acknowledge his debt to Treuer's work, probably because the two had fallen out in the midst of controversy during the 1570s. Treuer's *Little Bell of Prayer* remained the masterwork, however, and in the last decades of the sixteenth and throughout the succeeding centuries, others turned to his volume as they produced their own collections in order to aid contemporaries in turning to their providential God through the model of Martin Luther.[59]

Whereas Luther's consolatory writings were written for lay use, much of Luther's heritage was repackaged for pastoral use as well. In 1582 Conrad Porta (1541-1585), a pastor who had never studied under Luther but who had voraciously devoured his writings as a student at the University of Rostock, prepared a handbook of pastoral care which consisted largely of citations from Luther. In *Pastorale Lutheri* Porta assembled citations from Luther's works in twenty-four chapters on various aspects of the pastoral ministry. Porta believed that his volume provided a valuable and necessary addition to the literature on the exercise of the pastoral office because Luther, "a second Paul, whom God had raised up out of his unmerited grace and mercy, as the world now declines," had been able to say more in a paragraph or a few lines than most others could in several pages.[60] Porta does not seem to have grasped the distinction of law and gospel and the pastoral approach of Luther that goes with it. Porta's book reflects an official, institutional view of the office of public ministry, much concerned with legal forms for pastoral activities, and therefore it does not convey a finely focused image of the kind of pastor

---

[59]See Frieder Schulz, *Die Gebete Luthers, Edition, Bibliographie und Wirkungsgeschichte* (Gütersloh: Mohn, 1976), esp. 20-27 and the bibliography, 79-135.

[60]Conrad Porta, *Pastorale Lvtheri, Das ist, Nützliche vnd noetiger Vnterricht vnd den fuernemsten stuecken zum heiligen Ministerio gehoerig, Vnd richtige Antwort auf mancherley wichtige Fragen von schweren vnd geferlichen Casibus . . . Fuer anfahende Prediger vnd Kirchendiener zusammenbracht* (Eisleben: Petri, 1582; I have used the 1591 edition) cc/r. See Robert Kolb, "Luther the Master Pastor: Conrad Porta's *Pastorale Lutheri*, Handbook for Generations," *Concordia Journal* 9 (1983): 179-87.

Luther hoped to educate for the Lutheran church, the kind of pastor he himself had been.

By Porta's time, the publication of florilegia of Luther's written thought had become commonplace. Many of them aided polemical efforts. This use of Luther's words began in the same period when Rörer and Cruciger were editing their collections of consolation, the period in which German Lutherans stood under the severe threat of imperial suppression, the period during which Rabus produced his martyrology and the Magdeburg *Centuries* were written. When Emperor Charles V finally began to muster forces to enforce the Edict of Worms and thereby provoked the Smalcald War, he set the stage for a propaganda battle, launched primarily by the Wittenberg professors to justify the Evangelical princes' armed resistance to the emperor. Luther was frequently cited in behalf of the cause, above all through the republication of his *Warning to His Dear Germans* of 1531, with a suitable preface by Philip Melanchthon.[61]

The Smalcald War and the promulgation of the Augsburg and Leipzig Interims in 1548 set the stage anew for internal controversies within Luther's following. In these controversies, another kind of assembly of Luther-citations was fashioned, again chiefly for a clerical audience, although also in some cases designed for a wider public. The Wittenberg prophet's understanding of justification through faith was clarified through the republication of several sermons, newly aimed against the apostate Andreas Osiander.[62] In the dispute over the compromises of the Leipzig Interim, composed by Melanchthon and his Wittenberg colleagues to insure harmony between their new prince, Moritz, and his ally in the Smalcald War, Emperor Charles, the opponents of this

---

[61]*Warnunge D. Martini Lutheri an seine lieben Deudsche, vor etlichen Jaren geschrieben auff diesen fall, so die feinde Christlicher Warheit diese Kirchen vnd Land, darinne reine Lere des Euangelij geprediget wird, mit Krieg ueberziehen vnd zerstoeren wolten. Mit einer Vorrede Philippi Melanchthon* (Wittenberg, 1546); see Oskar Waldeck, "Die Publizistik des Schmalkaldischen Krieges," *Archiv für Reformationsgeschichte* VII (1909-1910): 1-55; VIII (1910-1911): 44-133.

[62]For example, two anonymous publications, *Drei Sermon D. Martini Lutheri, darin man spueren kan wie ein Herlicher Prophetischer Geist in dem manne gewesen ist, das er das, was itzt vngoetlich, vom Andrea Osiandro geleret wird, lengst zuuor, als wuerd es bald geschehen gesehen hat* (Frankfurt/Oder: Eichorn, 1552) and *Christlicher vnd Gruendtlicher bericht, Von der Rechtfertigung des Glaubens, Einwonung Gottes vnd Christi in vns. Der Ehrwirdigen, Gottseligen herrn vnnd Euangelischer warheyt Lehrern. D. Martini Luthers heyliger gedechtnuss, Johannis Brentzij, vnnd Vrbani Regij Seligen* (n.p., n.d.), and the edition of Bernhard Ziegler, *Zwo Predigten des Ehrwirdigen herren Doctoris Martini Lutheri . . .* (Leipzig: Hantzsch, 1551).

Evangelical Interim made available to the public Luther's warnings about the judgment of God to come following the apostasy of his followers after his death.[63] As this contention among Lutherans over adiaphoristic compromises with the papacy widened into disputes over the role of good works in salvation and the freedom of the will, Luther's words became a favorite weapon, wielded primarily by the more radically Lutheran Gnesio-Lutherans rather than by their Philippist opponents.[64]

The controversialists of the period not only republished catena of Luther quotations in behalf of their causes, but also they turned to Luther as an authority and source of argument to supplement their use of Scriptural authority in defense of their teaching. Luther's own polemical stance in the first decades of the Reformation movement had provided a model for his students' understanding of the theological process. The situation produced by the Smalcald War and the promulgation of the two Interims forced them to follow that model. Little wonder that they turned to Luther then as an authority and as a source for constructing their polemics. At first, the Philippists tried to bolster their defense of the Leipzig Interim with appeals to Luther's pacific approach to papal customs in 1522; but the Gnesio-Lutherans replied with volleys of Luther's anti-papal statements and his insistence on forthright confession. From the appeal to Luther as their common preceptor, the Gnesio-Lutherans, under the leadership of the Mansfeld clergy with Spangenberg at its center, moved towards appealing to the sainted doctor because he was a special instrument of God. Thus, the words which they cited against their foes from Luther's writings strengthened their argument immensely.[65]

----

[63]Joachim Westphal, *Sententia Reverendi Viri D. M. Luth. Sanctae memoriae de Adiaphoris ex scriptis illius collecta* (Magdeburg: Lotther, 1549); in German, *Des Ehrwirdigen vnd thewren Mans Doct. Marti. Luthers seliger gedechtnis meinung von den Mitteldingen* (Magdeburg: Lotther, 1550); Matthias Flacius Illyricus, *Etliche Brieffe des Ehrwirdigen Herrn D. Martini Luthers seliger gedechtnis an die Theologos auff den Reichstag zu Augspurg geschrieben, Anno M.D.XXX. Von der vereinigung Christi vnd Belials . . .* (Magdeburg: Roedinger, 1549).

[64]For example, on good works, Albert Christian, *Dispvtatio Reverendi Patris D. Martini Lutheri, de operibus legis & gratiae . . .* (Magdeburg: Lotther, 1553); on freedom of the will, *Warhafftige vnd bestendige meinung vnd zeugnis Von der Erbsuende vnd dem freien willen Des Ehrwridigen tewren Mans Gottes D. Martin Luthers* (Jena: Rebart, 1560).

[65]Robert Kolb, " 'Perilous Events and Troublesome Disturbances,' The Role of Controversy in the Tradition of Luther to Lutheran Orthodoxy," in Kyle C. Sessions and Phillip N. Bebb, eds., *Pietas et Societas, New Trends in Reformation Social History, Essays in Memory of Harold J. Grimm* (Kirksville: Sixteenth Century Journal Publishers, 1985) 181-201.

Directly out of such use of Luther's words, perhaps, sprang another kind of florilegium, the doctrinal *Loci communes,* which attempted in a single volume to systematize Luther's thought by topics. These appeared first in the 1560s, and newly edited *Loci* of Luther appeared again in 1581 and the 1590s.[66] The arrangement in each of the *Loci* was different, but an overview of Luther's thought was presented in each; and each grew out of and furthered the perception of Luther as a special man of God, saintly because he brought the power of God's Word to bear on contemporary life. In addition, of course, Luther's *Small Catechism* became the basic text of instruction in Christian doctrine for Lutheran children, serving a host of functions as it was reprinted in many editions during the later-sixteenth century.[67]

Luther's words offered guidance on other concerns of the church beyond doctrinal issues. In an effort to guide pastors through the problems of biblical interpretation remaining for those who had used and then abandoned the allegorical approach to the Scriptures, the south German pastor, Jacob Hertel, collected Luther's comments on biblical passages considered difficult to interpret.[68] Luther's guidance on marriage, usury, and the responsibilities both of governmental authorities and their subjects all seemed valuable to compilers during the third quarter of the century.[69] In the controversy over the proper appraisal of Melanchthon's

---

[66]Johannes Corvinus, *Loci communes Doct: Mart: Lutheri totius Doctrinae Christianae. Das ist Heubtartickel Vnsers Christlichen Glaubens vnd rechtschaffener Lere, aus D. Mart. Luthers Schrifften* (Ursel: Heinrich, 1564); Timotheus Kirchner, *Thesavrvs: explicationvm omnivm articvlorvm ac capitvm, catholicae, orthodoxae, verae ac piae doctrinae Christianae . . . ex reverendi vereque Dei viri ac summi Theologi, D. Martini Lutheri . . . operibus* (Frankfurt/Main: Rhebart and Feyeraben, 1566) and *Deutsche Thesavrvs, Des Hochgelerten weitberumbten vnd theuren Manns Gottes D. Mart. Luthers . . .* (Frankfurt/Main: Schmid and Feyerabendt, 1568); Michael Neander, *Theologia megalandri Lvtheri . . .* (Eisleben: Gaubisch, 1581); Theodosius Fabricius, *Loci communes D. Martini Lvtheri viri Dei et Prophetae Germanici . . .* (Magdeburg: Gena, 1594).

[67]See Robert Kolb, "The Layman's Bible: The Use of Luther's Catechisms in the German Later Reformation," in David P. Scaer and Robert D. Preus, eds., *Luther's Catechisms—450 Years* (Fort Wayne IN: Concordia Theological Seminary Press, 1978) 16-26.

[68]Jacob Hertel, *Allegoriarum, Typorum, et exemplorvm veteris & noui Testamenti Libro duo: Nunc primum ex omnibus Latinis operibus reuerendi Patris D. Martini Lvtheri Theologi collecti* (Basel, 1561).

[69]Johann Pfeil, *Schatzkammer Vnd Heuratsteur dess heiligen Geistes Darinnen zu lehrnen, alles was einem jeden Christen Menschen vom heiligen Ehestande zu wissen von noeten ist, Auss den Operibus dess Ehrwirdigen Hochgelarten Herrn, Doctor Martini*

person and teaching that arose in the wake of the Formula of Concord and the overthrow of his "crypto-Calvinist" disciples in Saxony in the 1570s, Melanchthon's defenders collected favorable attestations of his character and teaching from a number of individuals but published them under the title *Testimonies of Dr. Martin Luther concerning His Comrade in Work and Danger, Philip Melanchthon.*[70]

This interest in what Luther had to say and in his almost apostolic authority produced another type of book, the index of his writings, designed to facilitate access to the major editions of his works being published at the time.[71] Some compilers went beyond merely providing an index and formulated counsel and plans for the reading of Luther's works. Joachim Mörlin (1514-1571) prepared such a volume. Luther should be read, he observed, because Luther's understanding of the Scriptures was thorough and fundamental and because his comments on them were well-expressed and well-grounded. Mörlin then suggested that the reader begin with Luther's *Small Catechism*, which contains law, gospel, and the table of Christian responsibilities. The reader should continue to the *Large Catechism*, the Schwabach Articles of 1529, Luther's *On the Lord's Supper, Confession* of 1528, the Smalcald Articles, the *Instruction for Visitors*, and the Augsburg Confession and its Apology. (Like Spangenberg and other contemporaries, Mörlin attributed these three documents to Luther as well as to Melanchthon because he believed that Luther had shaped Melanchthon's theology.) Mörlin's list continued with Luther's lectures on Galatians of 1531-1532, the *Last Words of David, On the Councils and the Church,*

Lutheri seligen . . . zusammengezogen (Frankfurt/Main: Reffeler and Feyerabendt, 1565); anonymous, *Vom wucher vnd widerkeuifflichen Zinsen. D. Martinus Luther* (Magdeburg: Lotther, c. 1552); Georg Walther, *Vom ampt der weltlichen Oberkeit, nach ordenung der Zehen Gebot, aus Gottes wort, vnd Buechern Doct. Lutheri, gestellt* (Jena: Richtzenhan, 1559).

[70]*Testimonia D. Martini Lvteri de socio laborvm et pericvlorvm svorvm Philippo Melanchthone* (Görlitz: Fritsch, 1580).

[71]Christoph Walther, *Register aller Buecher vnd Schrifften des Ehrnwirdigen Herrn Doctoris Martini Lutheri seliger gedechtnis welche in die Eilff Deudsche Teil, vnd in die sieben Latinische Tomos, zu Wittemberg gedruckt sind* (Wittenberg: Lufft, 1558). Sigismund Schwob [Schwabe], *Register Deudsch vnd Latinisch, aller Buecher vnd Schrifften des Ehrnwirdigen Herrn D. Martini Lutheri, gerichtet zu gleich auff die Wittenbergische, vnd X.I.I. Jhenischen Tomos, des Alten vnd newen Drucks* (Wittenberg: Seitz, 1564), and *Index omnivm librorvm et scriptorvm Reverendi Patris D. Martini Lvtheri* (Wittenberg: Seitz, 1564). Timotheus Kirchner, *Index oder Register vber die acht deudsche tomos . . .* (Jena: Richtzenhan and Robart, 1564).

19. The Wittenberg Edition of Luther's Works,
German Part, Volume 5

Against Hans Wurst, and the Genesis lectures.[72]

Conrad Porta composed a similar volume. He suggested six reasons why Luther's works should be read: (1) Luther had been called and raised up by the Holy Spirit. (2) His works treat every article of Christian teaching with singular skill and provide the most efficacious approaches to consolation. (3) They treat their subject matter with the most appropriate and well-selected words. (4) They evaluate the works of the teachers and writings of that time and are more useful than them all. (5) They and their author were miraculously preserved in the greatest and gravest of dangers. (6) They were issued and defended with singular consistency. Porta developed a thematic overview of and introduction to Luther's thought, reminding his readers that Luther, having rejected the language of the philosophers, had used simple biblical language to get the heart of the Scriptural message into the hearts of his people.[73]

Luther's disciples viewed him first as a man of the Word, orally proclaimed by him and set for all time in his writings. They believed that God had chosen Luther as a special instrument to give unique testimony to the pure gospel set down by the biblical writers centuries earlier. God's power had come in its most special and vital way to Germany, to Christendom, through Luther. Luther, therefore, had provided in a number of ways a one-of-a-kind example for the personal piety of individual believers, families, and—above all—pastors.

But does all this qualify Luther for the label "saint"? Is a man of the Word—the Lutheran Man of the Word—a saint in anything like the medieval sense of the term?

It is important to note the caution of James Weiss, who argues that Luther's students did not follow the model of medieval hagiography in recording his life and rehearsing his deeds.[74] In celebrating Luther's contributions to the church, Rabus turned to a martyrological form that followed ancient models of reciting the history of God's people, rather than to the form of medieval "saints' legends," and two of his contemporaries

---

[72]Joachim Mörlin, *Wie die Buecher vnd Schrifften, des thewren vnd seligen Manns Gottes D. Martini Lutheri nuetzlich zu lesen. Fuer einfeltige frome Pfarherrn vnd andere Christen Liebhaber vnd Leser, der Buecher D. Martini Lutheri* (Eisleben: Petri, [1565]).

[73]Conrad Porta, *Oratio continens adhortationem, ad assidvam Lectionem scriptorum Reverendi Patris & Praeceptoris nostri D. Martini Lvtheri, vltimi Eliae & Prophetiae Germaniae* (Jena: Richzenhan, 1571; reprint Helmstedt: Schnor, 1708).

[74]See note 4. Weiss continues his work on this topic which he began in his doctoral dissertation, "Friendship and Rhetoric: The Development of Humanists' Biographies in Sixteenth-Century Germany," (University of Chicago, 1980).

turned to sermonic biography. Mathesius, the most influential of Luther's early biographers, wrote under the influence of the humanistic principles he had learned both at Melanchthon's feet and, most clearly and completely, from Melanchthon's biographical sketches of his Wittenberg colleague. The successors who relied chiefly on him came out of a literary world that Melanchthonian or Wittenberg humanism had shaped. They celebrated Luther not so much as one who had performed great deeds—certainly not as one who had performed or could still perform miracles in behalf of his suppliants—but rather as one through whom God had performed the greatest of all deeds, the proclaiming of his forgiving and liberating Word.

If a saint was, however, a human being of special religious stature and powers, many among Luther's students did regard him as a true saint—one on whom the divine power, authentically dwelling in the Word of God, rested, one who therefore offered a sterling example of the pious Christian life.

Scholars disagree on precisely when and how Luther's personality became less important and this image—together with the mythic dimensions of his career—became the center of biographical interest. Horst Stephan even thought that Mathesius had "no congenial understanding of Luther's spirit," although his biography retained a certain liveliness and a touch of human reality, which, however, was lost when those died who had personal memories of the reformer.[75] The disposition to venerate Luther as "super-human"[76] is reflected very early in the tradition, beginning as early as the funeral oration that Melanchthon delivered in February 1546 (in spite of his efforts to mute this urge); in the account of Luther's death by Aurifaber, Jonas, and Coelius; and even tucked in among the excerpts collected by Rabus. Yet "super-human" is not quite the right word—certainly not "super-human" in the sense of the medieval wonderworkers, for even Mathesius regarded Luther as no more than the superlative human instrument whom God had selected to accomplish the work of his redeeming gospel.

Nonetheless, Luther's students and their students in the sixteenth century did indeed regard him as a saint, as their kind of saint. He was

---

[75]Horst Stephen, *Luther in den Wandlungen seiner Kirche* (Giessen: Topelmann, 1907) 14-15. But Zeeden, *Martin Luther,* 22, points out that in 1546 the image of Luther was already beginning to be reduced to a stereotype that was larger than life. Even Rabus, who certainly had memories of Luther from his Wittenberg sojourn, included no personal anecdotes in his account.

[76]Ibid., 41, and Brückner, "Luther," 273, use the term.

"of blessed memory," and his life was described in special religious genres: the martyrology and the sermon. He was cited in their disputes as one with saintly authority. Lutheran theology left no place for a wonder-worker or a super-human intercessor; the Reformation saint's sole task was to point to God through word and example. In the view of Luther's followers, the reformer's heroic confession of faith and his faithful testimony to the biblical message had qualified him as the saint of the Lutheran church.

CHAPTER FIVE

The Saints and the Lord in the Faith of Late-Reformation Lutherans

THE ACKNOWLEDGMENT OF THE SAINTS
IN LATE-REFORMATION WORSHIP

LUTHER WAS, OF COURSE, not the only saint to be revered and treasured in the German Lutheran churches during the Late Reformation. Religious practices change slowly on the level of popular belief. There is no reason to think that the German peasants and townsmen who came to love and revere Martin Luther as a saintly figure cast off their allegiances to ancestral patrons without some feeling of loss. Furthermore, their pastors and theologians left in place some of the system that commemorated the saints. The Evangelical constitutions composed for the churches of each Lutheran city or state usually fixed certain days as formal festivals and often indicated that services should be held on other days in commemoration of individuals or events in the history of God's people.

A great diversity in the number and kinds of celebration existed among Evangelical principalities. Local practices ranged from the rather conservative retention of a number of festivals in the Brandenburg constitution of 1540, to the radical displacement of almost all the medieval festivals (naturally not those connected with the life of Christ, including the Annunciation and the Purification, which celebrated the Virgin Mary as well as Jesus) in the ecclesiastical constitution of the dukedom of Prussia of 1525. The Brandenburg constitution specified celebration of the festivals of the Apostles, of All Saints, and of Saints Katherine, Martin, Lawrence, Mary Magdalene, John the Baptist, and Michael the Archangel, as well as the five Marian holidays: the Annunciation, the Visitation of Mary to Elizabeth, the Nativity, the Purification of Mary, and her Assumption.[1]

Early definitions of Lutheran observances of saints' days are found in the Homberg church constitution, formulated for the lands of Philip of Hesse in 1526, and in the articles which the Wittenbergers prepared for the visitation of electoral Saxony in 1528. The Hessians ordered that full worship services—that is, including the observance of the Lord's Supper—be celebrated on all the traditional Christological feasts, plus the three Marian holidays associated with Christ's birth—the Annunication, the Visitation, and the Purification. In addition, special preaching services were to be held on the festivals of Saint Stephen, the conversion of Saint Paul, and both the birth and the beheading of John the Baptist. The Saxons celebrated the three Marian festivals, along with those of the Apostles, Mary Magdalene, Michael and All Angels, and the birth of John the Baptist.[2]

The distinction between special, full festival services and preaching services is to be found in a number of church constitutions of the period that classify festivals in two categories of more or less significance. Where this distinction was made, the Christological feasts always were observed with full services, those of the saints with preaching services; or the biblical saints were celebrated with full services while the non-bib-

---

[1]Emil Sehling, ed., *Die evangelischen Kirchenordnungen des 16. Jahrhunderts* (Leipzig: Eisland, 1902-) IV:35 for Prussia, III:86-87 for Brandenburg. Robert Lansemann, *Die Heiligentage, besonders die Marien-, Apostel-, und Engeltage in der Reformationszeit, betrachtet im Zusammenhang der reformatorischen Anschauung von den Zeremonien, von den Festen, von den Heiligen, und von den Engeln* (Göttingen: Vandenhoeck & Ruprecht, 1939) 196-97, presents a table which sets forth the variance in the official Evangelical saints' days in sixteen selected sixteenth-century Lutheran ecclesiastical constitutions. For selected north German ecclesiastical constitutions, cf. Johannes Moritzen, *Die Heiligen in der nachreformatorischen Zeit* (Schriften des Vereins für schleswig-holsteinische Kirchengeschichte 7; Flensburg: Wolff, 1971) 16-30.

[2]Sehling, *Kirchenordnungen*, VIII,1:45-50 for Hesse; I:164 for Saxony.

lical saints were accorded the simpler, preaching service.[3] Other constitutions moved the observance of the day of the apostle or other saint to the nearest Sunday.[4] The most frequent celebrations apart from the days of the Apostles were those of John the Baptist's birth and, less frequently, his beheading; Mary Magdalene; the conversion of Paul; and Michael and All Angels. Several Lutheran churches also continued to observe long-time German favorites, such as the days of Saint Lawrence, the third-century Roman martyr, and of Saint Martin, the fourth-century bishop of Tours.[5]

The full medieval festival calendar was sometimes used for general dating in some ecclesiastical constitutions of the period. Some constitutions specifically singled out one particular festival in the struggle against medieval practice. In many parts of Germany, 15 August—the Assumption of the Blessed Virgin—had been celebrated as a day of Thanksgiving. Lutheran practice often moved this celebration—by specific prescription in certain places—to the day of Michael and All Angels, 29 September.[6] Some constitutions also pointedly rejected the celebration of Corpus Christi, although in Brandenburg (1540) and Anhalt (1532), territories with initially very conservative reformations, *Fronleichnam* remained in their first Lutheran constitutions.[7]

German Lutheran pastors also continued to preach on the days of the saints. Early in his career, Luther preached on a number of saints' days.

---

[3]Ibid., examples include Hesse (1526, 1532, 1566) VIII:49-50, 75, 308; Brieg in Silesia (1592), III:445; Verden (1606), VII,1:66; Danzig (1612), IV:204.

[4]Ibid., examples include Hamburg (1529), V:513-15; Buxtehude (1552), VII,1:78-79; Brandenburg (1558), III:91; Schwarzburg/Thur (1587), II:137.

[5]Ibid., examples of these lists can be found in constitutions from Hadeln (1526), V:466; Hamburg (1529), V:513-15; Pomerania (1535, 1569), IV:343, 440; Albertine Saxony (1539), I:174; Calenberg-Göttingen (1542), VI,2:797; Reuss (1552), II:555; Gera (1556), II:158-59.

[6]Ibid., I:627; the constitution of Oschatz (1555) retained the full medieval calendar for scheduling certain payments; Saint Michael's and All Angels became the day of thanksgiving in, for example, Göttingen (1531), ibid., VI,2:911; Prussia (1544), IV:68-69; Mecklenburg (1552), V:200-201; Oldenburg (1573), VII,2/1:1096-97; and Hoya (1581), VI,2:1186.

[7]Ibid., III:86-87, Brandenburg (1540); Anhalt (1532), II:542. The 1568 constitution removed the celebrations of Corpus Christi and Mary's assumption from Anhalt's official list, as the county was moving in a Calvinist direction. Note also that in the constitution of Northeim (1539), ibid., VI,2:934-35, Corpus Christi was preserved for political and social reasons but "all non-Christian ceremonies" connected with it, above all the procession, were abolished. The constitution of Oldenburg (1573), ibid., VII,2;1:1097, prescribed preaching against traditional practices on the Sunday nearest Corpus Christi.

Toward the end of his career, he preached quite regularly on the Annunciation, the Visitation, and the Purification of Mary, as well as on the days of John the Baptist and Saint Michael and All Angels. Luther ignored most other days connected with the saints. However, the postils of many of Luther's associates and students contain sermons not only for the days which Luther had celebrated with sermons but also for other saints' days: Paul's conversion; Saint Stephan, the Holy Innocents, Mary Magdalene, All Saints, and occasionally for other saints' days.[8]

One example is the collection of sermons issued by Nikolaus Selnecker in 1577, the same year in which he and five others completed their work on the Formula of Concord. Selnecker composed sermons for the festivals of the Twelve Apostles and a few others in the order in which they fell during the church year, beginning with Andrew (November 30) and concluding with Martin (November 11). He included the festivals of Stephen, John, the conversion of Paul, and the Baptism of Christ, perhaps because they fall together in the period between Christmas and Lent. He treated the Annunciation, the Visitation, and the Purification, the birth of John the Baptist, the days of Mary Magdalene and Michael and All Angels; and he noted that the festival of Philip and James the Less (May 1) was also the festival of Walpurgis—sister of Wilibald, the ninth-century missionary—an important day in northern Germany. Selnecker appended to his sermons for the festivals of the saints an account of the life of Martin Luther, fixed to his baptismal day under the name of Martin of Tours. Selnecker thus observed Luther among the saints, without placing him in exactly the same category, by providing a sermon for the observation.[9]

A book on feasts and festivals written by Matthaeus Dresser (1536-1607) gives a broader picture of the Lutheran observance of saints' days around 1580. Dresser indicated that some of Luther's followers were not only observing the great festivals of the church and celebrating the appointed days of great confessors of the patristic period, such as Polycarp and Basil, but also they were remembering the feasts of Lawrence; Gregory the Great, the late-sixth-century pope whom many Lutherans regarded as the founder of many of the evil practices of the papacy; Kilian, the seventh-century Irish monk who brought the gospel to Franconia; Margaret, the third-century martyr; Nikolaus, the fourth-century bishop,

---

[8]Lansemann, *Heiligentage*, 198-201.

[9]Nikolaus Selnecker, *Epistolarum et evangeliorum dispositio, quae diebus Festis B. Mariae semper virginis, & S. Apostolorum usitate in Ecclesia proponuntur & explicantur* (Frankfurt/Main, 1577).

and others vital to medieval piety. Dresser also felt compelled to treat the
Marian festivals, the festival of the Holy Cross, and even Corpus Christi,
although he utilized these holy days as the occasion for polemic against
them and their medieval significance. Dresser's polemic, in a Latin volume prepared probably for clergy use, might have been directed against
Roman Catholic foes; but the volume was intended as a practical handbook for pastors, and it seems likely that Dresser also intended to help
them continue the battle against the medieval love of the festivals still
present among their people. Certainly the mention of saints' days, even
that of Pope Gregory the Great, indicates that the pastors were encoun-
tering observances of these days in some form.[10]

This impression is supported from the thirty sermons on the pe-
ricopes for the days of certain holy martyrs and confessors of Christ, published by Johann Habermann (1516-1590), a pastor in Zeitz, Saxony, and
superintendent of the foundation at Naumburg. In addition to sermons
for the festivals of James, the Holy Innocents, Mark, and Luke from among
the biblical saints, he also composed sermons for Saints Nikolaus, George,
Margaret, Anne (the mother of Mary and a German favorite), Lawrence,
and Katherine, as well as for the festivals of All Saints, All Souls, Mary's
birth, Mary's ascension, and Corpus Christi.[11] The last-named again offered more occasion for polemic than for edification; but the fact remains
that a Lutheran postil did contain sermons preached on these days.

Intended to help other pastors deal with these festivals and the
practices surrounding them, such treatments of these medieval holy days
indicate that Evangelical pastors were having to combat the entrenched
rhythm of ecclesiastical observances on special days of the year, including the days of saints of dubious use in the Evangelical effort to restruc-
ture the piety of daily life. This must mean that among the Lutheran
populace at the time of the publication of the Book of Concord, remnants
of medieval practices regarding the saints and their days were still lively
and relatively strong. A quarter-century later, the *Ecclesiastical Calendar* cast
in homiletic form by Martin Behm (1557-1622), pastor in Silesia, again ad-

---

[10]Matthaeus Dresser, *De festis et praecipvis anni partibvs Liber, non solvm nomina
& historias, sed vsum etiam Exercitationibus scholasticis indicans* (Erfurt: Mechler, 1584).

[11]Johann Habermann, *Dreissig Predigten Vber die Epistel vnd Euangelien, so an den
tagen etlicher heiligen mertern vnd Bekennern Christi etc. vor zeiten sind gelesen vnd gebraucht worden* (Wittenberg, 1585).

dressed such festivals[12]—further indication that the traditional holy days of the medieval church still retained significance for his seventeenth-century parishioners and their neighbors in surrounding lands, even if that significance may have been shifting under the impact of Evangelical preaching.

The hymnody of the period also reflects the continued role of the ancient apostolic saints and their festivals in Lutheran worship. Early in the Reformation, propagandists had used hymns to combat the veneration of the saints[13] and to celebrate heroic confessors, martyrs both of the ancient church and of the contemporary Reformation movement.[14] As Lutheran liturgies were established, hymnists composed texts to be used on specific Sundays and festivals. The Saxon pastor Caspar Löner provided the public with an "instruction" on how to celebrate saints' days with song in a hymnal that he prepared in 1527. His single verses recall an outstanding fact or two to be remembered on the days of the apostolic saints of the church year, Simon and Jude, Bartholomew, Peter, Andrew, Paul, John, Philip, James the Less and James the Greater, Matthew, Matthias, Thomas, John the Baptist, Stephan, Michael and All Angels, and All Saints. To these he added Mary, the sister of Martha. Each verse offered the the contemporary singer a word of admonition or consolation

---

[12]Martin Behm, *Kirchen Calendar, Das ist, Christliche Erklerung Des Jahres vnd der zwoelff Monaten: Allen Pfarherrn, Schuldienern vnnd Haussuaetern in 13. Predigten verfasset vnd abgehandelt* (Wittenberg: Schmidt, 1608); see Moritzen, *Die Heiligen* 65-66.

[13]The Breslau reformer Ambrose Moibanus (1494-1554) composed "A Spiritual Song and Instruction on the Invocation of the Saints," published in 1527, in which he directed through paraphrases of biblical passages that God alone be worshiped and insisted that Christ alone mediates between God and his human creatures; the text is found in Philipp Wackernagel, ed., *Das deutsche Kirchenlied von der ältesten Zeit bis zu Anfang des XVII. Jahrhunderts* 5 vols. (Leipzig: Teubner, 1864-1877), 3:551-52.

[14]See, for example, the poetic summary, "From the History of Eusebius, on the Ten Persecutions and the Destruction of Christendom," by the Wittenberg student, later disciple of Caspar Schwenckfeld, Adam Reusner (1496/1500-c. 1575/ 1582), ibid., 3:150-55; and see the hymns on the apostles who suffered for proclaiming the gospel and on "all martyrs and confessors of Jesus Christ," by Michael Weisse, Luther's disciple and a pastor of the Bohemian Brethren, ibid., 3:339-43. Nikolaus Selnecker wrote a hymn in a similar vein on the theme, "The Blood of the Saints is the Seed of the Church," a half century later, ibid., 4:292-93. Veit Hurtlein's poetic narrative of the martyrdoms of Matthias Waibel and Caspar Tauber, two men whose confession is celebrated in Rabus's pages, provides examples of sixteenth-century hymnic martyrology, ibid., 3:433-38.

based on the saint's example.[15]

Exactly a half-century later, Nikolaus Selnecker issued a new book of worship for electoral Saxony, his *Christian Psalms, Songs, and Hymns, in which Christian Teaching is Comprehended and Explained.* It contained a number of hymns that he had prepared for use on specific festivals, among them Saints Stephen, John, John the Baptist, Peter and Paul, Mary Magdalene, Bartholomew, Michael and All Angels, Simon and Jude, Andrew, and Thomas. These hymns rehearsed biblical stories and ancient legends regarding the saints, placing the saints' deeds within God's economy of salvation and protection of his people. After these poetic accounts of the continuing struggle between Satan and God's angels, Selnecker printed a prayer to Christ for church, school, government, homes, and the Christian congregation, that they might have all temptation turned away from them and that Christ's people might receive the blessing of Christian living and dying under the protection of the angels. For that, Selnecker's singers joined with the angelic hosts in thanking the Holy Trinity.[16]

In this same hymnal Selnecker included four-line stanzas written by Joachim Reubold. These 147 rhymes summarized the gospel lessons for Sundays and festivals (in some cases, a given day had two stanzas) or a gospel lesson for the evening service preceding days such as Christmas or Epiphany. Reubold's verses were intended for children to memorize. His festivals included the days of the apostolic saints and, in addition, Saints Barbara, Nikolaus, Mary Magdalene, and Lawrence, as well as four Marian holidays.[17] The Brandenburg pastor Bartholomaeus Ringwald (c. 1530–c. 1599) also composed hymns for the gospels of several saints' days, among them Saint Katherine.[18] Individual hymns for Marian festivals and the festivals of John the Baptist and of Saint Michael and All Angels may also be found among the hymnic heritage of the Lutheran Late Reformation.[19]

---

[15]Ibid., 3:623-26.

[16]Ibid., 4:326-27, 331-37.

[17]Ibid., 5:105-16.

[18]Ibid., 4:964-75.

[19]Cyriakus Spangenberg may have prepared a medieval hymn for the festival of the Annunciation and placed it in the Mansfeld hymnal of 1568, ibid., 4:1066. (N.B.: All of the following references are to *Das deutsche Kirchenlied* . . . as well.) From the 1520s we have Michael Weisse's hymns of the mother of the Lord, which specifically condemn trust in Mary, 3:343-44. This theme is found in the poetic

    In German Lutheran lands, the saints were present in the minds of the people also because, in many cases, they were present before their eyes in the ecclesiastical art of altars and church buildings. In comparison to other areas where the Reformation became established, Lutheran Germany experienced relatively little iconoclasm; many images of the saints of post-biblical church history remained alongside the medieval images of prophets and apostles. In some cases images associated with local miracles—few though they were in Lutheran areas—were eradicated early in the developing Reformation, and there are examples of the latter-day destruction of statues of Saint Christopher in the early seventeenth century. But, in general, as the Reformation moved into the period of Protestant orthodoxy, depictions of a wide variety of saints remained. Those of the Blessed Virgin and the Apostles encountered no objections because they were biblical; but other saints also retained their places in the decorative art of the churches. Some did so because they were the patrons of the church; others offered worthy examples or stories for the cultivation of piety. Later in the seventeenth and eighteenth centuries, some Lutherans were forced to defend the presence of holy statuary by arguing that the images of the saints reminded the people of the heathen practices which the Reformation had brought to an end. But the retention of these images, in spite of the radically different theological function which they could perform as adornments to Lutheran worship, did not seem so contradictory to most sixteenth- and seventeenth-century Lutherans that the statues required special justification.[20]

    In more prosperous parishes, particularly in mercantile cities, new art was developed for the churches in the late-sixteenth and early-seventeenth centuries. Most of the chancel art of this period reflects the highly Christocentric nature of Lutheran theology, with scenes of the crucifixion and resurrection most popular. But the saints, the heroes of the proclamation of God's Word, were not forgotten completely. The choir stalls built in the closing years of the sixteenth century for the Church of Saint Ulrich, a formerly Franciscan church in the city of Braunschweig, cele-

---

retelling of the Annuciation by Valentin Triller, a Breslau reformer, 4:47-48; see also the Marian hymns by Cunrad Michael of Nordhausen, 4:131; Ludwig Helmbold, 4:643 (for the Visitation); and Bartholomaeus Ringwald, 4:956-57 (on the gospel for the Visitation). Triller, 4:48, Georg Oemler, 4:126-28, Helmbold, 4:643, and Otto Moyse, 4:725, composed hymns for the festival of John the Baptist; and Helmbold, 4:676, Georg Barth, 4:900-901, and Ringwald, 4:967-68, for that of Michael and All Angels. These hymns all date from the 1550s and 1560s.

    [20]Moritzen, *Die Heiligen*, 30-34; Martin Scharfe, *Evangelische Andachtsbilder. Studien zur Intention und Funktion des Bildes in der Frömmigkeitsgeschichte vornehmlich des schwäbischen Raumes* (Stuttgart: Müller & Gräff, 1968) 146-49, 155-81.

brate the chain of witnesses to God's Word by depicting forty-six key post-biblical confessors of that Word, which was finally being preached also in that parish. The majority were patristic figures and most were doctors of the church, including some regarded with suspicion by some Lutherans: Ignatius of Antioch, Polycarp, Justin Martyr, Irenaeus, Clement of Alexandria, Origen, Tertullian, Lawrence, Cyprian, Lactantius, Eusebius of Caesarea, Athanasius, Hilary, Basil of Caesarea, Gregory of Nazianzus, Ambrose, Epiphanias, Jerome, Theophilactus, Augustine, Chrysostom, Cyril, Theodoret, Leo I, Fulgentius, Gelasius I, Vigilius, John of Damascus, and Gregory the Great. The chain of witnesses continued with medieval figures, Anselm of Canterbury, Bernard of Clairvaux, Bonaventure, Hugh of Paris, Jean Gerson, and (out of chronological order) the Venerable Bede. Like Ludwig Rabus, the designer of the Saint Ulrich's choir stalls recognized John Hus and Jerome of Prague as the key late-medieval figures who had led to Martin Luther and Philip Melanchthon—all four of whom were depicted on stalls. The series concludes with Johann Bugenhagen, Luther's colleague and the author of the first Evangelical ecclesiastical constitution of Braunschweig; three Evangelical superintendents of the Braunschweig churches from the late-sixteenth century, Joachim Mörlin, Martin Chemnitz, and Polycarp Leyser; and two other prominent Lutheran theologians of that period, Aegidius Hunnius and Georg Mylius. It is significant to note that two other series of paintings also graced Saint Ulrich's, one an overview of biblical history, the other a presentation of the passion of Christ. Further, depiction of the confessors of the church spread to two other churches within the city. During the seventeenth century, both the Church of Saint Katherine and the Church of Saint Magnus introduced depictions of the confessors of the church into their worship areas. Saint Katherine's included twenty-three confessors, representing the entire span of church history; at Saint Magnus were depicted only the "moderns": Hus, Luther, Bugenhagen, Mörlin, Chemnitz, and Leyser.[21]

It is impossible to measure the impact that retention of the visible remnants of medieval veneration of the saints had on the pious of the parish. Lutheran pastors and teachers attempted to shift the attention of their hearers and pupils away from the visual to the verbal, with the ef-

---

[21]Dietrich Mack, *Bildzyklen in der Brüdernkirche zu Braunschweig (1596-1638)* (Stadtarchiv und Stadtbibliothek Braunschweig Kleine Schriften 10; Braunschweig: Waisenhaus-Buchdruckerei, 1983) 9-28. See also the observations on other artistic depictions of Evangelical theologians by R. W. Scribner, *For the Sake of Simple Folk, Popular Propaganda for the German Reformation* (Cambridge: Cambridge University Press, 1981) 227.

fect of diminishing the impact that ecclesiastical art had on popular belief—this, in contrast to the Late Middle Ages, when no print and little
verbal instruction was available to teach the faithful through words rather
than pictures. The Reformation had initially attacked the "salvific
display"[22] of the period with its own use of woodcuts and other artistic
forms in a massive counteraction against medieval piety, including veneration of the saints. Heavy emphasis on the spoken Word of preaching
and teaching altered the way in which iconic salvific display shaped the
minds of the believers; and concentration on a theology and piety that
tended to displace veneration of the saints gradually caused the popular
mind to become detached from the faith that medieval depictions once
had cultivated. As a result, few new depictions of the saints were painted
or sculpted, polemic against the icons and what they stood for continued
into the seventeenth century, and even the magnificent array of patristic,
medieval, and contemporary confessors at Saint Ulrich's may be interpreted as an attempt to refocus attention away from devotion to the saints
and towards their confession instead. These few depictions must have
made a positive contribution to the shaping of Evangelical understanding
of what really makes a Christian "hero," namely, the proper proclamation and confession of the Word of God.

Treatments of the festivals of the Christian church in song or in
sermons continued to be occasions to criticize the abuses long connected
with remembering the saints; but, at the same time, these treatments were
also recognitions of the value of remembrance, so long as it focused on
the power that God had loosed through his Word in the saints' proclamation and confession and in the piety of their holy lives.

THE PROVIDENCE OF GOD AND THE CALLING
OF THE CHRISTIAN AS SUBSTITUTES
FOR THE VENERATION OF THE SAINTS

Lutheran theologians and pastors had to replace the saints; that is,
they had to ensure that the functions that the saints had performed for
medieval Christians would be performed in other ways for their parishioners. They had to make certain that Lutherans understood that although holy power is not mediated through the saints, God, the provident
Creator, nevertheless brings his omnipotent concern for his people to bear
on every aspect of daily life. Lutheran preachers and authors had to develop an image of the saint as a model for Christian behavior, a vehicle
for admonition and encouragement, without confusing that role of the

---

[22]Ibid., 4-5.

saint with the role that lay alongside it in the medieval perception of the holy person—that of mediator and dispenser of super-human power. The Lutheran leaders of the sixteenth century apparently failed to recognize the need to address the problem of holy time, of the propitious day, of the power associated with the celebrated time at which the holy person's power was strongest. Because they did not recognize the problem clearly, they dealt with holy time only obliquely, if at all.

The medieval veneration of the saints had been, above all, a means whereby divine power was mediated and applied in the daily lives of the people; this work of the saints on behalf of the pious was, for many, more important than their prayers for the ultimate deliverance of souls from purgatory. Rudolf Schenda has suggested that this issue was vital for popular piety in the era of the Reformation, because the stories of the saints and of the exercise of their power carried with them an argument for the legitimacy of the entire doctrinal system and worldview of which they were a part. The religion of the saints thus served both as a stabilizing factor in the midst of religious turmoil and cultural questioning and as a means for indoctrinating norms and values.[23] The Protestants of the sixteenth century countered the belief in the ability of the saints to mediate divine power in human lives on the theological level with a strong emphasis on God's providence. Hymns, catechetical instruction, prayerbooks, and sermons served to cultivate in the pious this trust in a loving and fatherly God, who had revealed his ultimate care and concern in his Son, Jesus Christ, and who would take care of his chosen people in the smallest details of their lives.

As these various kinds of literature brought the positive power of God into the consciousness of the pious Lutheran parishioner, so other kinds of works reinterpreted the negative powers at work in the world in new ways and made them subject directly to the power of the loving God. Collections of stories of wonders on earth and in the heavens had been popular throughout the century.[24] A broadsheet literature developed in evangelical circles, advertising specific, miraculous events and defining their significance as exhibitions of the presence of God's wondrous power

---

[23]Rudolf Schenda, "Die protestantisch-katholische Legendenpolemik," *Archiv für Kulturgeschichte* 52 (1970):44-48.

[24]An introduction to and bibliography of this literature is provided by Rudolf Schenda, "Die deutschen Prodigiensammlungen des 16. und 17. Jahrhunderts," *Archiv für Geschichte des Buchwesens* IV (1963):637-710. See also Miriam Usher Chrisman, *Lay Culture, Learned Culture, Books and Social Change in Strasbourg, 1480-1599* (New Haven: Yale University Press, 1982) 260-64, on published materials reflecting this element of religious belief.

in sixteenth-century Germany.[25] Several leading Lutheran authors of the latter half of the century interpreted such wonders in some cases as the works of Satan but in other cases as signs of the judgment of God and a summons from his merciful hand to the repentance that would bring the believer into the safety of God's grace. According to the compilers of these collections, the wondrous signs pointed to the coming Last Day; their compilations—along with tracts and books of other genres—give evidence among the Lutheran populace of strong eschatological expectations of God's imminent deliverance of his people from all evil through Final Judgment. Eschatological sermons and tracts similarly reminded the people of the nearness of God's ultimate power. This popularity of literature on the Endtime indicates that the proclamation of the immediate approach of Christ to judge the living and the dead was quenching, at least in part, the thirst to trust in the mediated power of God to intervene through saints in the midst of his world. The reformers and their successors told their parishioners that the eschaton would complete the earthly dimension of the tender care for his people of the loving Creator and Father.[26] Belief in that message eliminated the need to trust the power of the saints.

Even apart from eschatological deliverance, the message of faith in a provident God undoubtedly had the same effect among German Lutherans that Keith Thomas states it had among English Protestants.[27] The magic that the wonderworking saints of medieval religion had performed had been set in a partial worldview, but it was less adequate than the Reformers' belief in a unified universe under one Creator God. The faith preached by the Reformers offered a framework for dealing with all life's problems, placing the solution to all problems firmly and comprehensively in the hands of a God whose love had displayed itself in his own incarnation and death on his people's behalf. Evil could be better explained—albeit not always utterly—with reference to human responsibility; evil's end rested not on the ability of its victims to manipulate the saints in just the right way but rather on the constancy of God, who hates

---

[25]Numerous woodcuts depicting prodigies and signs may be found in Walter L. Strauss, *The German Single-leaf Woodcut, 1550-1660* (New York: Abaris, 1975) 86, 98, 99, 106, 107, 110-111, 112-13, 115, 116, 120, 124, 194, 195, 236, 350, 351, 359, 362, 363, 364.

[26]Robin Barnes, "Prophecy and the Eschaton in Lutheran Germany, 1530-1630" (Ph.D. dissertation, University of Virginia, 1980) passim.

[27]Keith Thomas, *Religion and the Decline of Magic* (New York: Scribner, 1971) 636-38.

evil.

With a world thus secured by God's providence, saints could remain in a role as passive exhibitors of the power of God. Wittenbergers from Luther and Melanchthon through Rabus and Flacius had so used them; and the Reformers' heirs continued to pay attention to saints and particularly to martyrs for the same purposes. Scholars continued to treat the saints into the eighteenth century in their scholarly disputations with various historical and moral interests.[28] While popular, broadsheet journalism in Lutheran areas paid close attention to persecution in other parts of Europe during the latter decades of the sixteenth century,[29] martyrs often were seen as evidence for God's providence rather than as examples calling believers to stalwart confession. But the persecution of the faith did return to German Lutheran lands in the seventeenth century, the martyrs' theme was renewed. Although Rabus's work was not revived or republished, other treatments of martyrdom were issued. These reports sprang not only from theologians but also from historians and dramatists. Infrequent historical accounts of contemporary martyrs commanded the interest of the German reading public, particularly in travel literature of the time, with stories about those who gave their lives rather than renounce the Christian faith for the Muslim religion. For example, Rudolf Stadler, who died in Persia because he refused to convert to Islam, was heralded as a martyr and champion of the Christian faith by Adam Olearius.[30]

In a significant turn from history to fiction indicative of the influence of the Baroque in Lutheran circles, the historical account of martyr-

---

[28]For example, *Ex antiquitate martyrologica Dissertatio accademica*, Martin Lubath, presiding (Halle: Salfeld, 1693); *Disputatio publica sollenis de Persecutionibus et Martyriis Christianorum veterum*, Johann Meisner, presiding (Wittenberg: Wendt, 1564); *In paucitatem martyrum Antiquioris Christi Ecclesiae*, Christian Wilhelm Loescher, presiding (Wittenberg: Kreusig, 1697); *Dissertatio historico-theologica de autocheiria Martyrum*, Heinrich Klausing, presiding (Leipzig: Titius, 1720). See also such varied works as the brief lecture by Johann Christoph Ortlob and Georg Christoph Hentschel, *Martyres furori gentilium ultra mortem expositios . . .* (Leipzig: Titius, 1699); the larger volume by Caspar Sagittarius, *De martyrum cruciatibus in primitiua ecclesia Liber* (Jena: Bauhofer, 1673; second edition, Frankfurt/M, Leipzig: Crocher, 1696); and the treatment of biblical martyrs by Georg Weinrich, *Martyrologii Sanctorum ex XI. Cap. ad Hebr.* (Leipzig: Lantzenberger, 1606). All these were intended for a Latin-reading audience.

[29]Chrisman, *Lay Culture*, 267-68.

[30]Adam Olearius, *Vermehrte Newe Beschreibung Der Muscowitischen vnd Persischen Reyse, Schleswig, 1655*, Dieter Lohmeier, ed. (Tübingen: Niemeyer, 1972) 520-23.

dom became less prominent than the imaginative during the seventeenth century. The widely read poet and dramatist, Andreas Gryphius (1616-1664), himself experienced the Habsburgs' strong effort to suppress the Lutheran faith in his native Silesia, and he reflected his convictions concerning the necessity of confessing the faith in both his poetry and his drama. His dramatic treatment of Christian confession in *Catherina of Georgia*—the story of a Christian queen who resists the pressures of her Persian captors to forsake Christ for the Islamic religion—won wide popularity in Orthodox Lutheran Germany.[31] Indeed, such vernacular literary efforts seem to have provided German Lutherans with a substitute for the popular presentation of heroic confessors that the martyrbooks of Foxe, Crespin, and van Haemstede continued to be in other Protestant lands.

In seventeenth-century Germany, where theology found expression largely in Latin, popular literary forms, including poetry and drama, flourished in the vernacular. Seventeenth-century Lutherans were offered a large number of meditative and devotional works in addition to drama and poetry, and in these they found the comfort, encouragement, and admonition that Rabus had wanted to offer through his book of confessors and martyrs. Fiction, as well as history, could present the heroic human figures that the persecuted in Silesia, and later in Salzburg, needed to help them endure harrassment and exile for Luther's faith. Drama and poetry reinforced catechetization and preaching in the effort to engender courageous confession and create trust in a loving and caring God.

Theologians in this period tended to use martyrs less to encourage public confession and more to strengthen faith in God's providence in daily life. This trend had been heralded by the publication of a German translation of the collection of martyr stories assembled by Hieronymus Weller (1499-1572), a student at Wittenberg in the early 1530s, who served

---

[31]Much has been written in the twentieth century on Gryphius; see, for example, Adolf Strutz, *Andreas Gryphius, Die Weltanschauung eines deutschen Barockdichters* (Hörgen Zurich: Münster-Presse, 1931) esp. 78-87; Werner Eggers, *Wirklichkeit und Wahrheit im Trauerspiel von Andreas Gryphius* (Heidelberg: Winter, 1967); Harald Steinhagen, *Wirklichkeit und Handeln im barocken Drama. Historisch-ästhetische Studien zum Trauerspiel des Andreas Gryphius* (Tübingen: Niemeyer, 1977); and Wolfram Mauser, *Dichtung, Religion und Gesellschaft im 17. Jahrhundert. Die "Sonnete" des Andreas Gryphius* (Munich: Fink, 1976) esp. 111-14, on Gryphius's use of sonnets for confession against the Roman Catholics in Silesia. Peter N. Skrine, *The Baroque, Literature and Culture in Seventeenth-Century Europe* (London: Methuen, 1978) 53-66 places Gryphius in the context of Baroque treatments of martyrdom, the exaltation of which he labels "a major and central concern of the baroque world," p. 54.

nearly his entire ministry in Freiburg, Saxony. Weller's *School of the Cross* was prepared in Latin shortly before his death, published posthumously in 1580, and reprinted in 1607. Each chapter begins with a biographical sketch focusing on the confession and death of the martyr, after which the author presented the lessons that he wanted his reader to draw from the events depicted. From the story of Saint Lucia, for example, Weller taught those who had come to the school of the cross that faith cannot rest unless it is confessing, that God provides for his people, that faith puts complete trust in God. In this story Weller also called attention to the wondrous power of God that kept the fire from burning Lucia. Weller told the story of Polycarp to teach Christian contemplation in the midst of persecution: Polycarp had withdrawn from his congregation only when he saw that his exile would bring no danger nor disadvantage to his church.

After some fifty didactic recitals of events and admonitory applications, Weller's work in the 1607 version offered the reader nearly forty pages of comforting passages from Scripture for various tests and trials; thirty-one letters written by Weller, about half specifically intended to comfort fellow believers; and a group of aphorisms also designed to strengthen the Christian in the midst of trial. Weller's work illustrates the later-Lutheran reluctance to deal with contemporary saints and martyrs; he used only the examples of the ancient church. Like the earliest authors of Lutheran lives of the saints—Hermann Bonnus, Georg Major, and Georg Spalatin, who published their works in the 1540s (see chapter 1)—Weller apparently imagined that his work was best directed to the Latin-reading public, probably the clergy, although Weller's applications of the stories suggest that he believed that the pastors who read his book would use the stories in their sermons to teach their parishioners lessons about God's providential love and care from the lives of the saints.[32]

Weller's long-time associate and friend, Michael Hempel, prepared a preface for the 1607 edition. This preface indicates that in Hempel's mind the book would fulfill its purpose if it aroused its readers to resist Satan's pressures both in the persecutions that might fall upon the church from the Turk's sword and also in the deceit of human reason. The threat from the papacy or from the Roman Catholic emperor was ignored; the threat from false doctrine—one which Rabus also had perceived—Hempel saw as standing alongside that source of imminent

---

[32]Hieronymus Weller, *Creutz-Schule, Oder Etlicher Maertyrer und andere vornehme Historien, mit ihren Lehren, Trost-Spruechen, Schrifften, Episteln, und geistreichen Spruechen* (Halle: Zeitler, 1697; other editions in German appeared in Magdeburg, 1580; Freiburg/Saxony, 1607; and Halle, 1700).

persecution, the Turk. Above all, the book was designed to give consolation and instill faith in God's providence; from its stories the readers
would see, according to Hempel, "the presence, majesty, and omnipotence of the true God."[33]

This use of history as exhortation to trust in God's providing care
was a change in the function of martyr stories from the use to which Rabus put them in 1551. By the late seventeenth century, Wilhelm Will, a
pastor in Bechtheim, on the Rhine, composed a collection of stories about
those who had died piously in order to help his people face the assault of
pestilence. Will presented his subjects as "models and examples of dying
saints and believers from Christ's birth to these times, who departed this
world with heroic, comforting words and prayers." Will held up these
glimpses from the history of God's people so that his readers might themselves die well; he was not concerned with rallying them against a human
persecutor to public confession.[34] The purpose of martyrology had been
transformed. Rabus's call to resistance against papal tyranny through
stalwart, public confession of the Evangelical faith seemed less relevant
after 1555; now, the martyrs and other Christian heroes treated in the
works of authors like Weller offered examples and models for a broader
range of Christian attitudes and actions.

The transformation from Rabus's concern with martyrs as models
for individual confession of the faith to Will's use of martyrs as models
for pious dying further illumines a more general change in the tone and
purpose of German-Lutheran treatment of saints and martyrs. Collections of examples of pious conduct were not restricted to biographical
forms; some arranged by theme—for example, under headings dictated
by the Ten Commandments—also became popular among German Lutherans in the 1570s and after. The prefaces of these works, for instance
that of Andreas Hohndorf, reflected a confidence in the value of historical examples to admonish and encourage the faith of his own age—the
same confidence that Rabus had possessed as he embarked on the pub-

---

[33]Ibid. (1697 edition) b3-[c7], esp. b4v.

[34]Wilhelm Will, *Legenda pie defunctum, Das ist: Fuerbildt vnd Exempel, etlicher
sterbenden heiligen vnd christglaeubigen Menschen von Christi Geburt an, biss auff diese
zeit so mit Heldenmuth Trostreichen worten vnd Geberden von dieser Welt abgeschieden*
(Frankfurt/Main: Bassaeus, 1696).

lication of his martyrology, although with a different goal in mind.[35]

Pious admonition and encouragement provided support for the typical Christian in his or her responsible exercise of the assignments or callings that God had given in the three estates of home, community, and church. Luther's theology of the Christian's calling and his understanding of the priesthood of all believers were proclamations that all believers are saints and that all human activity performed by the believer, both in the religious sphere and also in the profane realms of family and occupational life, of political duties and obligations, are godly.[36] Sebastian Schwan's apologies for not including examples of heroic Christians from among the princes and housefathers in his edition of the lives of the ancient fathers demonstrates that Luther's thoughts on sainthood had made an impression on his followers (see chapter 1).[37] But when all are saints and all activities are saintly, there is less reason to put the spotlight on any individual saint or calling.

Arguing that the role of the saint is determined by the expectations of a group's religious norms and the sanctions growing from these norms, Martin Scharfe points to a narrowing of the number of serviceable saints and useful elements in saints' lives within the German Reformation.[38] The thrust of Luther's vision of sanctity in the callings of all Christians did more than that, however; it actually worked to eliminate a need for, or the ability to be comfortable with, any heroic Christians at all. Increasingly, the role of the confessor was reserved for the clergy, who alone could properly confess, in the pulpit; heroic testimony in the face of oppressive, tyrannous, and cruel persecutors of the faithful did not invite imitation in the daily lives of most heirs of Luther's cause. True piety, rather, found its ideal expression in the exercise of the commonplace. This meant that identification of the exemplary Christian according to the old patterns of

---

[35]Andreas Hohndorff, *Promptvarivm exemplorvm. Das ist, Historien vnd Exempelbuch, nach ordnung vnd Disposition der heiligen zehen Gebott Gottes. . . . zusammen getragen* (Frankfurt/Main: Schmidt, 1572), and Zacharias Rivander (1553-1594), *Der Ander Theil promptvarii exemplorvm* (Frankfurt/Main: Feyerabendt, 1587) are good examples of these books; see Ernst Heinrich Rehermann, "Die Protestantischen Exempelsammlungen des 16. und 17. Jahrhunderts," in Wolfgang Brückner, ed., *Volkserzählung und Reformation* (Berlin; Schmidt, 1974) 579-645, and Heidemarie Schade, "Andreas Hohndorffs Promptuarium Exemplorum," ibid., 647-703.

[36]See Gustaf Wingren, *Luther on Vocation*, Carl C. Rasmussen, trans. (Philadelphia: Muhlenberg, 1957).

[37]See ch. 1, n. 67.

[38]Martin Scharfe, "Der Heilige in der protestantischen Volksfrömmigkeit," *Hessische Blätter für Volkskunde* 60 (1969): 93-106, esp. 97-103.

magical power or extraordinary good works had become impossible. The ground once commanded by the medieval saints, half-way between us and God, had been preempted both by God and us.

CONCLUDING REMARKS

Sixteenth-century Lutheranism, like every other Protestant movement, had to deal with the medieval beliefs and practices surrounding the veneration of the saints. Luther and his followers attacked that veneration on the basis of their belief in the providence of God and in the sufficiency of Christ's mediating work on behalf of sinners. The Lutheran Reformation turned all believers into saints and emphasized that saints serve God by hearing and proclaiming his Word and by carrying out their divinely-assigned callings in daily life, within their households, their political communites, and their churches.

The focus on God's providence, Christ's intercession, and the believers' callings in daily life came to be common among Calvinists, Puritans, and Lutherans alike. On the basis of these doctrinal foundations all three Protestant confessions criticized the medieval veneration of the saints and sought to replace the old reliance upon the saints with new conceptual frameworks for faith and discipleship. Each confession used a variety of polemical and pedagogical tools to accomplish this, among them the martyrology.

All Protestants had their own martyrologies, because Ludwig Rabus initiated a common phenomenon. If he had not, certainly someone else would have moved from the recital of individual Protestant martyrs' stories to a compilation of these stories. The need for heroes of their cause, the tradition of Christian martyrology, and the polemical and edificatory usefulness of these stories made this development inevitable.

The differences in the role that Rabus's martyrbook played among his fellow German Lutherans and the role that Foxe's, Crespin's, and van Haemstede's played , respectively, among the Puritans, Huguenots, and Dutch Calvinists can be attributed to several causes. One is the differing political situations in these Reformation lands. None escaped some persecution; but England, France, and the Netherlands all witnessed much more severe and dramatic persecution of Protestants than did Germany during the sixteenth century. Foxe's, Crespin's, and van Haemstede's readers found a martyrology more immediately meaningful, more relevant, than did Rabus's readers.

Second, this pattern of persecution seems to have coincided with different attitudes toward the saints in the late-medieval population. Evidence suggests that at least the northern Germans had had few of their own, native saints to venerate. They did venerate the saints, but without the same kind of attachment to local heroes present in the cultus of other Western-European areas. This also means that they were less practiced in finding heroes of the faith among their own kind; thus they proved less disposed to look for new heroes in the Reformation movement.

Third, the German Lutheran Reformation left in place more remnants of medieval respect for the saints than did other Protestant movements—in the liturgical year and preaching, in hymns, and in the artwork of their churches. Thus, Lutherans had more contact at least with the biblical saints—and a few selected old favorites from church history, as well. This slightly diminished their need for newer heroes.

Fourth, the Lutherans did have one contemporary saint whose stature among them fulfilled much of their need for a demonstration of God's power in their midst. No single Puritan hero, no Calvinist saint, stood so tall among the sixteenth-century Protestants as Luther, towering, as he did, over the European landscape and, above all, over the German landscape, because of his heroic confession of the faith at Worms and his key role in all the Reformation movements of the sixteenth century.

Moreover, Luther's understanding of the nature of God's Word, as working through human speech, indirectly taught his followers to subsume energies formerly directed towards the venerated saints into a veneration for the new prophet, the new Elijah, the new doctor of the church, Martin Luther himself. His concept of the living voice of the Gospel permitted his followers to hear a special manifestation of God's power at its most powerful present in human proclamation. They believed that the Scriptures not only infallibly point to the divine truths of heaven but also that the Scriptures continue to inform the speaking of the Gospel, making God's power really present. No exhibition of God's power is more significant than the forgiveness of sins and recreation of believers as children of God. Therefore, Luther's disciples were prepared to hear God's power exhibited in the mouths of the proclaimers of the Word. Among their contemporaries in this category, they knew of no one comparable to Luther. Among the prophets of God throughout history, they recognized few comparable to Luther.

Lutherans, in fact, were more interested in the source of God's power coming into their lives through the Word than in the effects of divine power manifested in the lives of heroic confessors. They were more interested in the history of the proclamation, the confession of faith itself, and less interested in the history of the proclaimers, the confessors themselves; Lutherans preferred a history of dogma (the Magdeburg *Centuries*) to a history of martyrs (Rabus's *Accounts*). One example—the paramount example in Luther—of God's gift of a hero of the Word almost sufficed for them.

Lastly, in Protestant lands, the veneration of the saints gave way under the advance of new conceptions of reality. At the heart of a new conceptual framework for Christian thinking lay faith in the God who provides for everything—above all, salvation through Jesus Christ alone. For Lutherans, the power to bestow salvation was being actualized in their villages and towns through God's forgiving and recreating Word, present in preaching, absolution, the sacraments, and mutual conversation and consolation among believers.

Although trust in the saints' powers undoubtedly waned only gradually in German villages and guild halls, the teaching of that new German hero, prophet, and martyr, Martin Luther, would not abide trust in anything but the Word of God. The old saints, with their extraordinary deeds and their supernatural powers, had lost a place in Luther's new scheme of things. According to that scheme, God's power in his Word was sufficient for his people, who lived out saintly lives doing the ordinary tasks to which God had called them through the strength of his Word.

Appendix

THE ANCIENT MARTYRS
OF RABUS'S FIRST (GERMAN) EDITION

James [the Greater], Apostle, cxxiij/r
James [the Less], Apostle, cxxiiij/r
John the Baptist, cxxviiij/r
John, Apostle and Evangelist, cxxix/v
Ignatius, Bishop of Antioch, cxxxiij/r
Justinus, cxxxv/r
Julianus, cxxxvj/v
Ischirion, cxxxviiij/r
Juventius, armorbearer of Emperor Julian, cxxxviiij/v
Isaaces, clxiij/v
Julitta, clxiiij/v
Lucius, cxlvij/v
Lucianus, cxlviij/v
Liberatus, a physician, with his wife, clj/r
Lawrence, a deacon, clij/v
Machabeus, with six brothers and their mother Solomona, clvij/r
Marinus, clxxvj/v
Macedonius, clxxviiij/r
Marcus, Bishop of Arethusa, clxxix/r
Milles, clxxx/v
Masculas, clxxxj/v
Muritta, a deacon of Carthage, clxxxij/r
Metras, a priest or elder of Alexandria, clxxxiiij/r
Nemesion, an Egyptian, clxxxvj/r
A citizen of Nicomedia, clxxxvj/v
Nisibener, clxxxviiij/r
Nestabus with two brothers, Eusebius and Zeno, clxxxviiij/v
Nestor, clxxxix/v
Numidicus, a priest or elder of Carthage, clxxxix/v
Origen, cxcij/v
Polycarp, Bishop of Smyrna, cxcv/r
Peter, Apostle, ccij/r
Paul, Apostle, ccvj/v
Pothinus, Bishop of Lyons, ccix/r
Ptolemus, ccx/v
Potamiena, a virgin, ccxij/r
Peter, a young prince of Emperors Diocletian and Maximian, ccxij/v

Philoromus, an imperial prince in Alexandria, ccxiij/v
Peter, Bishop of Alexandria, ccxv/v
Paphnutius, ccxv/v
Publia, ccxvij/r
Pusices, chief superintendent of King Saporis in Persia, ccxviiij/r
The Forty Soldiers, ccxx/v
Quinta, ccxxvij/r
Romanus, ccxxviiij/v
Stephan, ccxxxj/r
Sanctus, ccxxxij/v
Serapion, ccxxxiiij/v
Suenes, ccxxxv/r
Symeon, Archbishop of Seleucia, ccxxxv/v
Sebastian, a count, ccxxxix/r
Saturus, ccxl/r
Seven brothers, ccxlj/v
Theodorus, ccxlvij/v
Trabula, ccl/r
Two natural brothers in Tanbaia, ccij/r
Typasa, a city in Mauritania, cclij/r
Vetius Epagathus, ccliij/r
Urbanus, cclv/v
Valentinianus, cclvij/r
Usthazares, cclviij/r
Victoria, cclx/v
Victorianus, a mayor of Carthage, cclxj/r
Vitalis, cclxij/r
Zacharias, son of Barachiah, cclxiiij/r

Volume II

Jeremiah, j/r
Amos, v/r
The Jews of Alexandria, vj/v
Thomas, Apostle, xiij/v
Agbarus, xvj/v
Bartholomew, Apostle, xix/v
Matthias, Apostle, xxvj/r
Simon Zelotes, Apostle, xxxiiij/r
Mark, Evangelist, xl/r
Luke, Evangelist, xliij/r

BOOK ONE OF THE SECOND EDITION
OF RABUS' MARTYROLOGY (OLD TESTAMENT)

I. Abel, 1r
II. Zacharias, a son of Jehoida or Barachiah, 8v
III. Elisha the Prophet, 11r
IV. Amos the Prophet, 21v
V. Isaiah the great and faithful Prophet, 25r
VI. Jeremiah, the Prophet whom evil tormented, 33r

VII. Hananiah or Shadrach, Mishael or Mischach, and Azariah or Abednego, 48v
VIII. Daniel the Prophet, 55v
IX. Two Jewish Women, who with two of their sons and children, were thrown over the wall to their death for having the children circumcised according to the law, 64r
X. Eleazar, 65v
XI. Seven brothers and their mother [the Maccabees], 68r

BOOK TWO OF THE SECOND EDITION
OF RABUS'S MARTYROLOGY
(NEW TESTAMENT AND PATRISTIC)

MEDIEVAL MARTYRS
IN RABUS'S FIRST EDITION

BOOK THREE OF THE SECOND EDITION
OF RABUS'S MARTYROLOGY
(FIFTEENTH CENTURY)

CONTEMPORARY MARTYRS
IN RABUS'S FIRST EDITION

Patrick Hamilton, ccxciiij/r-ccxcv/r

Volume V

Gallus Korn, j/r
Hans von Salhausen, vj/v
The city of Miltenberg, xx/v
Arsatius Seehoffer, xxxiiij/v
Argula von Grunbach, ciij/v
Paul Speratus, cxxix/r
Wolfgang Schuch, cxliij/r
Peter Spengler, cliiij/v
Matthias Devay, clx/v-cclxxiiij/v

Volume VI

Johannes Voyt, j/r
Caspar Tauber, xxij/v
Nicolaus of Antwerp, xxxvj/r
Louis Berquin, xxxvij/r
Three Tracts of Consolation for Georg von
    Brandenburg by Martin Meglin, xxxviij/r
The city of Hildesheim, lxxxj/v
Joannes of Cadurco, cvj/v
Joannes Ponitet, cviij/v
The City of Orleans, cix/v
The French Persecution of 1535, cxiiij/v
Martin Gonin, cxxj/r
Franciscus Landrus, cxxvj/r
Peter Bruly, cxxx/r
Jacob Chobard, cl/v
Driander, clj/v
Peter Clericus, cliij/r
Simon Walder, clxij/v
"A Joyful Admonition . . . " by Civilius, an
    Italian, clxxij/r
The exiled citizens of Leipzig, clxxxj/r
The exiled pastors of Bohemia and Lausitz,
    cxcviij/v

Franciscus and Nicolaus Thiessen, ccij/v-ccix/
    v

Volume VII

Johannes Apell and Friedrich Fischer, j/r
Wolfgang Ruoss, xx/v
Hanna von Draschwitz, Milia von Olsnitz,
    Urusula von Feilitschin, xxv/v
Lampert Thorn, xxvj/v
Florentina von Oberweimar, xxviij/v
Ursula, Duchess of Munsterburg, xxxv/r
Simon Grynaeus, lvj/v
The citizens of Oschatz, lxiij/r
The citizens of Louvain, lxv/r
Persualdus, lxxxvij/r
Peter de Lerma, xciij/r
Justus Imbssberger, xcvij/v
Franciscus San Romanus of Burgos, cxiiij/v
Aegidius of Brussels, cxxix/v
Rochus of Brabant, cliiij/r
Peter Alexander, clvj/r
Francisco Enzinas, clxxvj/r
Robert Agnus, Jacob Ranald, Jacob Venator,
    William Andreae, and an Honorable
    Woman named Helena, ccxxxj/r
Hoste or Joerg of the Catelyne, ccxxxiiij/r
John Hess's translation of the account of Jo-
    hannes [Esch] and Heinrich [Voes] of
    Brussels, ccxlv/r-cclvj/v

Volume VIII

The Bishop of the Lochau, j/r
Matthias Zell, vij/r
The Provosts and Prior of the Augustinians
    in Nuremberg, ccxxij/r
Herman von Wied, ccxxiiij/v-ccxcvj/v

BOOK FOUR OF THE SECOND EDITION
OF RABUS'S MARTYROLOGY (1517-1529)

I. Martin Luther, 110r
II. The Bishop of Lochau, 211v
III. Jacob Probst, Augustinian, prior at Ant-
    werp, 214r
IV. Gallus Korn, Dominican of Nuremberg,
    220r
V. Hans von Salhausen, 221v
VI. Matthaeus Zell of Kaisersberg, pastor of
    the Cathedral at Strassburg, 226v
VII. Johannes Voyt, Franciscan of Weimar,
    317v
VIII. Johannes Appel and Friedrich Fischer,
    two doctors, 326r
IX. Wolfgang Russ of Otting in Bavaria, 333v
X. Hanna von Draschwitz, Milia von Ols-
    nitz, Ursula von Felitschin, 335v

XI. Johannes Esch and Heinrich Voes, two
    Augustinians of Brussels, 336r
XII. The pastors of Schonbach and Buch,
    345v
XIII. Master Arsatius Seehoffer of Munich,
    348r
XIV. Argula von Grunbach, nee von Stauf-
    fen, 375r
XV. The City of Miltenberg, 383r
XVI. Paul Speratus, doctor, 388r
XVII. Lampert Thorn, 393v
XVIII. Florentina von Oberweimar, 394v
XIX. Two Provosts and a Prior of the Au-
    gustinian Order of Nuremberg, 397r
XX. Caspar Tauber, a citizen of Vienna in
    Austria, 398r

BOOK FIVE OF THE SECOND EDITION
OF RABUS'S MARTYROLOGY (1530-1555)

Bibliography

PRIMARY SOURCES

Allsdorf, Johann. *Warhaffter vnd bestendiger bericht von dem Christlichen ende . . . des Hochwirdigsten Herrn Hermans, Ertzbischoffen zu Coelln vnd Churfuersten. . . .* Leipzig: Gunther, 1553.

Amsdorf, Nikolaus von. *Grund vnd vrsach auss der Cronicke, Warumb Johannes Huss vnd Jeronimus von Prag verbrant seyn.* Magdeburg, 1525.

_____. *Vom Bapst vnd seiner Kirchen, das sie des Teufels, vnd nicht Christi vnsers lieben Herrn Kirche sey.* N. p., 1551.

_____. *Ein gut newe Jar, den grossen Herrn in dieser Welt geschanckt.* Jena: Roedinger, 1554.

Amsterdam, Johannes. *Prophetiae aliqvot vere: Et sententiae insignes reuerendi patris Domini Doctoris Martini Lutheri, Tercij Helie. . . .* Magdeburg: Lotther, 1552.

_____. *Etliche warhafftige weissagung, vnd fuerneme spruche des Ehrwirdigen Vaters, Hern Doctor Martini Luthers, des dritten Helie. . . .* Magdeburg: Lotther, 1552.

Aurifaber, Johann (Breslau). *Chronica des Ehrwirdigen Herrn D. Mart. Luth. Deudsch.* Wittenberg: Lufft, 1550. Reissued by Lufft, 1559.

Aurifaber, Johann (Saxony), Justus Jonas, and Michael Coelius. *Vom christlichen Abschied aus diesem Leben des Reverendi Dr. Martini Lutheri.* Wittenberg: Lufft, 1546.

Baumgarten, Hermann, ed. *Sleidans Briefwechsel.* Strassburg: Trübner, 1881.

Behm, Martin. *Kirchen Calendar. . . .* Wittenberg: Schmidt, 1608.

Die Bekenntnisschriften der evangelisch-lutherischen Kirche. 5. ed. Göttingen: Vandenhoeck & Ruprecht, 1963.

Bernays, J. and Harry Gerber, eds. *Politische Correspondenz der Stadt Strassburg im Zeitalter der Reformation.* Heidelberg: Winter, 1933.

Beuther, Michael. *Calendarium Historicum.* . . . Frankfurt am Main: Zephel, 1557.

Bonnus, Hermann. *Farrago praecipvorvm exemplorvm de Apostolis, Martyribus, Episcopis, & Sanctis Patribus ueteris Ecclesiae.* . . . Schwäbisch Hall, 1539.

Büttner, Wolfgang. *Epitome Historiarum.* Leipzig: Apel, 1596.

Carion, Johann. *Chronica durch Magistrum Johan Carion vleissig zusamen gezogen.* Philip Melanchthon, ed. Wittenberg: Rhau, 1532.

Catalogus Nouus ex nundinis vernalibus Francofurti ad Moenum, Anno M.D.LXXI. Frankfurt/Main: Corvinus, 1571.

Christian, Albert. *Dispvtatio Reverendi Patris D. Martini Lutheri, de operibus legis & gratiae.* . . . Magdeburg: Lotther, 1553.

Chytraeus, David. *Onomasticon theologicvm recente recognitvm.* . . . Wittenberg: Crato, 1558.

————. *Onomasticon Theologicum Davidis Chytraei. Erklerung aller Manns vnd Weibes Personen Namen.* . . . Valentin Beyer, trans. Eisleben: Gross, 1605.

Coccius, Paul. *Gross Martyrbuch vnd Kirchen-Historien.* . . . Hanau: Anton, 1606.

Corvinus, Johannes. *Loci communes Doct: Mart: Lutheri totius Doctrinae Christianae.* . . . Ursel: Heinrich, 1564.

Crespin, Jean. *Actiones et Monumenta Martyrum.* . . . Geneva: Crespin, 1560.

————. *Maertyrbuch Darinnen merckliche denckwuerdige Reden vnd Thaten vieler heiligen Maertyrer beschriben werden.* Herborn: Rab, 1590.

————. *Recveil De Plvsiervs Personnes qui ont constamment enduré la mort pour le Nom de nostre Seigneur Iesus Christ depuis Iean Hus iusques a ceste anne presente M.D.L IIII.* Geneva: Crespin, 1554.

Cruciger, Caspar, ed. *Etliche Trostschriften vnd Predigten für die, sie in Todes vnd ander Not vnd anfechtung sind.* Wittenberg: Creutzer, 1545.

Dresser, Matthaeus. *De festis et praecipvis anni partibvs Liber.* . . . Erfurt: Mechler, 1584.

Eber, Paul. *Calendarivm historicvm conscriptvm.* Wittenberg: Rhau, 1550.

Enzinas, Francisco de. *Mémoires de Francisco de Enzinas, Texte Latin Inédit.* Ch. Al. Campan, ed. Brussels: Société de l'histoire de Belgique, 1862-1863.

Fabricius, Theodosius. *Loci communes D. Martini Lvtheri viri Dei et Prophetae Germanici.* . . . Magdeburg: Gena, 1594.

Fecht, Johannes, ed. *Historiam Ecclesiasticae . . . Supplementum . . . Epistolis ad Joannem, Erasmum et Philippum Marbachios.* Frankfurt/Main and Speyer, 1684.

Flacius, Matthias Illyricus. *Catalogus testium veritatis, qui ante nostram ae-tatem reclamarunt Papae.* Basel: Oporinus, 1556.

———. *Catalogus testium veritatis. Historia der zeugen, Bekenner vnd Mar-terer.* . . . Conrad Lautenbach, trans. Frankfurt/Main, 1573.

———. *De vocabulo fidei et aliis quibusdam vocabulis explicatio vera et utilis, sumta ex fontibus ex Ebraica.* Wittenberg: Creutzer, 1549.

———. *Etliche Brieffe des Ehrwirdigen Herrn D. Martini Luthers . . . an die Theologos auff den Reichstag zu Augspurg geschrieben.* . . . Magde-burg: Roedinger, 1549.

———. *Historia Ioannis Hussi et Hieronymi Pragensis . . . Monumenta.* Nu-remberg, 1558. Reprint, Nuremberg: Gerlach/Montanus, 1583.

Foxe, John. *Commentarii rerum ecclesia gestarum, maximarumque per totam Europam persecutionum, a Wiclevi temporibus ad hanc usque aetatem descriptio.* Strassburg: Wendelin Rihel, 1554.

———. *Rerum in ecclesia gestarum, quae postremis et periculosis his tempo-ribus evenerunt.* . . . Basel: Brylinger and Oporinus, 1559.

Funck, Johann. *Chronologia hoc est, omnivm temporvm et annorvm ab initio mvndi vsque ad resvrrectionem Domini nostri Iesv Christi computatio.* Nuremberg: Wachter, 1545.

Gloccer, Georg. *Warhafftige Historia Vnd grundlicher Summarischer Bericht von der Lehr, Leben.* . . . Strassburg: Bertram, 1586.

Goebel, Johann Conrad. *Christianus Vapulans. Oder Marter-Chronick.* . . . Mühlhausen: Eibel, 1699.

Goltwurm, Kaspar. *Ein Newes lustig Historisch Calendarium.* . . . N.p., 1553.

———. *Kirchen Calendar.* . . . Frankfurt am Main: Egenolff, 1559.

Habermann, Johann. *Dreissig Predigten Vber die Epistel vnd Euangelien, so an den tagen etlicher heiligen mertern vnd Bekennern Christi etc. vor zei-ten sind gelesen vnd gebraucht worden.* Wittenberg, 1585.

Hertel, Jacob. *Allegoriarum, Typorum, et exemplorvm veteris & noui Testa-menti Libro duo.* . . . Basel, 1561.

Hohndorf, Andreas. *Calenderivm historivcm. Oder, Der heiligen Marterer Historien.* . . . Frankfurt am Main: Feyerbendt, 1575. Reissued as *Calenderivm Sanctorum et Historiarum.* . . . Leipzig: Berwaldt, 1579.

———. *Promptvarivm exemplorvm. Das ist, Historien vnd Exempelbuch, nach ordnung vnd Disposition der heiligen zehen Gebott Gottes . . . zusammen getragen.* Frankfurt/Main: Schmidt, 1572.

Josephus. *Flauij Josephi . . . Alle Buecher.* Caspar Hedio, trans. Strassburg: Emmel, 1553.

Kirchner, Timotheus. *Deutsche Thesavrvs, Des Hochgelerten weitberumbten vnd theuren Manns Gottes D. Mart. Luthers.* . . . Frankfurt/Main: Schmid and Feyerabendt, 1568.

————. *Index oder Register vber die acht deudsche tomos*. . . . Jena: Richtzenhan and Robart, 1564.

————. *Thesavrvs: explicationvm omnivm articvlorvm ac capitvm . . . ex reverendi vereque Dei viri ac summi Theologi, D. Martini Lutheri . . . operibus*. Frankfurt/Main: Rhebart and Feyerabendt, 1566.

Klausing, Heinrich. *Dissertatio historico-theologica de autocheiria Martyrum*. Leipzig: Titius, 1720.

Kyriander, Wolfgang. *Persequutiones ecclesiae, quas secundum historicos & Chronographos . . . Collatio*. Ingolstadt: Weissenhort, 1541.

Landolff, Erhard, pseud. *Billiche Antwort zum vorsprung, allein auff die Vorrede des schmaehbrieffes, welchen Katharina Zellin wider Doctor Rabum offentlich hat lassen aussgehn*. . . . N. p., 1558.

Lappaeus, Johannes. *Warhafftige Prophezeiungen des thewren Propheten, vnd Heiligen Manns Gottes, D. Martini Lutheri*. . . . Ursel: Heinrich, 1578.

Loescher, Christian Wilhelm. *In paucitatem martyrum Antiquioris Christi Ecclesiae*. Wittenberg: Kreusig, 1697.

Lubath, Martin. *Ex antiquitate martyrologica Dissertatio accademica*. Halle: Salfeld, 1693.

Luther, Martin. *Christlicher vnd Gruendtlicher bericht, Von der Rechtfertigung des Glaubens, Einwonung Gottes vnd Christi in vns*. . . . n. p., n. d.

————. *Colloqvia oder Tischreden Doctor Martini Lutheri*. Frankfurt/Main: Schmidt, 1568.

————. *Drei Sermon D. Martini Lutheri, darin man spueren kan wie ein Herlicher Prophetischer Geist in dem manne gewesen ist*. . . . Frankfurt/Oder: Eichorn, 1552.

————. *D. Martin Luthers Werke*. Weimar: Böhlau, 1883-.

————. *Der erste [-achte] teil aller Buecher vnd Schrifften . . . Doct. Mart. Lutheri*. Jena: Richtzenhan, 1555-1559.

————. *Der erste [-zwelffte] Teil der Bucher d. Mart. Luth.* Wittenberg: Lufft, 1539-1561.

————. *Luther's Works*. Saint Louis: Concordia; Philadelphia: Muhlenberg/Fortress, 1955-1973.

————. *Testimonia D. Martini Lvteri de socio laborvm et pericvlorvm svorvm Philippo Melanchthone*. Görlitz: Firtsch, 1580.

————. *Tomus primus [-septimus] omnivm opervm reuerendi domini Martini Lutheri*. Wittenberg: Lufft, 1545-1561.

————. *Vom Wucher vnd widerkeufflichen Zinsen*. Magdeburg: Lotther, c. 1552.

————. *Warhafftige vnd bestendige meinung vnd zeugnis Von der Erbsuende vnd dem freien willen*. . . . Jena: Rebart, 1560.

_____. *Warnunge D. Martini Luther an seine lieben Deudsche.* . . . Wittenberg, 1546.

_____. *Zwo Predigten des Ehwirdigen herren Doctoris Martini Luther.* . . . Bernhard Ziegler, ed. Leipzig: Hantzsch, 1551.

Major, Georg. *Vitae patrom, in vsvm ministrorvm verbi, qvo ad eivs fieri potuit repurgatae.* Wittenberg, 1560.

Marbach, Johann. *Von Mirackeln vnd Wunderzeichen. Wie man sie auss vnnd nach Gottes Wort fuer waar oder falsch erkennen soll.* . . . Strassburg, 1571.

Mathesius, Johann. *Historien Von des Ehrwirdigen in Gott Seligen Thewren Manns Gottes, Doctoris Martini Luthers anfang, lehr leben vnd sterben.* . . . Nuremberg, 1566; Nuremberg: Berg, 1580.

Meisner, Johann. *Disputatio publica sollenis de Persecutionibus et Martyriis Christianorum veterum.* Wittenberg: Wendt, 1564.

Melanchthon, Philip. *Corpus Reformatorum, Philippi Melanthonis opera quae supersunt omnia.* Halle: Schwetschke, 1834-1860.

Mörlin, Joachim. *Wie die Buecher vnd Schrifften, des thewren vnd seligen Manns Gottes D. Martini Lutheri nuetzlich zu lesen.* . . . Eisleben: Petri, [1565].

Musculus, Andreas. *Thesavrvs: Hochnutzlicher tewr Schatz vnd Guelden Kleinot.* . . . Frankfurt/Oder: Eichorn, 1577.

_____. *Das Erste [-Vierte] Theil des Gueldenen kleinots.* . . . Frankfurt/Oder, 1561-1562.

Neander, Michael. *Theologia megalandri Lvtheri.* . . . Eisleben: Gaubisch, 1581.

Nicolai, Philip. *Commentariorum de regno Christi.* Frankfurt/Main: Spies, 1597.

_____. *Historia dess Reichs Christi.* Gothard Artus, trans. Nuremberg: Endten, 1629; Jena: Hertel, 1659.

Olearius, Adam. *Vermehrte Newe Beschreibung Der Muscowitischen vnd Persischen Reyse, Schleswig, 1655,* Dieter Lohmeier, ed. Tübingen: Niemeyer, 1972.

Ortlob, Johann Christoph and Georg Christoph Hentschel. *Martyres furori gentilium ultra mortem expositios.* . . . Leipzig: Titius, 1699.

Osiander, Lukas. *Epitomes Historiae ecclesiasticae Centuria I. II. III. 2.* ed. Tübingen: Gruppenbach, 1607.

Otto, Anton. *Etliche Propheceysprueche D. Martin Lutheri, Des dritten Elias.* Magdeburg: Lotther, 1552.

Pantaleone, Heinrich. *Martyrum Historia . . . Pars secunda.* Basel: Brylinger, 1563.

_____. *Prosopographiae herorum atque illustrium virorum totius Germaniae, Pars tertia.* Basel: Brylinger, 1566.

Petrarch, Francesco. *Das der Bapst mit seinem Hoffe die rechte Babilon vnd Babilonische Hure sey.* Magdeburg: Roedinger, c. 1550.

Pfeil, Johann. *Schatzkammer Vnd Heuratsteur dess heiligen Geistes.* . . . Frankfurt/Main: Reffeler and Feyerbendt, 1565.

Pilicarius, Johannes. *Trostspiegel der armen Suender . . . Aus den Buechern des Ehrwirdigen Herrn D. Martini.* . . . Leipzig: Berwald, 1556.

Porta, Conrad. *Oratio continens adhortationem, ad assidvam Lectionem scriptorum . . . D. Martini Lvtheri.* . . . Jena: Richzenhan, 1571; reprint, Helmstedt: Schnor, 1708.

———. *Pastorale Lvtheri.* . . . Eisleben: Petri, 1582.

Preisenstein, Jodocus. *Eine Christliche Leichpredig, Bey der Leich vnd Begrebnuss des Ehrwuerdigen vnd Hochgelehrten Herrn Ludouici Rabi.* . . . Tübingen: Hock, 1593.

Probus, Anton. *Oratio de vocatione et doctrina Martini Lutheri Doctoris Magni & Prophetae Germaniae ultimi.* Leipzig: Baerwald, 1583.

Rabus, Ludwig. *Christliche Bettbüchlins.* . . . 2 vols. Frankfurt/Main, 1565, 1568.

———. *Ein Christliche Predig, Von dem Eingesatzten H. Euangelischen Kirchendienst, Lehr vnd Predigampt.* Ulm: Ulhart, 1573.

———. *Conciliationes locorum S. Scripturae in specie pugnantium. Ex Libris D. Aurelii Augustini.* . . . 2 vols. Nuremberg: Montanus and Neuber, 1561.

———. *Euangelium am XX. Sontag nach Trinitatis: Matthei am XXII. Von der Koeniglichen Hochzeyt, vnd Hochzeytlichem Kleyd.* Strassburg: Emmel, 1567.

———. *Historiae de S. Abele, Ecclesiae militantis in veteri Testamento Protomartyre, Ex sacris literis . . . collecta & conscripta.* Strassburg: Emmel, 1567.

———. *Der Heyligen ausserwoehlten Gottes Zeugen, Bekennern vnd Martyrern . . . Historien.* . . . 8 vols. Strassburg: Balthasar Beck, 1552; Samuel Emmel, 1554-1558.

———. *Historien der Martyrer.* . . . 2 vols. Strassburg: Josias Rihel, 1571, 1572.

———. *Ein kurtze vnd Christliche Predig von notwendigem vnnd einfaltigem verstand der Sechs Hauptstuck vnsers Christlichen Catechismi.* Ulm: Varnier, 1560.

———. *Wider Neun fuerneme Haubtlaster . . . Ein kurtze vnd Christliche Predig.* Nuremberg: Berg, 1561.

Rivander, Zacharias. *Der Ander Theil promptvarii exemplorvm.* Frankfurt/Main: Feyerabendt, 1587.

Rörer, Georg, ed. *Vieler schoenen Spruche aus Goettlicher Schrifft auslegung, daraus Lere vnd Trost zu nemen, Welche der ehrnwirdige Herr Doctor Martin Luther seliger, vielen in jre Biblien geschrieben.* Wittenberg: Lufft, 1547.

Sagittarius, Caspar. *De martyrum cruciatibus in primitiua ecclesia Liber.* Jena: Bauhofer, 1673; 2. ed., Frankfurt/Main, Leipzig: Crocher, 1696.

Saur, Abraham. *Diarivm historicvm. Das ist, Ein besondere tägliche Hauss und Kirchen Chronica.* . . . Frankfurt/Main: Bassaeus, 1582.

Savonarola, Jerome. *Der Li. Psalm Dauids Misere mei Deus durch Hieronymum Sauonarolam.* . . . Johann Spangenberg, trans. Leipzig: Wolrab, Augsburg: Ulhart, 1542. Reprint, Leipzig: Voegelin, 1561; translated into Low German, Magdeburg: Kirchener, 1562.

_____. *Der LXXX. Psalm.* . . . Johann Spangenberg, trans. Leipzig: Wolrab, 1542.

Schelhorn, Johann Georg. "Nachricht von dem Leben D. Ludwig Rabus, eines wolverdienten Gottesgelehrten in dem 16 Jahrhundert," *Nuezliche und angeneme Abhandlungen aus der Kirchen-Buecher-und Gelerten-Geschichte.* Johann Bartholomaeus Riederer, ed. Altdorf: Ammermueller, 1768.

Eine Schoene Historia, vom standhaftigkeit des Heiligen Basilij, beschrieben in der Tripartitia Historia. . . . Magdeburg: Roedinger, 1549.

Schulz, Frieder. *Die Gebete Luthers, Edition, Bibliographie und Wirkungsgeschichte.* Gütersloh: Mohn, 1976.

Schwob, Sigismund [Schwabe]. *Index omnivm librorvm et scriptorvm Reverendi Patris D. Martini Lvtheri.* Wittenberg: Seitz, 1564.

_____. *Register Deudsch vnd Latinisch, aller Buecher vnd Schrifften des Ehrnwirdigen Herrn D. Martini Lutheri.* . . . Wittenberg: Seitz, 1564.

Sehling, Emil, ed. *Die evangelischen Kirchenordnungen des 16. Jahrhunderts.* Leipzig: Eisland, 1902-.

Eine sehr schoene histori, von der standhafftigkeit in Bekentnis vnd leiden, des heiligen manns Simeonis. . . . Magdeburg: Roedinger, c. 1550.

Selnecker, Nikolaus. *Epistolarum et evangeliorum dispositio, quae diebus Festis B. Mariae semper virginis, & S. Apostolorum usitate in Ecclesia proponuntur & explicantur.* Frankfurt/Main, 1577.

_____. *Oratio Historica de Initiis, Causis et Progressu Confessionis Augustanae et de Vita ac Laboribus D. D. Martini Lutheri.* Jena: Steinman, 1592.

Senarcleus, Claude [pseud., for Francisco de Enzinas?]. *Historia vera de morte sancti uiui Ioannis Diazij Hispani.* . . . Basel: Oporinus, 1546.

Sleiden, Johannes. *De statu religionis et reipublicae Carolo Quinto Caesare commentarii.* Strassburg: Wendelin Rihel, 1555.

Spalatin, Georg. *Magnifice consolatoria exempla, & sententiae, ex Vitis & passionibus Sanctorum & aliorum summorum Virorum.* Wittenberg: Schirlentz, 1544.

Spangenberg, Cyriakus. *Cythara Lvtheri. Die schoenen, Christlichen trostreichen Psalmen vnd Geistliche Lieder . . . D. Martini Lutheri.* Erfurt: Georg Bawman, 1570.

————. *Die Achte Predigt. Von dem werden Gottes Manne, Doctor Martin Luther, Das er der fuertrefflichst vnd groessest THEOLOGVS gewesen, von der Apostel zeit her.* Erfurt: Georg Bawman, 1566.

————. *Die dritte Predigte, von dem heiligen Gottes Manne, Doctore Martino Luthero, Sonderlich von seinem Prophetenampte. . . .* Erfurt: Georg Baumann, 1564.

————. *Die XXI. Predigt. Von D. Martin Luther, dem Werden Gottes Manne, Das er ein weiser vnd fuersichtiger Richter auff dem Berge des Herrn gewesen.* Frankfurt/Main: Nicolaus Bassaeus, 1574.

————. *Die Fuenftte Predigt, Von dem Apostelampt des trefflichen Mannes, D. MARTIN. LVTHERS.* N. p., 1565.

————. *Historia. Vom Leben, Lere vnd Tode Hieronymi Sauonarole. . . .* Wittenberg: Seitz, 1556.

————. *Die Neunde Predigt, Von dem heiligen Manne Gottes, D. MARTINO LVTHERO, Das er ein rechter Engel des Herrn, vnd eben der Engel, dauon Apocal. 14. geschrieben stehen, gewesen sey.* Eisleben: Petri, 1568.

————. *Die sechste Predigt. Von dem werden Gottes Lerer: Doctor Martin Luther. Das er ein rechter PAVLVS gewesen.* Erfurt: Georg Bawman, 1565.

————. *Theander Lutherus.* Ursel, 1589.

————. *Die vierde Predigt Von dem grossen Propheten Gottes, Doctore Martino Luthero, das er ein rechter Helias gewesen.* Erfurt: Georg Bawman, 1564.

————. *Die Zehende Predigt, Von dem thewren Bekenner D. MARTINI LVTHER. Das er ein rechtschaffen heiliger MARTYRER vnd Bestendiger Zeuge Jhesu Christi gewesen.* Eisleben: Petri, 1568.

————. *Die XX. Predigt: Von Doctore Martino Luthero, wie ein getreuwer vnd erfahrner Geschworner er auff vnsers HERRN Gottes Berge gewesen.* Frankfurt/Main: Nicolaus Bassaeus, 1574.

Stumpf, Johannes. *Des grossen gemeinen Conciliums zu Costentz kurtze doch grundtlichere vnd volkommnere dann vor nie in Teütsch gesähen Beschreybung.* Zürich: Forschauer, 1541.

Surius, Lorenz. *De probatis sanctorum historiis. . . .* 6 vols. Cologne: Colinius and Quentel, 1570-1575.

Van Bracht, Tieleman Janszoon. *Het bloedigh tooneel der doops-gesinde en weerelosse Christinen.* Dordrecht: Braat, 1660.

Van Haemstede, Adrien. *De Geschiedenisse ende den doodt der vromer Martelaren, die om ghetuyghenisse des Euangeliums Haer bloedt ghestort hebben.* [Antwerp?], 1559.

Voyt, Johan. *Eyn Sermon von Newen Jare . . . . Darumb er als ein Ketzer von den selben seinen Brudern geacht vnd mit vil verfolgung veriagt.* Zwickau: Gastel, 1523.

Wackernagel, Philip, ed. *Das deutsche Kirchenlied von der ältesten Zeit bis zu Anfang des XVII. Jahrhunderts,* 5 vols. Leipzig: Teubner, 1864-1877.

Walch, Johann Georg. *Bibliotheca historiae ecclesiasticae.* 4 vols. Jena: Crocker, 1762.

Walther, Christoph. *Register aller Buecher vnd Schrifften des Ehrnwirdigen Herrn Doctoris Martini Lutheri. . . .* Wittenberg: Lufft, 1558.

Walther, Georg. *Beicht vnd Bettbuechlein Darinn schoene vnd kurtze erklerung, in Frag vnd antwort, aus dem Catechismo Lutheri vnd andern Schrifften gezogen.* Frankfurt/Main: Feyerabent, 1581.

_____. *Trostbuchlein, Auss der heiligen Schrifft, vnd. D. Martini Lutheri Buechern, von wort zu wort gestellet.* Nuremberg: Berg and Newber, 1559.

_____. *Vom ampt der weltlichen Oberkeit, nach ordenung der Zehen Gebot, aus Gottes wort, vnd Buechern Doct. Lutheri, gestellt.* Jena: Richtzenhan, 1559.

Weinrich, Georg. *Martyrologii Sanctorum ex XI. Cap. ad Hebr.* Leipzig: Lantzenbergert, 1606.

Weller, Hieronymus. *Creutz-Schule, Oder Etlicher Maertyrer und andere vornehme Historien, mit ihren Lehren, Trost-Spruechen, Schrifften, Episteln, und geistreichen Spruechen.* Halle: Zeitler, 1697; Magdeburg, 1580; Freiburg/Saxony, 1607; Halle, 1700.

Westphal, Joachim. *Sententia Reverendi Viri D. M. Luth. Sanctae memoriae de Adiaphoris ex scriptis illius collecta.* Magdeburg: Lotther, 1549.

_____.*Des Ehwirdigen vnd thewren Mans Doct. Marti. Luthers seliger gedechtnis meinung von den Mitteldingen.* Magdeburg: Lotther, 1550.

Wied, Hermann von. . . . . *Appellation . . . . Auss dem Lateinischen verteutscht.* Bonn: von der Muellen, 1545.

_____. *Bestendige Verantwortung des Bedenckens vonn Christlicher Reformation . . . Anno M.D.XXXXV.* N.p., n.d.

_____. . . . . *einfeltigs bedecken, warauff ein Christliche in dem wort Gottes gegrünte Reformation . . . . anzurichten sey.* Bonn: von der Muellen, 1543.

Wigand, Johann. *De persecvtione impiorvm. . . .* Frankfurt/Main: Corvinus, 1580.

_____ et al. *Ecclesiastica Historia.* Basel, 1559-1574.

Will, Wilhelm. *Legenda pie defunctum, Das ist: Fuerbildt vnd Exempel, etlicher sterbenden heiligen vnd christglaeubigen Menschen.* . . . Frankfurt/Main: Bassaeus, 1696.

Witzel, Georg. *Chorus sanctorum omnium.* . . . Cologne: Quentel, 1554.

Zell, Katherine. *Ein Brieff an die gantze Burgerschafft der Stadt Strassburg von Katherina Zellin* . . . . *Betreffend Herr Ludwigen Rabus* . . . . N. p., 1557.

SECONDARY LITERATURE

Abray, Lorna Jane. *The People's Reformation, Magistrates, Clergy, and Commons in Strasbourg, 1500-1598.* Ithaca: Cornell University Press, 1985.

Aigren, René. *L'Hagiographie. Ses sources, ses méthodes, son histoire.* Paris: Bloud and Gay, 1953.

Althaus, Paul, Sr. *Forschungen zur evangelischen Gebetsliteratur.* Gütersloh, 1927; Hildesheim: Olms, 1966.

Althaus, Paul, Jr. *The Theology of Martin Luther.* Robert C. Schultz, trans. Philadelphia: Fortress, 1966.

Barnes, Robin B. "Prophecy and the Eschaton in Lutheran Germany, 1530-1630." Ph.D. dissertation, University of Virginia, 1980.

Brady, Thomas A., Jr. *Ruling Class, Regime and Reformation at Strasbourg, 1520-1555.* Leiden: Brill, 1978.

Brown, Peter. *The Cult of the Saints. Its Rise and Function in Latin Christianity.* Chicago: University of Chicago Press, 1981.

————. "The Rise and Function of the Holy Man in Late Antiquity," *Society and the Holy in Late Antiquity.* Berkeley: University of California Press, 1982, 103-52.

Brückner, Annemarie and Wolfgang, "Zeugen des Glaubens und ihre Literatur, Altväterbeispiele, Kalenderheilige, protestantische Märtyrer und evangelische Lebenszeugnisse," *Volkserzählung und Reformation.* Wolfgang Brückner, ed. Berlin: Schmidt, 1974, 520-78.

Brückner, Wolfgang. "Luther als Gestalt der Sage," *Volkserzählung und Reformation.* Wolfgang Brückner, ed. Berlin: Schmidt, 1974, 260-94.

Cargill Thompson, W. D. J. "The Problems of Luther's 'Tower Experience' and its Place in his Intellectual Development," *Religious Motivation: Biographical and Sociological Problems for the Church Historian.* Studies in Church History 15. Derek Baker, ed. Oxford: Oxford University Press, 1975, 187-211.

————. *Studies in the Reformation, Luther to Hooker.* E. W. Dugmore, ed. London: Athlone, 1980.

Chrisman, Miriam Usher. *Lay Culture, Learned Culture, Books and Social Change in Strasbourg, 1480-1599.* New Haven: Yale University Press, 1982.

_____. *Strasbourg and the Reform, a Study in the Process of Change.* New Haven: Yale University Press, 1967.

Clemens, Otto. *Luther und die Volksfrömmigkeit seiner Zeit.* Dresden: Ungelenk, 1938.

Conquerel, Ath. fils. "Vie et mort du martyr Wolfgang Schuch, brulè á Nancy, le 21 Juin 1525," *Bulletin de la Société de l'histoire du Protestantisme française* 2 (1854):632-48.

Crew, Phyllis Mack. *Calvinist Preaching and Iconoclasm in the Netherlands, 1544-1569.* Cambridge: Cambridge University Press, 1978.

Dedeke, Gerhard. "Die protestantischen Märtyrerbücher von Ludwig Rabus, Jean Crespin und Adriaen van Haemstede und ihr gegenseitigen Verhältnis." Licentiate dissertation, University of Halle-Wittenberg, 1924.

Delehaye, Hippolyte. *Les origines du culte des martyrs.* Brussels: Société des Bollandistes, 1933.

_____. *Sanctus, Essai sur le culte des saintes dans l'antiquité.* Brussels: Société des Bollandistes, 1927.

Delius, Walter. "Luther und die Marienverehrung," *Theologische Literaturzeitung* 79 (1954): 410-14.

Deneke, Bernard. "Kaspar Goltwurm, Ein lutherischer Kompilator zwischen Überlieferung und Glaube," *Volkserzählung und Reformation.* Wolfgang Brückner, ed. Berlin: Schmidt, 1974, 125-77.

Dickens, A. G. *Contemporary Historians of the German Reformation.* London: Institute of Germanic Studies, University of London, [1978].

_____. and John M. Tonkin, with Kenneth Powell. *The Reformation in Historical Thought.* Cambridge: Harvard University Press, 1985.

Diener, Ronald E. "The Magdeburg Centuries, A Bibliothecal and Historiographical Analysis." Th.D. dissertation, Harvard Divinity School, 1978.

Dru, Alexander, ed. *The Journals of Søren Kierkegaard.* New York: Oxford University Press, 1938.

Dubois, Jacques. *Les martyrologes du moyen âge latin. Typologie des sources du Moyen Âge occidental* fasc. 26. Turnhout: Brepols, 1978.

Ebeling, Gerhard. *Luther, an Introduction to his Thought.* R. A. Wilson, trans. Philadelphia: Fortress, 1970.

Edwards, Mark U., Jr. *Luther and the False Brethren.* Stanford: Stanford University Press, 1975.

Eggers, Werner. *Wirklichkeit und Wahrheit im Trauerspiel von Andreas Gryphius.* Heidelberg: Winter, 1967.

Endriss, Julius. *Die Ulmer Kirchenvisitation der Jahre 1557-1615.* Ulm: Hohn, 1937.

Fick, C. J. *Die Märtyrer der Evangelisch-Lutherischen Kirche, Bd. 1.* Saint Louis: Niedner, 1854.

Fraenkel, Peter. "Revelation and Tradition. Notes on Some Aspects of Doctrinal Continuity in the Theology of Philip Melanchthon," *Studia Theologica* 13 (1959): 97-133.

_____. *Testimonia Patrum, The Function of the Patristic Argument in the Theology of Philip Melanchthon.* Geneva: Droz, 1961.

Frend, W. H. C. *Martyrdom and Persecution in the Early Church.* New York: New York University Press, 1967.

Friedensburg, Walter. *Johannes Sleidanus, Der Geschichtsschreiber und die Schicksalmächte der Reformationszeit.* Leipzig: Heinsius, 1935.

Fritz, F. *Ulmische Kirchengeschichte vom Interim bis zum dreissigjährigen Krieg (1548-1612).* Stuttgart: Scheukele, 1934.

Gilmont, Jean Françôis. "La genèse du martyrologue d'Adrien van Haemstede (1559)," *Revue d'histoire ecclesiastique* LXIII (1968): 379-414.

_____. *Jean Crespin, un éditeur réformé du XVIe siècle.* Geneva: Droz, 1981.

Halkin, Leon E. "Hagiographie Protestante," *Analecta Bollianda* 68 (1950): 153-63.

Haller, William. *The Elect Nation, The Meaning and Relevance of Foxe's Book of Martyrs.* New York: Harper, 1963.

_____. "John Foxe and the Puritan Revolution," *The Seventeenth Century, Studies in the History of English Thought and Literature,* Richard Foster Jones, ed. Stanford: Stanford University Press, 1951, 209-24.

Hartfelder, Karl. *Philipp Melanchthon als Praeceptor Germaniae.* Berlin: 1889; Nieuwkoop: De Graaf, 1964.

Hauffen, Adolf. *Johann Fischart, Ein Literaturbild aus der Zeit der Gegenreformation.* Berlin: De Gruyter, 1921.

Headley, John M. *Luther's View of Church History.* New Haven: Yale University Press, 1963.

Hebenstreit-Wilfert, Hildegard. "Märtyrerflugschriften der Reformationszeit," *Flugschriften als Massenmedium der Reformationszeit,* Hans-Joachim Köhler, ed. Stuttgart: Klett, 1981.

Hermann, Wolfgang. "Die Lutherpredigten des Cyriacus Spangenberg," *Mansfelder Blätter* 39 (1934/35): 7-95.

Hieber, Wolfgang. "Legende, protestantische Bekennerhistorie, Legendenhistorie, Studien zur literarischen Gestaltung der Heiligenthematik im Zeitalter der Glaubenskämpfe." Doctoral dissertation, University of Würzburg, 1970.

Hoyer, Siegfried. "Jan Hus und der Hussitismus in den Flugschriften des ersten Jahrzehnts der Reformation," *Flugschriften als Massenmedium der Reformationszeit*, Hans-Joachim Köhler, ed. Stuttgart: Klett, 1981, 291-308.

Hubert, Friedrich. *Vergerios publizistische Thätigkeit*. Göttingen: Vandenhoeck & Ruprecht, 1893.

Joachimsen, Paul. *Geschichtsauffassung und Geschichtsschreibung in Deutschland unter dem Einfluss des Humanismus, 1. Theil*. Leipzig: Teubner, 1910.

Kantzenbach, Friedrich Wilhelm. "Aspekte zum Bekenntnisproblem in der Theologie Luthers," *Lutherjahrbuch* 30 (1963), 70-96.

Kelley, Donald R. "Martyrs, Myths, and the Massacre: The Background of St. Bartholomew," *The Massacre of St. Bartholomew. Reappraisals and Documents*. Alfred Soman, ed. The Hague: Nijhoff, 1974, 181-202.

Kittelson, James M. *Wolfgang Capito from Humanist to Reformer*. Leiden: Brill, 1975.

Klaiber, Wilbirgis. "Zur Wirkung von Theologie auf Hagiographie—im frühesten Versuch einer reformatorischen Bearbeitung der Antoniusvita bei Hermann Bonnus," *Heilige in Geschichte, Legende, Kult, Beiträge zur Erforschung volkstümlicher Heiligenverehrung und zur Hagiographie*, Klaus Welker, ed. Karlsruhe: Badenia, 1979, 63-75.

Koch, Ernst. "Lutherflorilegien zwischen 1550 und 1600," Sixth International Congress on Luther Research, Erfurt, German Democratic Republic, 1983.

Koenker, Ernst B. "Søren Kierkegaard on Luther," *Interpreters of Luther, Essays in Honor of Wilhelm Pauck*. Jaroslav Pelikan, ed. Philadelphia: Fortress, 1968.

Kolb, Robert. "German Lutheran Reactions to the Third Session of the Council of Trent," *Lutherjahrbuch* 51 (1984): 63-95.

———. "The Layman's Bible: The Use of Luther's Catechisms in the German Late Reformation," *Luther's Catechisms—450 Years*. David P. Scaer and Robert D. Preus, eds. Fort Wayne, Indiana: Concordia Theological Seminary Press, 1978, 16-26.

———. "Luther the Master Pastor: Conrad Porta's *Pastorale Lutheri*, Handbook for Generations," *Concordia Journal* 9 (1983): 179-87.

———. " 'Perilous Events and Troublesome Disturbances,' The Role of Controversy in the Tradition of Luther to Lutheran Orthodoxy," *Pietas et Societas, New Trends in Reformation Social History, Essays in Memory of Harold J. Grimm*. Kyle C. Sessions and Phillip N. Bebb, eds. Kirksville: *Sixteenth Century Journal* Publishers, 1985, 181-201.

Körsgen-Wiedeburg, Andrea. "Das Bild Martin Luthers in den Flug-schriften der frühen Reformationszeit," *Festgabe für Ernst Walter Zeeden.* Horst Rabe, Hansgeorg Molitor, and Hans-Christoph Rublack, eds. Münster: Aschendorff, 1976, 153-77.

Lackmann, Max. *Verehrung der Heiligen: Versuch einer lutherischen Lehre von den Heiligen.* Stuttgart: Schwabenverlag, 1958.

Lang, Peter. *Die Ulmer Katholiken im Zeitalter der Glaubenskämpfe: Lebens-bedingungen einer konfessioneller Minderheit.* Frankfurt/Main: Lang, 1977.

Lansemann, Robert. *Die Heiligentage, besonders die Marien-, Apostel-, und Engeltage in der Reformationszeit. . . .* Göttingen: Vandenhoeck & Ruprecht, 1939.

Lerner, Robert E. *The Heresy of the Free Spirit in the Later Middle Ages.* Berkeley: University of California Press, 1972.

Lienhart, Marc. *Luther: Witness to Jesus Christ. Stages and Themes of the Re-former's Christology.* Edwin H. Robertson, trans. Minneapolis: Augsburg, 1982.

Lilje, Hanns. *Luthers Geschichtsanschauung.* Berlin: Furche, 1932.

Lucius, Ernst. *Die Anfänge des Heiligenkults in der christlichen Kirche.* Gus-tav Anrich, ed. Tübingen: Mohr/Siebeck, 1904.

Mack, Dietrich. *Bildzyklen in der Brüdernkirche zu Braunschweig (1596-1638).* Stadtarchiv und Stadtbibliothek Braunschweig Kleine Schriften 10; Braunschweig: Waisenhaus-Buchdruckerei, 1983.

Manns, Peter. "Luther und die Heiligen," *Reformatio Ecclesiae . . . Fest-gabe für Erwin Iserloh.* Remigius Bäumer, ed., Paderborn: Schön-ingh, 1980.

Martin Luther und die Reformation in Deutschland, Ausstellung zum 500. Ge-burtstag Martin Luthers, Veranstaltet vom Germanischen Nationalmu-seum Nürnberg. . . . Frankfurt/Main: Insel, 1983.

Massner, Joachim. *Kirchliche Überlieferung und Autorität im Flaciuskreis. Studien zu den Magdeburger Zenturien.* Berlin: Lutherisches Verlags-haus, 1964.

Maurer, Wilhelm. *Der junge Melanchthon, 1. Der Humanist.* Göttingen: Vandenhoeck & Ruprecht, 1967.

Mauser, Wolfram. *Dichtung, Religion und Gesellschaft im 17. Jahrhundert. Die "Sonnete" des Andreas Gryphius.* Munich: Fink, 1976.

McGrath, Alister E. *Luther's Theology of the Cross.* Oxford: Basil Blackwell, 1985.

McNeill, John T. "John Foxe: Historiographer, Disciplinarian, Tolera-tionist," *Church History* 43 (1974): 216-29.

Michaelis, Otto. *Protestantisches Märtyrbuch.* Stuttgart: Steinkopf, 1917.

Moeller, Bernd. "Religious Life in Germany on the Eve of the Reformation," *Pre-Reformation Germany*, Gerald Strauss, ed. New York: Harper & Row, 1972. [Translated from "Frömmigkeit in Deutschland um 1500," *Archiv für Reformationsgeschichte* 56 (1956): 5-31.]

Momigliano, Arnaldo. "Historiography on Written Tradition and Historiography on Oral Tradition," *Studies in Historiography*. London: Weidenfeld and Nicolson, 1966.

————. "Pagan and Christian Historiography in the Fourth Century," *Essays in Ancient and Modern Historiography*. Oxford: Blackwell, 1977, 107-26.

Moreau, G. "Contribution à l'Histoire du Livre des Martyrs," *Bulletin de la Société du l'Histoire du Protestantisme français* 103 (1957): 173-99.

Moritzen, Johannes. *Die Heiligen in der nachreformatorischen Zeit, I.* Flensburg: Wolf, 1971.

Mozley, J. F. *John Foxe and His Book*. London: SPCK, 1940.

Olson, V. Norskov. *John Foxe and the Elizabethan Church*. Berkeley: University of California Press, 1973.

Pelikan, Jaroslav. "Luther's Attitude Toward John Hus," *Concordia Theological Monthly* 19 (1948): 747-63.

Piaget, Arthur, and Gabrielle Berthoud, *Notes sur le Livre des Martyrs de Jean Crespin*. Neuchâtel: Secretariat de l'Université, 1930.

Pijper, Fredrik. *Martelaarsboek.* 's Gravenhage: Nijhoff, 1924.

Pinomaa, Lennart. *Die Heiligen bei Luther*. Helsinki: Luther-Agricola Gesellschaft, 1977.

Piper, Ferdinand. *Die Zeugen der Wahrheit, Lebensbilder zum evangelischen Kalendar*. Leipzig: Tauchnitz, 1874.

Preuss, Hans. *Die Vorstellungen vom Antichrist im späteren Mittelalter, bei Luther, und in der konfessionellen Polemik*. Leipzig: Hinrich, 1906.

Quellen zur Ketzergeschichte Brandenburgs und Pommerns. Berlin: de Gruyter, 1975.

Quentin, Henri. *Les martyrologes historiques du Moyen Âge. Étude sur la formation du martyrologue romain*. Paris, 1908; Aalen: Scientia, 1969.

Rehermann, Ernst Heinrich. "Die Protestantischen Exempelsammlungen des 16. und 17. Jahrhunderts," *Volkserzählung und Reformation*. Wolfgang Brückner, ed. Berlin: Schmidt, 1974, 579-645.

Reu, Johann Michael. *Quellen zur Geschichte des Katechismus-Unterricht*. Gütersloh: Bertelsmann, 1904.

Rohner, Ludwig. *Kalendargeschichte und Kalendar*. Wiesbaden: Athenaion, 1978.

Rothkrug, Lionel. "Religious Practices and Collective Perceptions: Hidden Homologies in the Renaissance and Reformation," *Historical Reflections/Réflexions historiques* 7,1 (1980).

Scarisbrick, J. J. *The Reformation and the English People*. London: Basil Blackwell, 1984.

Schade, Heidemarie. "Andreas Hohndorfs Promptuarium Exemplorum." *Volkserzählung und Reformation*. Wolfgang Brückner, ed. Berlin: Schmidt, 1974, 646-702.

Schaff, Philip. *Die Sünde wider den heiligen Geist und die daraus gezogenen dogmatischen und ethischen Folgerungen*. Halle: Lipper, 1841.

Scharfe, Martin. *Evangelische Andachtsbilder. Studien zur Intention und Funktion des Bildes in der Frömmigkeitsgeschichte vornehmlich des schwäbischen Raumes*. Stuttgart: Müller & Gräff, 1968.

————. "Der Heilige in der protestantischen Volksfrömmigkeit," *Hessische Blätter für Volkskunde* 60 (1969): 93-106.

Scheible, Heinz. *Die Entstehung der Magdeburger Zenturien, Ein Beitrag zur Geschichte der historischen Methode*. Gütersloh: Mohn, 1966.

Schenda, Rudolf. "Die deutschen Prodigiensammlungen des 16. and 17. Jahrhunderts," *Archiv für Geschichte des Buchwesens* IV (1963): 638-710.

————. "Hieronymus Rauscher und die Protestantisch-katholische Legendenpolemik," *Volkserzählung und Reformation*. Wolfgang Brückner, ed. Berlin: Schmidt, 1974, 178-258.

————. "Die protestantisch-katholische Legendenpolemik," *Archiv für Kulturgeschichte* 52 (1970): 28-48.

Schmidt, Martin. "Luthers Schau der Geschichte," *Lutherjahrbuch* 30 (1963): 17-69.

Scribner, R. W. *For the Sake of Simple Folk, Popular propaganda for the German Reformation*. Cambridge: Cambridge University Press, 1981.

Sepp, C. *Geschiedkundige nasporingen*. Leiden, 1873.

Seyboldt, Robert Francis. "Fifteenth Century Editions of the Legenda Aurea," *Speculum* 21 (1946): 327-48.

Siggins, Ian D. Kingston. *Martin Luther's Doctrine of Christ*. New Haven: Yale University Press, 1970.

Skrine, Peter N. *The Baroque Literature and Culture in Seventeenth-Century Europe*. London: Methuen, 1978.

Steinhagen, Harald. *Wirklichkeit und Handeln im barocken Drama. Historischästhetische Studien zum Trauerspiel des Andreas Gryphius*. Tübingen: Niemeyer, 1977.

Stephen, Horst. *Luther in den Wandlungen seiner Kirche*. Giessen: Topelmann, 1907.

Strauss, Gerald. "The Course of German History: The Lutheran Interpretation," *Renaissance Studies in Honor of Hans Baron*. Anthony Molho and John A. Tedeschi, eds. DeKalb: Northern Illinois University Press, 1971, 663-86.

Strauss, Walter L. *The German Single-leaf Woodcut, 1550-1600.* New York: Abaris, 1975.

Strutz, Adolf. *Andreas Gryphius, Die Weltanschauung eines deutschen Barockdichters.* Hörgen Zürich: Münster-Presse, 1931.

Thomas, Keith. *Religion and the Decline of Magic.* New York: Scribner, 1971.

Van der Haeghen, Ferdinand ed. *Bibliographie des martyrologes protestantes Néerlandais.* LaHaye: Nyhoff, 1890.

Volz, Hans. *Die Lutherpredigten des Johannes Mathesius: Kritische Untersuchung zur Geschichtsschreibung im Zeitalter der Reformation.* Halle: Waisenhaus, 1929.

Wagenmann. "Rabus, Ludwig," *Allgemeine Deutsche Biographie.* Leipzig: Duncker & Humblot, 1898, 27:97-99.

Waldeck, Oskar. "Die Publizistik des Schmalkaldischen Krieges," *Archiv für Reformationsgeschichte* VII (1909-1910):1-55; VIII (1910-1911):44-133.

Weinrich, William C. *Spirit and Martyrdom, A Study of the Work of the Holy Spirit in Contexts of Persecution and Martyrdom in the New Testament and Early Christian Literature.* Washington, D.C.: University Press of America, 1981.

Weinstein, Donald, and Rudolph M. Bell, *Saints & Society, the Two Worlds of Western Christendom, 1000-1700.* Chicago: University of Chicago Press, 1982.

Weiss, James Michael. "Erasmus at Luther's Funeral, Melanchthon's Funeral Oration for and Biography of Luther," *The Sixteenth Century Journal* XVI, 1 (1985): 91-114.

————. "Friendship and Rhetoric: the Development of Humanists' Biographies in Sixteenth-Century Germany." Ph.D. dissertation, University of Chicago, 1980.

————. "Luther and His Colleagues on the Lives of the Saints," *The Harvard Library Bulletin* 33 (Spring 1985): 174-95.

Weyrauch, Erdmann. *Konfessionelle Krise und soziale Stabilität, Das Interim in Strassburg (1548-1562).* Tübingen: Klett-Cotta, 1978.

White, Helen C. *Tudor Books of Saints and Martyrs.* Madison: University of Wisconsin Press, 1963.

Wingren, Gustav. *Luther on Vocation.* Carl C. Rasmussen, trans. Philadelphia: Muhlenberg, 1957.

Wolgast, Eike. "Der Streit um die Werke Luthers im 16. Jahrhundert," *Archiv für Reformationsgeschichte* 59 (1968): 177-202.

————. "Die Wittenberger Luther-Ausgabe, Zur Überlieferungsgeschichte der Werke Luthers im 16. Jahrhundert," *Archiv für Geschichte des Buchwesens* IX, 1/2 (1970): 1-336.

Zahrnt, Heinz. *Luther deutet Geschichte, Erfolg und Misserfolg im Licht des Evangeliums.* Munich: Mueller, 1952.

Zeeden, Ernst Walter. *Martin Luther und die Reformation im Urteil des deutschen Luthertums.* Freiburg/Breisgau: Herder, 1950.

Index